DEDICATED TO YOU, THE READER

"You're creative, whether you think so or not. You have things that make you click. You see life in a way that no one else has before. You have potential. You have gifts that you have mastered, and some that you haven't even realized yet. You are attractive, strong, and unique. You fit some molds and break others. You know beauty differently than anyone. You are hilarious. You are meaningful. You are instrumental in a plan made by Someone who loves you.

You have times of peace, times of anger, times of hurt, times of joy, times of sorrow, and times of love. But in all times, you are something this world has never seen the likes of before. And you are so influential that you sometimes change it without noticing.

You are something totally new, something amazing, and something mind-blowing.

You are incredible."

Mark Rodriguez

Taken from "About You" on
www.markrodriguezphotography.com

The Extraordinary Ordinary Life of Mark Rodriguez

by Mark Rodriguez
with Leigh Ellen Rodriguez

ISBN 978-1-63393-098-8

Published by

köehlerbooks™

210 60th Street
Virginia Beach, VA 23451
212-574-7939
www.koehlerbooks.com

THE EXTRAORDINARY ORDINARY LIFE OF MARK RODRIGUEZ

MARK RODRIGUEZ
WITH LEIGH ELLEN RODRIGUEZ

VIRGINIA BEACH
CAPE CHARLES

TABLE OF CONTENTS

PREFACE

This will most likely be painful to read. It certainly is to write. But you need to know what happened that horrible, beautiful night to fully understand the importance of Mark's words. But before I recount the events of May thirtieth, please allow me to share a memory of something that happened about four days before Mark was killed. I think it will make it easier for all of us.

It was one of those May nights that hinted summer is near. Carlos and I were on the screened-in porch, lingering after dinner while our three younger kids played in the pool. Mark, barely seventeen years old, came bounding onto the porch, bouncing like he did when he was excited about something. The conversation went something like this:

"I have this idea that is gonna sound crazy, but I really feel like I am supposed to do it."

Carlos and I exchanged a smile, as the last time this happened, he talked us into letting him go to Nicaragua for a month.

"Okay, shoot. What is it?"

"Okay," with more enthusiastic gestures, "I really want to get some time away alone with God. I want to go away for two or three nights and just take my guitar, Bible, and journal and head out into the woods to worship and pray."

"And which woods would these be?"

"I don't know yet. But it would be nice if there was a river or something."

"Honey, great idea, but, if you remember, you are a minor, have no way to protect yourself, no outdoor survival training, can't use a compass, and basically quit Boy Scouts as a Tenderfoot."

Mark, with a big smile, said, "I know. It will be okay, Mom. I just know I really want this time alone with God."

Carlos and I exchanged another look and I think we both knew we wouldn't really win this fight. This kid could talk us into anything.

"Okay, how about this? We will ask Grammy about you camping on her farm where you would get the full sense of being alone, but wouldn't be far from help if you need it; or we could look into a retreat center or something."

"Sweet." And off he went.

A few minutes later, we see Mark running, fully clothed toward the pool, with a Batman mask on. As his siblings screamed, he cannonballed them to their delight. This was Mark. An extraordinary, ordinary kid. That memory is a treasure now. I would do anything to see that crazy Batman cannonball again.

• • •

It was a Friday about five days later. School had let out for the summer so Mark slept in and then joined us for lunch. Mark's Oklahoma grandparents, Carlos' mom and dad, were in town for a visit so they took Carlos, me, and Mark out for his first experience with Vietnamese food. As for most teenage boys, food is love, so Mark was very content and happily caught up his grandparents on his summer plans.

Afterwards, Mark and I left lunch to run a few errands together. He agreed to keep me company while I stopped into a nail salon. He was easily bribed with a Frappuccino.

While we waited for my nail appointment, he asked me to make sure that the place wasn't a cover for human trafficking. We talked about his passion to bring women and children out of the dark places of forced prostitution and slavery.

We talked about his call to lead worship. I distinctly remember telling him that I also felt he had the gift of public speaking and that I thought God would use that along with his heart of worship.

Then we played a game against each other on our phones. He took great delight in kicking my butt. He was so happy.

Mark had finished his junior year with exceptional grades and fantastic SAT scores. He had turned his love of photography into a business and he had already taken some senior portraits and booked his first wedding. He had money in his pocket and he helped buy his own car. And, for him, the icing on the cake was he had finally joined a band he was regularly practicing with as lead vocalist and guitarist. The summer stretched out before him like a reward for his hard work. He was ready to celebrate his friends' graduation that night. It was a perfect day.

Because he was rushing to get to graduation, I didn't see him very much after we got home. He quickly went to his room to get ready for the night. I do remember him running down the steps and a blurred image of him going out the front door. In the haste, however, I did notice he was wearing his favorite Dr. Pepper T-shirt and khaki shorts, which prompted me yelling, "Are you sure you want to wear that to graduation?" My words fell flat. "I'm late, Mom, gotta go! I'll text you later." More blur of rushing as I shouted after him, "I love you... don't speed... better to be late!" And off he went to watch his older friends graduate.

That was the last time I saw him.

Throughout the night, he texted me. I know he enjoyed graduation, and then he headed to a late dinner with one of his good friends, Joseph. And at 10:36 p.m., he texted me he had dropped off Joseph and was heading home.

I waited up for him. At 11:00 p.m., I anxiously listened for him; by 11:15 p.m., I was frustrated; did he stop somewhere and not tell me? By 11:30 p.m., I was terrified. He wasn't answering calls or texts, and this was not like him. So I texted Joseph, who didn't know where he was. I woke Carlos and he jumped in the car to go retrace Mark's route while I called hospitals and the police department. Carlos tried to assure me that his phone probably just ran out of battery and maybe he had a flat tire, but I could hear the tension in my husband's voice. We stayed on the phone as he drove Mark's route; our panic increased. The nightmare only got worse when Carlos came upon the scene around midnight. We were on the phone together when he told me he could see Mark's van, obviously crashed, airbag deployed, police and emergency personnel everywhere, and an ambulance pulling off. We prayed on the phone together, and I remember saying, "No matter what, we will worship," and we begged God for Mark's life. I hustled to get my clothes on to head to the hospital, panicked. My mind raced. Head injury? Spinal injury?

And then I could hear in the background an officer saying, "Sir, get in the car… SIR, get in the car… you can't go over there."

And Carlos said, "Honey, I'll call you right back. I'm going to find out what is going on."

A few minutes later Carlos called and said the words that still shoot panic through my soul, "Honey, sit down. Our son is gone. Our son is dead. Our son is deceased."

And all I could think of was I had to get to Carlos.

Thankfully, Carlos' parents were still with us visiting, so I woke up my mother-in-law, since I needed to leave the younger kids sleeping. She amazingly kept her composure and positioned herself in the kitchen in case she was needed. Next, I called my mom and told her the news. She began to cry, and I told her I needed her to collect herself so that she and Dad could prepare to come as quickly as possible. I heard her take a deep breath as she controlled her crying and made herself sound strong for me. They would start the five-hour drive as soon as possible. It breaks my heart that a grandparent would ever have to hear the words I said that night. But both grandmothers are praying women, strong-in-the-Lord women, and they held us in prayer throughout the night.

I called my friend Karen who drove me to meet Carlos. I regret what she had to experience with me that night, but am so thankful for her. She loved Mark, too. As Carley's mom, his best friend and girlfriend of five years, she knew Mark well, and we had become close friends. She wisely wouldn't let me drive to meet Carlos. And while we drove, we learned what had really happened. Carlos called and told me that Mark had been shot. Shot?! We would find out more details later, but we learned that James Brown, a twenty-nine-year-old man, had been sitting in a parking lot near where Mark had dropped Joseph off. When Mark made a U-turn to come home, James Brown pulled out behind him and with two shots, one to the head and one to the back, from a revolver, instantly killed Mark. Witnesses said that he shot him from behind and that Mark would not have ever even seen him coming. The detectives would later remark how impossible it seemed that a crazed person in a moving vehicle could fatally shoot someone who was also in a moving vehicle, especially considering he used his nondominant hand. As Mark veered off the road, Brown drove by and continued to shoot the sides of the car. When Carlos called to tell me Mark was shot, Karen and I thought the shooter was still on the loose. So, we prayed for safety, but also for the shooter's soul. I remember saying that I was going to choose to forgive him right then, because I might not be able to later. God has honored that decision. I believe that my son's killer must have been a very troubled soul; to have that much rage in his body and mind must have been hell. I leave it to God to sort out things with him. And Carlos and I believe wholeheartedly that God numbers our days, that "no power of hell, no scheme of man can ever pluck us from His hand." God was sovereign that night, as always. He was present with Mark every second of the way Home. And that is what makes that horrible night beautiful.

We found out later that James Brown continued to shoot at everything he passed as he drove to his home. Miraculously, Brown didn't kill any other civilians. But there was another casualty. Officer Brian Jones arrived at Brown's home and attempted to get Brown to surrender. Brown fired shots through the front window and then came outside and continued to fire an assault rifle at Officer Jones, who was struck multiple times in the chest, piercing his ballistic vest. The police officer was killed, leaving behind his wife, Rebekah, and children Bryson, Mariah, and Kyler. Officer Curtis Allyson, who came to his aid, was also shot and badly injured. Officer Toofan Shahsiah pursued Brown as he fled from his home, and when Brown attacked him and tried to grab his weapon, Officer Shahsiah shot and killed him. Officer Shahsiah's actions have been deemed justified. I am convinced his actions saved many lives that night.

We have never really gotten an answer as to why James Brown did what he did that night. Toxicology reports showed he was not drinking or using drugs. Criminal records confirm Brown pleaded guilty to a misdemeanor assault charge in January 2011. The records show the charge was originally a felony charge for assaulting an officer, before it was reduced.

Brown was sentenced to one year in the Norfolk City Jail and ordered to be of uniform good behavior for two years.

Despite the sentence and order from a judge, Brown was cited for carrying a firearm in public in July 2012.

In August 2012, Brown pleaded guilty to the charge which accused him of carrying a handgun loaded with more than twenty rounds.

He was known in his neighborhood as "Wyatt Earp" because he would open-carry his firearm. One detective said he thinks he just "cracked and wanted to take down as many people as he could on the way out." We found out later from one of his family members that he was possibly off his medication for Bipolar Disorder and was likely psychotic that night.

As we watched morning dawn on the thirty-first, we faced the horrible task of having to tell Mark's siblings he was dead. And not because his car crashed, not because he was robbed, not because he was caught between someone else's dispute, but because someone just decided to randomly shoot him.

I sat waiting to hear them stir and received a text from a friend saying, "Have you seen Mark's heaven blog?"

It was then that we learned that shortly before his death, he had posted the following:

HEAVEN
4-5-14

I've been meditating on heaven a lot lately, and I must say, it wells my eyes with tears of joy every now and then. What a beautiful thought that one day, I will be completely in the presence of God and will actually be able to feel the magnitude of all his love and peace with no earthly fears or worries to distract me. The joy that I feel now, the serenity I feel now, will finally be made perfect.

The presence of God here on earth is enough to make me shudder in wonder. I've had some incredible moments in life that can only be explained as miracles where I see my Abba, my Father move in love for me so powerfully; it brings me to my knees in amazement. To think that one day, I will be perfectly and totally in His presence... I'm definitely going to need a heavenly body because the joy He fills me with now sometimes makes me feel like I'm about to explode!

I love the image of Heaven because it is perfect, perfect peace. Every quarrel, every hurt, it's all gonna be resolved. All of God's children will be together and we won't hurt each other anymore; we'll finally understand how to love perfectly. And the fact that we'll all be worshiping the Lord together in one place, forever... that amazes me.

It makes me so excited to think of the wedding feast awaiting us when we go to be with the Lord. I imagine streets filled with rejoicing, loud trumpets, wedding bells... I'm sure it'll be far more incredible than I can comprehend now, and I love that.

God is super good. I can't wait to be with Him forever.

When we arrive at eternity's shore
Where death is just a memory and tears are no more
We'll enter in as the wedding bells ring
Your bride will come together and we'll sing
You're beautiful

"You're Beautiful" Phil Wickham

Mark's death at times seemed senseless and wasteful. But we learned through his death just how extraordinary our seemingly ordinary son had been. We received streams of supportive and sympathetic emails, cards, and phone calls. But it was the stories of how Mark helped others, quietly and unassumingly, that revealed what an exceptional person our son had been.

After reading his blog, we recalled the countless times we had seen Mark grab his journal, cup of coffee and Bible, and realized that he had left us more of himself in those journals. Carlos and I collected all of Mark's blogs and other writings and sat on the floor that day, reading obsessively and marveling at the amazing gift God had left us.

A close family friend, Kathy, has been wheelchair-bound for years and often feels life is an uphill climb. She had a huge fondness for Mark and after his death said, "When I was with Mark, I was royalty."

Donna Carroll, a parent of one of Mark's good friends, wrote:

"Mark blessed my life many times over the ten years I was privileged to know and love him. Though he was young, he became a man after God's heart, and I was proud to have been led by Mark closer to the presence of God. Even a child is known by his deeds."

One older student wrote:

"Mark was a huge inspiration in my life. His love for God and for others was truly amazing, and I strive every day to be full of passion and faith, just as he was. I knew I could always count on his 'hey dude what's up' in the hallway to bring me joy and cheer me up if I needed it. He is my brother, and I love him so much."

Another student expressed:

"Your son changed my life. His love and passion for God shined through everything he did."

And there are hundreds more where those came from. No one talked about his grades, SAT scores or potential. They talked about his love.

Shortly after he was killed, I remembered that Mark wanted time alone away with God. You know, the two-to-three day retreat? Well, he got what he wanted in an amazing way—to be with God.

As you read his journals, blogs, and poems, you may notice, as I did, that God seems to be calling him closer and closer to Himself as his death neared. Did he know he was going to die? I don't think so, but I think his desire to be with God was growing as God prepared him to go Home.

Like Mark, we can have that same intimate and loving relationship with God. When we ask, He makes the ordinary extraordinary. May the words of Mark, a seventeen-year-old ordinary kid, help you to experience this extraordinary ordinary life with God.

"God is Super Good."

LEIGH ELLEN RODRIGUEZ

PROLOGUE

When Mark was twelve years old, Mark and I decided to run his first official race together. It just so happened that our fall vacation to Bald Head Island coincided with their annual Maritime Classic Road Race. The race was a perfect fit. The scenery is beautiful, and it was a place we both loved.

I had learned that as my boy was getting older and more independent, running was something I could continue to share with him. When we trained together, he would share stories from school, and I was able to hear the latest events happening in the Percy Jackson books he loved. It gave me a chance to encourage him as he learned to pace himself, and I knew it would not be long before he could easily outrun me.

I remember the pre-race nerves as we gathered with the other runners at the start. My family was all there on the sidelines; my brother and sister, their spouses and children, and my parents were there, hanging out with Will, Daniel, and Maria. We had a lot of support. But because of the nature of the island, there would only be a couple of places we would see them, and much of the course we would run without any spectators.

The gun sounded, and we took off. We were mindful of the starting adrenaline and tried to manage our pace. It was exhilarating. My family was cheering and dancing as we passed them, and we felt great. But as the race went on, the course turned onto a part of the island that is one rolling hill after another. We would not see our family until the finish line.

We had not trained for hills, and my body wasn't loving the incline. Mark kindly slowed his pace a bit and started telling me more stories. It was then that it occurred to me that I hadn't seen many young boys running. And as he slowed to accommodate his old mama, I told him, "Hon, I am thinking you need to run ahead. I haven't seen many other boys running, and I think you might have a chance to place in this race." At first, he refused. He said we had trained together, and he didn't want to leave me. I assured him I would be fine and that I really, really, wanted him to run his best race. I told him I would see him at the finish line and to TAKE OFF! And he did. As I saw his small frame sprint ahead, I eventually lost sight of him and was left to finish my race alone.

BEFORE YOU READ THIS JOURNAL

In order to get the most out of Mark's writings, you need to understand how it is organized. We have left the entries in their original form as much as we could. Very little has been left out and few corrections have been made. Sometimes, it takes a few days for his thoughts to develop on a certain topic. If a certain entry doesn't grab you, just keep reading. Enjoy the humor of a teenage boy as he delights in winning a game of Uno or gets excited about his favorite band's new release.

Watch how his relationship with God deepens as he gets older. And most of all, notice its simplicity and persistence. Mark repeats the same request over and over. "God, give me an intimate relationship with you." "God, teach me to love." And God answers those prayers in amazing ways. Those are prayers I can pray and you can pray. They are extraordinarily ordinary prayers.

We will explain things along the way if we think it will help you understand the context. But other than that, these are all Mark's words. One last thing: if something is in all caps, this is how Mark would emphasize that he felt God was telling him something.

INTRODUCTION TO PART I

We start with Mark's earliest journal. There is no date on some entries, but we know he wrote this in 2009, and most likely during the second part of sixth grade because of his references. This journal was kept separately from the others, wedged in the back of his bedside table.

Mark was a normal middle school kid when writing these thoughts, a regular kid who sometimes did silly stuff. I remember when he was in the fourth grade, he got into trouble at school for zooming around the classroom in a rolling chair. He also got called into the principal's office for shoving another student on the playground—to his defense, he was protecting a friend. His temperament was generally compliant, but if he didn't want to do something, you would have a hard time making him. For example, he really, really did not like Boy Scouts. He loved the friends, but could not get into the program. We were making him do it to help him learn the value of working to achieve one's goals. We faithfully drove him to every event, and he went without much fuss, but two years in we discovered that he had purposefully, in quiet rebelliousness, not advanced in the ranks and remained a Tenderfoot. That was the end of that.

Don't miss the significance of the subject of the first entry—Heaven. We have also included his prayers regarding publishing a book—a goal he did work toward. In middle school he created a story about an angel named Corinth but struggled to complete it. At the time he was writing his journals he had no idea they would ever be published. Now, this book is the culmination of his dream.

A PRAYER FOR PROTECTION

JULY 2009

Dear Jesus,

Thank You for the knowledge that I will eternally be with You in heaven. Those thoughts should keep me from the fears of this world. But without fear, how can there be bravery? Tonight, the night noises haunt me, causing me to pray for daylight. The night and day are both alike to You; let that be the same for me. Allow me to sleep soundly and contentedly without fear. Protect me, Lord Jesus. Please protect everyone else as well. Mom, Daniel, Maria, Dad, Will, Carley, Colin; protect them and everyone else.

I love You,
Amen

A PRAYER FOR CORINTH
AUGUST 2009

Dear God,

I pray for Corinth, my imaginary angel. I created him like You created us, and he seems to be a part of me. My prayer is that You would help me while I move his life. Make me into the spectacular writer that I want to be, but only if it is Your bidding. Please allow Corinth to become a best-selling story, something that truly moves people.

Thanks,
Mark

AUGUST 2009

Dear God,

Thank You for the wonderful gift of writing You have given me.

I love using this gift to create entirely different worlds. Thank You that I can write stories of Corinth, Saryn, Matt, and all those stories.

Love,
Mark

AUGUST 2009

Dear God,

Dad brought something to my attention today. I guess I've been kind of trying to get Corinth to work out as one big series, but Dad told me maybe I should just make it one book. I think that's a great idea; I just don't know how I'm going to fit ten years into one book. If I can finish this book and get it edited and published, I'll finally be an author. I want to use the gift of writing You gave me to its full extent, so please guide me in writing this book.

You rock,
Mark Rodriguez

AUGUST 2009

God,

I recently started a new book. Corinth wasn't really working out. It's better to have a short but great book than a big and bad one. Please bless this book and make me make You Lord of it.

Love,
Mark

Dear God,

You know, maybe I'm not cut out to be an author right now. Maybe when I'm older, but please guide me right now.

I love You,
Mark

Dear God,

You know how I want to be an author. I've written seventy pages now and expect I'll beat my page record. But God, I'm afraid I might not succeed. I don't want a repeat of last time. Please, give me the ideas to keep the story going. I need them, Lord. I want to accomplish my goal.

Thank You,
Mark

Note: Mark's sixth grade year ended with some major events. From March 27 through June 6, 2009, I was in Nicaragua with his little brother, Daniel, fostering their adopted sister, Maria. While I was gone, Mark and his brother, Will, stayed home with their dad so they could finish the school year. While I was gone, Mark turned twelve and won Norfolk Christian's Ambassador Award for being a good example what it looks like to be a true ambassador for Christ.

This is the highly dramatic and sweet note he wrote me on Mother's Day while I was still there:

Mom,

I miss you SO much. I need a mom really bad. I hope you will come home soon. I know not even death will stop you from coming to me. These words are of passion. I feel like I could cry. But, never, ever, ever forget that I LOVE YOU.

Happy Mother's Day,
Mark Rodriguez

I recently found the note I left for him to read when I departed for Nicaragua. It still echoes the cry of my heart today:

Son,

I want you to see how much you are like God in this situation. For Mark so loved Maria that he gave his one and only mommy that Maria would not perish… you are participating in saving Maria's physical life… you are my treasure. I don't know how I will live without you for this long. I will have to be very brave and trust God… When I see you again, I will kiss your face off.

A PRAYER FOR SUMMER
JUNE 2010

Dear God,

I have already seen You move many ways in my life this summer. Even today, when I had a swim meet, did You help me? I thought that butterfly was my worst stroke, yet I did better on it than any of my other strokes today.

I pray that my summer vacations would be fun, but I've got a problem with them. I don't want it to get in the way of me hanging out with Carley. Please make me still have plenty of fun this summer.

Amen

A PRAYER FOR THE INJURED
JUNE 2010

Dear God,

Thank You for curing Sam this week. He was in a lot of pain, but no matter how slowly, You're healing him. Please continue to save him. Grow him into a man of You. I pray for John Stone. Warren's already gone, but please save John. I pray for Mrs. Schanck. I pray all her diseases would leave, and that dear Carley and Carter wouldn't get them. Thank You for Mr. Schanck, who has been able to bless his kids with awesome talents. And lastly, I pray for me. Remove all darkness from me. Make me pure like Carley, she is truly a model of love and peace that I want to be like. May Your will be done in these matters.

Amen

Note: Sam is Mark's cousin, and he was born with a life-threatening intestinal blockage. Warren and John Stone are twins who were born to our friends Meade and Mary Elizabeth

Stone. Warren died shortly after he was born, and our family had been praying for their family. Mrs. Schanck is Carley's mom, and Mark knew she wasn't feeling well, but didn't really know why. So he prayed for her "diseases," which still brings a laugh when we read it today.

AUGUST 2010

Dear God,

Thank You that school is coming soon! I can't wait to go back. I pray all my classes get worked out. Please get me in a homeroom with Carley (Your decision, though). And thanks that we finally have lockers! Those should be great! I pray that Mrs. Stoner's baby would come out okay. And for Aunt Jessica's! Thanks for the new cousins!

Love,
Mark Rodriguez

AUGUST 2010

Dear God,

Thank You for the great trip I had, however, I pray my burn would heal. I pray that the new school year would work well. I pray Carley would be in my homeroom. I pray my teachers would be great, and that homework would work out.

Love,
Mark Rodriguez

A PRAISE FOR REDEMPTION

I fell from Your throne,
I dropped from heaven's seat
But when I gazed right back at You
Your eyes I did not meet

The path of sin I traveled down
The path of killers, thieves, and liars
I intentionally ran toward gates of Hell
To godless, lonely fires

But as I fell a maid caught me,
One of most pure virtue
Who called me back by saying,
"Hey, God wants to be with you"

I took her hand and now we walk
On Heaven's golden paths
We joke and laugh, for we are free
Of Satan's scarlet wrath

A PRAISE FOR CLEANSING

I stand in rain that's pouring down
Upon my blood-stained head
I rebelled and sinned against the Lord
My soul feels like it's dead

Who will lift me up from this pit
From this horrible, deadly hole
Away from tempters and idols of stone
Away from darkened sheol?

Lord, turn my water into wine
Cleanse my sinner's heart.
Change Red to White, Dark to Light
Save me from Satan's arts

My soul is cleansed from all my faults
No sin can now be seen
I feel the love of God surround
And now I'm truly clean

A PRAYER TO PURIFY

I look back at my life and hate what I see. I have committed many unrighteous acts. I hate them. If my friends heard of these, would they hate me? Perhaps. My Lord Jesus, I need You. I hate myself for what I have done, I need You to help me cast away the chains of my old life and embrace the new. For light and dark cannot abide within the same heart. I need You to take my hand and tell me You'll love me no matter what I've done. Oh, the way that makes me smile! I need not fear, for You fill my heart with holy joy. You died on a cross for no crime for me. I will not dishonor that. I shall not beat myself, for You made me. Your love for me is all that matters. When Satan's arrows fly towards me, may I block them with my shield of faith. May they bounce off my breastplate of righteousness. Purify me, O Lord. Your hand holds mine and will never let me go. I repent for what I've done, for every single sin. This song shows how I feel:

I need You, Jesus,
Come to my rescue,
Where else can I go?
There's no other name by
Which I am saved,
Capture me with grace
Adapted from "Rescue" by Eddie James

And here is my somewhat altered victory song, at least what I think it is:

Everlasting,
Who can understand Your ways,
Never ending
Your glory goes beyond all praise
But the cry of my heart
Is to bring You praise
From the inside out
Lord, my soul cries out
Heal me, Jesus

Adapted from "From the Inside Out"
Joel Houston and Hillsong United

Love,
Mark

SEPTEMBER 2010

Dear God,

I thank You for the friends You have given me. They are wise and good examples of how to be good Christians. But today, one of my wisest friend's wisdom turned out to be slightly frayed. She believes that I have been putting on an act for her about my relationship with You. Yet it is no act, I do love You. You are the only one who is always there for me. You helped me through one of my greatest problems. Give me the wisdom for this problem; control my mouth so that I can speak the right words. I love You very much.

Love,
Mark Rodriguez

SEPTEMBER 2010

Dear Heavenly Father,

I assume too much. From my last written prayer, I said that one of my friends didn't believe I was showing a true relationship with You. Yet, all I had to do was tell her how I felt about You. Thank You so much for giving her the ability to understand. She sees my assuming too much as a mere fault I have. Please help us continue to be good friends.

Love,
Mark Rodriguez

DELIVERY
OCTOBER 2010

God,

Even though I've given my life to You, temptation still follows me. I need You to help me when I'm about to fall, imbed Yourself in my mind so I don't sin. I need You more than anything else. If everybody hated me, You'd still love me.

Thanks,
Mark

CHRISTMAS BREAK 2010

Dear God,

Thank You for NCS. I love that school, and hope that is where the rest of my childhood is. Please make X-mas come soon. Please give the homeless homes for the winter.

Love,
Mark

THANKS FOR COMING DOWN
DECEMBER 25, 2010

Dear Jesus,

Happy Birthday!!! I know today probably isn't Your real birthday, but we're celebrating it. You've done and are doing a lot in my life, and without You I'd be nothing. Thank You for giving up Your throne to become a baby. I wouldn't have been able to do it.

Happy 2013th or something,
Mark

DECEMBER 31, 2010

Dear Lord,

This year has been filled with many events. It's been my most complicated year yet, and my years may just get more complicated. This year, my relationship with You has grown stronger. You're all I need, without You, I wouldn't be alive to write this.

I've also realized we live in a world of corruption. All around me are bad things. But there are people who follow a greater light in this land of distraction. I am one of them; the people I'm talking about are the Christians.

In the upcoming New Year, give me the strength to love You more than ever. No matter what bad or good things happen this year, You will be with me. I am never alone.

Love,
Mark

BE MY GUIDE AND LORD

JANUARY 2010

God,

You've done so much for me. Yet, unfortunately, I continue to sin. I need a guide, someone who will be my Lord and passion. At chapel, Mr. McAdoo asked us what our passion was, and You might not be mine. I want You as my passion, though. I want to honestly be able to say, without a doubt, that I love You first and foremost. Make that happen please.

I love You,
Mark

TRUTH IN THE WORD

Dear God,

As You know, I am currently in Romans. I have already finished Revelation, Genesis, and Exodus. I pray that with Romans I would be able to find life connections in it. That I'd see the truth in the word. Let me be able to apply it to my life so that I grow in wisdom and stature, and in favor with You and others.

Love,
Mark

A PLEA FOR UNDERSTANDING

Dear God,

Thank You for the guiding light You have given Your children. Our salvation is recorded in it, yet for some reason my mind cannot grasp the topic! While other books make sense to me, for some reason the Bible's verses just don't click in my head! Do I need more memorization of the Word? Maybe. Reveal this to me, Lord.

Love,
Mark

A PRAYER FOR PERSONAL RELATIONSHIPS

Dear Jesus,

Thank You for how much You care about me. You have given me good friends and a good home, and I'm thankful for that. My friends love me, but Your love for me would trump theirs, no contest. I pray that I would have more of a personal relationship with You; that when I pray, it would actually feel like I'm talking to You. I pray that I would want to tell others about You, that You would give me the strength of Paul and the bravery of martyrs. Be my guide, and make my body into a living temple, one that is clean and pure. I know my body already is a temple, but I pray it will continue to be pure.

Love,
Mark

A PRAYER FOR VISION

Dear God,

Thank You for the convicting Holy Spirit, He who shows me I've sinned. Lord, I pray that You would let me know right from wrong and help me to choose the right path. Like Wayne said, the same power that brought Christ back from the dead is in me, I can at least honor my parents. Make that power rise within me like a fire, dominating my sin. Make me like You God; someday I'll be perfect.

Love,
Mark

A PRAYER FOR NON-BELIEVERS

Dear God,

Tonight I thank You for the chapel speakers we had this week, who told us about the people who don't know You. God, I pray for those people. Let them hear about You, so they can spend eternity with You. Thank You.

Love,
Mark

Dear God,

Thank You for the amazing first thirteen years of my life. They've been awesome and fun, and I know You have much more for me. God, thank You for Carley. She is the best friend I've ever had, and I hope You have a ton in store for us.

Thanks again,
Mark

Note: These men gave Mark a blessing on his thirteenth birthday. Carlos gave him a dog tag with the verse Matthew 6:33 engraved on it "But seek first the Kingdom of God and his righteousness and all these things will be added to you."

Uncle Matt, Pop, Carlos, and Hillery Schanck (not pictured, Mark Bondi)

Dear God,

I need You. I need You more than food or water, air, friends, family, or pets. I may die, but You will always be here, in the hearts of those who serve You. God, help me to put on Your armor, may it guard me from bad thoughts and deeds. You can stop Satan's arrows from piercing my chest; sin is nothing to You. God, please make me make good choices.

Love,
Mark

Dear God,

Tonight I pray to be normal. Heck, maybe I am normal but just feel weird. God, allow me to be who I really am everywhere, all the time. God, allow me to face temptation and beat it. With Your power, I can do this. Thank You for always being there. Allow me to resist Satan.

Love,
Mark

A PRAISE TO MY CREATOR

Dear God,

Answer me when I call to You,
O my righteous God.
Give me relief from my distress;
Be merciful to me and hear my prayer.

Lord, I thank You. I thank You for Mom, Dad, Maria, Will, Daniel, Carley, and everyone else You've blessed me with. May they move my life to draw me closer to You. May Your light shine through me.

Love,
Mark

ENVIORNMENTAL CAMPING TRIP (ECT)

Dear God,

Yo. The day after tomorrow marks the start of ECT. I must say, it hasn't exactly turned out how I'd like, but You may have a reason for that. I pray that You would really move people during ECT. I pray that You'd move me as well, and my team. We need You more than anything, God.

Love,
Mark

ECT REFLECTION

Dear God,

Wow. This past week has been amazing. I'm happy to say that, even though the teams weren't what I would have chosen, I had a great time. Lord, I thank You so much for those that accepted You into their hearts. I ask that You would give me the strength to help them in their walk. God, I want to be a so-called "Jesus Freak." I want to burn for You and I want the world to see You through me. I threw my shame into the fire last night; illuminate my soul with Your Word so I can shine without fear.

I love You,
Mark

THE END OF SCHOOL
MAY 2010

Dear God,

I thank You for the wonderful year I just completed. I thank You for all the blessings You gave me. I pray that this summer I would live for You in all I do. I pray for peace of mind. I pray that I would have a great time with Carley. And I pray that next year, I'd grow in my relationship with You.

Amen

JOY

Hey God,

This week, in my devotions, it seems I was mostly reading about Joy. You are joy, and give it in abundance to those who follow You. You have joy when You see us working for You. Thank You for David. Allow me to grow into the godly man he was, so I may be on fire for You. Thank You for the joy You have when You see me.

Love,
Mark

NEED

Dear God,

I thank You for how much You care about me. You give me all I need. Even when I wrong You, You forgive me. When I praise You, You smile. You care more for me than anyone else does, a love that goes so far as that You died for me. Thank You for everything.

Love,
Mark

PATIENCE

Dear God,

Thank You for the freedom You have allowed our nation to have. With it, we are given the ability to worship You whenever we want.

God, I pray for patience. Patience with my brothers, when they tick me off. Patience so that I can see Your gifts to me. You have been patient with me, and I thank You for that.

Love,
Mark

Mark and his brother, Will

STRENGTH

Dear God,

This week, my devotions were about strength. I read that through my weakness You can accomplish great things. Look what You did with David after he sinned. God, strength is not my power, it is Your power in me. When I accepted You, You entered my heart with that power. May I use Your power to its greatest level.

Love,
Mark

SUMMER 2010

Dear God,

Thank You for the great trip I just had. Thank You for Claire and Sam*, for how cute they are. I pray they would grow up well. Thank You for all the beautiful wildlife I saw. Those bison were amazing. I pray that You would reveal Your beauty to other Montana visitors through nature.

Love,
Mark

*Claire and Sam are Mark's cousins

Mark and his sister, Maria in Montana

Dear God,

Thank You for my budgie, Alph. Thank You that he is already hand-tamed in the cage. God, I pray these weeks I'm gone won't have a poor effect on him. I pray that he has already bonded with me, and that he won't be too bored. Let him take advantage of his toys and have a good time while I'm gone. May mom have a good time with him and be good for him.

Thanks,
Mark

SUMMER CAMP REVIEW

Dear God,

Finally, the week of the latrine is OVER. I just finished my Boy Scout camp at Powhatan and am very glad to be home. However, there were good things there that I thank You for. For one: friends. Two: pretzels with cheese (I wouldn't mind those in Heaven) Three: Blobbing! That was awesome to do and watch. I thank You for all those things, and the world You gave us to experience them on. All in all, a pretty good week.

Amen,
Mark

8-2-10

Dear God,

I want to know how to put You in control. When temptation arises, do I fight it off? Or do I somehow let You deal with it? Tonight, when I read the Bible, please give me Your answer. Also, sometimes when I pray it kind of feels like I'm just talking to a brick wall. Please show Yourself, God; in the Bible, and music, and in other Christians.

Thanks,
Mark

8-4-10

A Psalm of Praise

You are amazing
For when I sin, even though
It hurts you
You forgive me and love me
Nothing I could do could make you love
me less.
You are love, My God
And you will never turn your
head from me for
my dross has been purged.
I lean my head on your
shoulder now, Lord
Take me under your
wing.
And for all the sins I've
ever done,
I once again say
"I'm sorry."

-Mark

8-26-10

Dear God,

I've been discovering some new things I enjoy lately. I've learned that I like playing guitar, and I don't think I'm as bad a singer as I say. God, I don't know where these gifts will take me, but perhaps I could take up a chapel leadership position. I would love to worship You using my talents. Please guide me in this path, Lord.

Love,
Mark

FIRST WEEK OF SCHOOL
AUGUST 2010

Dear God,

Thank You for a good first week of eighth grade. It was kind of crazy, but I'll get used to it. God, I need a better relationship with You. I'm a good kid, act like a Christian, but I'm not sure I have a relationship with You. Please make that book, *Grace Walk*, help me develop one. Thanks for people like Mr. G who can make us face the facts.

Love,
Mark

8-30-10

Lord, I pray about my latest speculation. Subconsciously, I've been searching for a defining gift. I realize that when people think of individuals in my class they think "popular cheerleader" or "amazing soccer player." God, I don't want to have a gift that defines me. I want YOU to define me. Nevertheless, if there some hidden talent I have, please show me, God.

Amen

9-4-10

God,
I found someone in the Bible who (besides You) may be a good role model for me. He's Elijah. A man of great faith and passion. Even in his tough times, when it was him against 450 prophets of Baal, he stood his ground because he put all his trust in You. That's how I want to be. Even though the people I face may only be gossipers rather than Baal prophets, I should be able to look them in the eye and say, "Stop." And I know You'll be there with me.

Love,
Mark

1-5-11

Dear God,

I once was blind, but now I see! God, I am free! Free in You, free from sin. No longer do the chains I struggle with bind me, for You have torn them away. All along, God, I wondered why You weren't saving me. When really, I had to choose my door, You or sin. I think last night may have been different because I poured out my feelings of pain and burden to Carley. Such a weight has been lifted from my heart! It is filled with Your spirit, and I know that's all I'll ever need.

All I had to do was give up myself. Now, I want to let You be my Lord, my Master. I've taken up Carley's New Year's resolution to be positive because I want to rejoice and every day You give me. You brought me to my lowest point to raise me up.

Thank you so much!

1-19-11

In Christ alone,
My hope is found...
Amazing Grace...
That saved a wretch like me...
Take this heart, take my life...
I once was blind...
But now I see...
All I need is you

Make me into the servant You want me to be, Lord. I love You so much more than anything!

In Christ alone,
Mark

1-19-11

Dear God,

My parents brought a good point to my eyes. So I want to enjoy life, how about I live? My life could be so much more than just reading. First, they're right in the fact that I need to try at school. It's sure not gonna come on its own, and I should not be satisfied with anything less than my best. You want my all, so I'll give it to You. Second, I want to have a strong and healthy body. I'm going to start working out again. I'm seriously a couch potato. God, I pray that by doing these things I wouldn't have the problems I've been having. If I do my best for You, what else do I need? Now and forever, I love You.

In Christ alone,
Mark

1-26-11

Horrible dream last night
Lived on hill, by a lake
Ran along path by lake, chased by "father" with a gun.
Shot twice in the heart, once in back?
In house—"father" pulls out machine gun and pommels me
Fall to ground want to die but can't, breathing constricted
He keeps shooting
Dying—a sudden pause, then lights go out like a power failure
Wake up two years later
Will—teenager, developing acne
See Carley teaching something
Like I missed them, even though I was dead
At school—people whisper they see me, "Isn't that…?"
Wonder if Wayne's wife is pregnant
See Wayne. He says, "Hey buddy, where you been?!"
I tell him I was dead
Walk with Harrison
New classrooms, new student—Olivia, dark skin and glasses
Ask teacher if I can take a break to organize thoughts
Parents live apart from us
I could feel the bullets hitting me
Could feel the want to die, could feel dying
Don't know age, grade, or year—have to ask
Terrible sense that world has changed incredibly

Note: When I found this in Mark's journal, my heart stopped. So many similarities to the way he died are foreshadowed here. Not just the way he died, but the age of his brother Will and his youth leader Wayne having a baby (they adopted a baby shortly after Mark's death). This is the only one of his nightmares he recorded.

2-7-11

God,
Here are some of the many blessings You have given me:
Parents
Hope
Resurrection
Home
Carley
Siblings
Entertainment
Clothes
Money
A good school
Freedom
Friends
Writing ability
Books
Movies
Music

2-27-11

Dear Jesus,

I have learned something about sin. You cannot give it a single thing, a single chance to enter your life, or it will. It took me months to realize this, but I finally understand. Thank You for showing me this, for it has affected me greatly.

God, I've been thinking lately. Carley seems to be called to serve, she wants to so bad. It seems to be her calling. What's my calling, God? Is there something I'm supposed to do? Is it what Carley does, constantly looking for a way to serve and impact specific people's lives? I definitely don't know. Maybe I haven't had my calling yet. I want to say I'll do whatever You want, but I'm not sure that's true. Some things are scary, God. Some things could kill me or have me imprisoned. I wish I was some heroic guy who would be able to walk into China and preach for You at the top of my lungs without fear. But that's not who I am. I'm definitely not perfect. I sin. I've lied, cheated, and done many other things. But I have Your power. The same power that walked on water, healed the sick, and raised the dead is in me. May You guide me with that power, Lord.

I am Your servant,
Mark

Isaiah 40:30-31

No matter how hard I ran,
I had to slow down.
No matter how far I crawled,
I could never escape.

Then, I was free. Free because you unlocked the chains.

Now, through you I can run forever.
The world may put up hurdles, but I can jump over them.

Thank you for your loving hand that forgives even the worst of men.

3-27-11

Father,

Life is choices. Who we are is determined by what road we choose to take. There are many roads, many choices.

I am faced with a choice.

At Norfolk Christian, I have love. I have some great friends I love hanging out with. But do I belong here?

Jesus, I've been questioning where my place is. I love Norfolk Christian because of my friends, girlfriend, and great teachers. However, I want to witness for You, God. I want Your love and light to shine through me, to pierce the darkness. And I don't know that I have the best opportunity at NCS.

At public schools, teachers are not allowed to openly support Christianity. Your light is being hidden at these places. I believe that this could be Satan trying to hide the light. God, I want to go there. I want to go and show people Your light and love. I want to show the people that are hurt and broken that there is a way to eternal life, and nothing in this world can offer that. I want to show You are the only way.

But God, I also want what I have at NCS. I want my friends. I want the safe environment NCS offers. If I left, people may be hurt. I want to witness for You to a world that hasn't heard. But I don't want to hurt my friends by leaving them. I don't know what to do, God.

You are all knowing and know the path I should take. I pray that You would guide me to the right way, and that I would follow Your guidance.

Your servant,
Mark

3-28-11

Dear Jesus,

Carley brought up a good point. Maybe I'm at NCS for a reason. When I last prayed, I thought I wanted to show people Your light and love in a place that is dark. However, NCS needs You as well. The light is clearly shown there, yet still some do not see. I was kind of scared to witness at NCS because I've already built a "rep" there. I was scared that if I suddenly started bringing up God and stuff, people would be uncomfortable. It is possible I could even lose some people I hold close. But Lord, the point is not my wants and comfort. The point is other people. God, please give me the strength to talk to my friends about You.

Good night,
Mark

3-31-11

You've created the universe that I am
But a speck in.
Yet You love me.
There are billions of people in the world.
Yet You love me.
I have betrayed You.
Yet You love me.
I've gotten angry at You.
Yet You love me.
You died for me.
I will love You.

4-1-11

You were jealous for me,
If love's like a hurricane, I am the tree,
Bending beneath the weight of Your wind and mercy.
Adapted from "How He Loves Me" by David Crowder Band

You are the key that unlocks the chains.
You're the ladder from the abyss to the clouds.
You are the dog that guides the blind.
You are amazing.

4-3-11

God,

It's interesting to think that all Christians have the same spirit within them. The same spirit that my spiritual gift comes from gave Carley her spiritual gifts. I guess this means we will all receive the spiritual gift that we're meant to have. For if You mean for something to happen, what can overthrow Your decision?

Mark

4-4-11

God,

Tonight I pray for the homeless. I pray for the poor souls whose minds have been destroyed. I pray for those who escaped domestic violence. I pray for the sick and the diseased. I pray for those who were born homeless.

These people are special, God. Special because You love them. You died for them God, so that they can have eternal life. Keep them safe in the biting cold spring sometimes brings. Thank You so much for the organizations that reach out to them.

Your son,
Mark

4-9-11 Mark's birthday

Dear God,

Thank You for these fourteen years You've given me on this planet. You've blessed me in so many ways, many of which I probably take for granted. Thank You for the great day I had today. Thank You so much, God, for everything.

Mark

4-18-11

Dear Jesus,

I just want to thank You so much for the father You've given me. In a time of darkness, he is there for me, to comfort and encourage me. Thank You that he is so understanding and loving. He cares about me. Many, many people do not have fathers that love them and care about them. Thank You for mine, God. Thank You for Dad.

Mark

5-1-11

Father,

May I sleep soundly tonight under the protection of Your wings. May I dream of beautiful things, God, things pleasing to You. Thank You for giving me a bed to sleep in. I pray for those who do not have homes or beds, that they would have shelter tonight.

Mark

5-10-11

Dear God,

I realize I haven't talked to You for a while, like really talked to You. I've been spending some great time in Your Word, but it's important for me to talk to You as well. I finished middle school, and am moving on to an exciting new chapter of life. God, with high school comes new challenges. Thank You that I have You to look to in times of need. As I get older, I will mature in my relationship with You, and I really look forward to that. Thank You for these three years, God.

Amen

INTRODUCTION TO PART 2

As Mark entered high school, his relationship with God matured and became more personal. From a young age his dad told him ***The Story*** about a Big God who loved him and gave him a part in it. Mark learned this Big God wanted to know him personally and be intimately involved in every aspect of his life. Carlos would say, "Do you know why I love you?" And then Mark would answer, "Because I am yours." We wanted Mark to know that we loved him unconditionally, and God does so even more. And this love was demonstrated when He sacrificed his son, Jesus, on the cross so we could be in a loving relationship with Him. The special thing about Mark was that he truly believed "The Great Story" and therefore experienced in extraordinary ways how God loved him.

12-9-11

I sometimes speak of the fallibleness (don't even know if that's a word) of humans. I guess it's just kind of one of those statements that's so brief but so true. You are perfect, humans are imperfect. God, I have no doubt as to my imperfection. I am a sinner. I sin against You, I dishonor Your sacrifice all the time. Whether it's in pride, in arrogance, in hate or in anything else, my deeds remind me constantly of my sins, my faults. I'm sorry. I don't really know a better way to say it than that. I am sorry, crazy sorry, for how much I dishonor You.

We have not loved
You with our whole heart,
We have not loved
Our neighbor as ourself.

God, maybe I'm not recognizing a sin that I am constantly committing. I pray they would show, Lord, that You'd convict me of them so that I'd ultimately become stronger in You.

Amen.

Note: This entry was made while Mark was on a retreat called "Camel Knees" led by his Youth leader, Wayne Patterson. The prayer is from *The Book of Common Prayer*.

12-10-11

Father,

Camel Knees is over. However, its vision is still in my heart: to become a person of prayer. It's obvious to me that prayer is something important, God. After all, it is direct communication with You.

Lord, it's such a crazy thought that my prayers are "powerful and effective." That statement just blows my mind, even if I don't fully get it yet. What I do get, however, is this: because of my prayers, something happens. My prayers **do** something. They have **impact**. That's such a crazy concept, Father, and I pray that I would come to understand it more.

It's also crazy just to think that I can pray. That I can commune with You. Before You took our sins upon You, communion with You was blocked by a veil. When You died that veil literally tore apart. A personal relationship with the God of the universe became possible for even the lowliest person. That's incredible, and like the other idea I mentioned, I don't completely get it. I don't think I'll ever be able to grasp it while I'm on earth. What I do understand of it blows my mind; it seems impossible that I, a sinner, could have an intimate relationship with the Lord, with the Ruler, with the Master of the universe. And that You want that relationship with me, well... it's amazing.

This relationship is far from developed. As I stated in my Camel knees notes, I am in a developing relationship with You. I pray that this relationship would grow deeper every single day.

Lord, on an entirely different note, I pray for this coming week and the next. Exams are almost upon me, and I've gotta say, I'm nervous. What I'm praying for is strength, God. Strength to study hard, strength to keep my nerve, strength to retain information. May I feel Your presence in every exam, giving me peace. I pray that I wouldn't get too stressed out as I study, trying to cram it all into my head.

I also pray for Carley, Father. She has the Biology exam Thursday, and they've just entered a new unit. I pray that she'd keep her head on, God, that she'd keep her nerve as she tries to drive this information into her head. Finally, I pray for my time with You, in the future, Lord. I pray that I would find time to pray often, Lord, and that I would seize those opportunities.

Amen

12-12-11

Lord,

Your love endures forever. What my parents have for me, You have a hundred fold. And You always will. No matter how many times I sin, Your love will not waver. You have set my heart free, Father. Even though I've committed adultery with the sinful nature for as long as I can remember, You died so I could be free of myself. So I could be free of the curse of man. There is no greater gift than the salvation You've given me, Lord. Thank You.

Lord, direct my footsteps according to Your Word. May Your decrees be constantly in my mind, out-screaming the lies of the world. I thirst for Your truth, and Your law is true. Therefore, fill my mind with Your law. May Your laws sustain me; let me live that I may praise You.

Amen

12-14-11

I love You, Father. I love the feeling of peace that comes over me when I sing songs of worship to You. You are all-powerful, unshakeable, immutable. Who can move You an inch from where You stand? Who can change Your mind? Nobody. You will never change. I am so grateful that I can rely on Your love; that I can trust every word You say. Father, I pray for peace. In this stressful time of exams, I pray that I would find time to breathe. I pray that the exams would be exactly as the teachers said it would be; that there would be no bad surprises.

God, fill me with Your peace. Give me a clear mind and a strong nerve. It's easy to freak out at exam time, but I pray that I will not lose my cool. Give me the strength to fight my way through these difficult times, so that I may emerge victorious on the other side when it's all finally over.

Thank You, Lord.
Amen

12-17-11

Lord,
Out of the chaos in this fallen world, You make beautiful things. Out of sickness, out of pain, even out of death you make beautiful things. Hope is springing up from darkness, Father. Thank you for your redemption, thank you for rebirth, thank you for release from the bonds that once held.

I love You.
Mark

12-18-11

I love You Lord; You heard my voice and my cry for mercy. You turned Your ear to me; I will call on You as long as I live. When I was entangled in the cords of death, when I was overwhelmed by the anguish of the grave, You saved me. Not because I was good enough, not because I went to church, not because I prayed before eating. No, You rescued me because of Your mercy, because of Your compassion. Because of Your love that transcends all understanding. God, in seven days the world will celebrate Christmas. I pray that I would remember what is important on that day, Father that I wouldn't get so swept up in gifts that I forget the true meaning. I love You, Father. Thank You for Christmas coming up.

Mark

12-19-11

Lord,

I can climb highest mountain; I can run through the fields; I can scale city walls searching. I can kiss honey lips; I can search for healing in a girl's fingertips; I can hold the devil's hand, searching. Father I could do all these things trying to find fulfillment, trying to find true pleasure, (joy), trying to find peace, trying to find purpose. But I will not find them. I can only find meaning in You, God. Nothing on earth can satisfy me but You. No matter what I do besides, I still won't find what I'm looking for.

You fulfill me, You give me joy, You give me peace, You give me purpose.

You broke the bonds and You
Loosed the chains
Carried the cross
Of my shame
Of my shame…

I love You, Father. Thank You for Your grace. Thank You for Your love. Thank You for saving me.

Mark

Adapted from "I Still Haven't Found What I'm Looking For"
by U2

12-22-11

Lord,

You are the light of the world.

The light that will never flicker, dim or go out. The light within; the light within me.

Like lost ships the people of this world wander. Seeking shelter, seeking home, seeking safety.

You are the lighthouse. You guide our paths, You lead us to safety. Father give Your light to my mouth, as it sings of hope, of You. Give

Your light to my hands, so they can play for You.

I long to sing to You a new song; to play skillfully, to shout for joy. I long to show people Your grace, Your love through music. Please, Father, make me into the best singer/guitarist I can be, so that I can serve You through song. This is what I long for. This is my dream.

I love You,
Mark

12-25-11

Jesus,

Happy Birthday! I love celebrating Your birth every year even though the world tries to hide You. Father, thank You so much for sacrificing Your heavenly throne and being born as a baby. Your sacrifice shows how much You love us. If You were willing to come into this broken, dark world to save us, You must really care for us. Thank You.

Thank You for the awesome day I had today, Father. I got some awesome stuff, got to eat donuts and monkey bread, hang with my awesome girlfriend, and be with my family. I had a great time, which

I'm sure will continue tomorrow when we have Christmas part 2. Father, I pray that I'd have fun at Gram's, but I also pray that my time apart from Carley will feel short. I'm gonna miss her, God, as always, and I pray that we'd have an awesome two days together when I get back. Thank You for her, God. Thank You.

I love You,
Mark

12-27-11

Father,

I confess that I have sinned. I sometimes allow bitterness to well up inside me against someone, and that bitterness becomes something like hatred. That really is what it is: hate. There are certain people that annoy me so much that I allow myself to only think negatively of them. And that's wrong.

I understand that I can choose if I think this way about people or not. And although it's really hard sometimes, I am called to choose to love others. I understand that I have a problem with that, Father, and I pray that You would guide me as I struggle with this issue. Thank You for Your eternal forgiveness, Father that I can confess without fear. I love You.

In Your name,
Amen

1-2-12

Father,

A new year has begun. This year, I turn fifteen, get my permit, and hopefully go to more awesome concerts.

I'm excited for what's in store. I love the beauty of growth, of creation. I can only imagine how I'll grow this year, Father. The mystery of the future is known only to You, God. You know my future. My future career, my future relationships, my future growth.

I have a dream. I dream to front a band, playing music that honors You. I dream to show Your hope Your joy, Your peace, Your love through music. I want this so bad, God, but I understand it may not be what You have in store for me. Whatever may come, please give me peace. Please give me contentment. Please give me joy. Guide me as I try to follow my dream, but show me if it is not Your plan.

Thank You.
Mark

1-8-12

Father,

You are amazing. You work in such powerful ways; the very day I was worried about not being able to make the first Nicaragua payment, I came home to letters containing the money I needed. And still I get more.

I'm so thankful for these donations, God.

Thank You so much for the trip coming up this summer, God. I'm incredibly excited to return to Nicaragua and to get to do Your work there. I have the feeling it's going to be an awesome experience.

On a completely different note, I pray for Will*, that he would heal quickly and wouldn't be in too much pain. Please let him be able to snowboard, because he'd be really upset if he wasn't.

Thank You,
Mark

*Will had broken his arm.

1-10-12

Father,

Your beauty is becoming very prevalent to me in nature. I look at the sunlight filtering through the trees, and it makes me think of You.

Thank You for all the ways I can see You and Your love.

God, I confess I feel like I haven't done much with my life and the future sometimes feels hopeless. When I look back at what I've done, I can't think of anything I've done for others that's big. Carley asked me what the most important thing I've ever done is, and I honestly don't know. I hate that: Looking back at my life and feeling like I haven't done anything massively important.

Father, CALL me. CALL me to serve You in a specific way, like You called Carley to give Olivia that bike. I long for a moment like that to look back and cherish, but I don't want to do it like something I just check off a list.

Father, on a grander scale; my music. Being in a band* is something I want to do, and I want to do it to serve You. But I understand that that might not end up happening. However, whatever I do in the future I want to do to serve You. And I know there's a wide range of things I can do. God, I just pray that You would guide me. I'm searching for MY mission, my purpose on this earth. And it's a scary, frustrating search. However, I know that what You have planned will come about.

I have desires, God, but Your desires are more important. Therefore, Your will be done. Not mine, but Yours. Guide me.

Mark

*Note: Mark joined a band just a few months before his death so his dream was fulfilled.

1-14-12

Dear God,

Everyone at school seems to build some type of a reputation. Some people are shy, some are outgoing, some are obnoxious. My reputation is this: People seem to think of me as a mature, respectful, responsible, Christian person. Some may think of me as carefree. Some may think of me as the perfect boyfriend.

Of course, it's great when people compliment me. That's not really the issue. The issue is my response. All these compliments make me prideful; well, really I make myself prideful. I view myself as this great person; and I sometimes find myself thinking I'm above other people. That's called arrogance.

I may not show my pride outwardly, but it's on the inside, sneakily eating me up. Father, if I continue on this path of false self-righteousness, it will change me, and the change will **not** be for the better. I can't let this continue. Show me how to be humble, **truly** humble, God. To put others above me; to not look at myself proudly and haughtily. If I don't destroy this, it **will** destroy me. Stand by me. Give me strength to kill this hypocritical perspective. This has got to be stopped. I've never realized how big an issue it is, but You've revealed to me my fault. Thank You.

Mark

Note: This explains a turning point in Mark's life that we witnessed, but didn't fully comprehend at the time. Up to this point, Mark was a rather introverted, one- or two-friend kind of guy. He was always pretty sweet and compliant but could be prone to melancholy and self-centeredness like many of us. When we were visiting his sister in Nicaragua a couple of years before, he turned his head away in disgust from the plate of food the orphanage had generously offered him. When I held it up to the Nicaraguan boys there and asked who wanted it, they swarmed me and tore it from my hands. I remember Mark's shocked expression when he realized how ungrateful he had been. But when he made this inner decision to be positive, what we saw on the outside was a joyful, social person coming to life.

When I went through a kale-eating phase, I remember serving up some kind of dinner that he clearly thought was hideous—the slow chewing and tiny bites made that obvious. I asked him what he thought, and he said, "It's alright. Thanks for making it, Mom." In the littlest of ways he demonstrated kindness and thankfulness, not because he was a nice guy, but because of a decision he had made to be grateful.

1-18-12

Father,

I've discovered something important: Life is a matter of perspective. When I wake up, if I look at my day as though it's going to be boring or hard or something like that, then I'll probably have a bad day. But if I look at it in a positive light, and focus on that as I live the day, I'll most likely have a good day. This is much more important than it seems. Perspective determines how you live, and in a way, who you are. I remember around this time last year I was living with a negative perspective. Then Carley told me she was going to start thinking more positively. I guess I realized that that was a good idea, so I made that decision as well. Now, I feel like

I fully understand the importance of positive thinking. Lord God, help me to see the beauty in all things. Not just in things I like, but things I don't as well. Be it something as small and trivial as food, or something deep and complex like people. You can't love someone if you have a negative perspective.

Thank You Father.
Mark

1-22-12

Father,

Your love is strong. You show Your love for me, for the world, through an uncountable amount of blessings. Lately, I've been sitting down and writing down a lot of those blessings. It's amazing how many there are.

Thank You for loving me, God. I, a sinner, who lived in death. You died for me; You took those lashes; You wore those thorns. It's amazing, the sacrifice You made. I'll never be able to fully understand it. I wish I somehow could so that I could be more thankful to You. You are the most precious gift, the most powerful sacrifice, the most courageous King.

Thank You.
Mark R

1-31-12

Father,

Thank You for Your Word. Thank You that even though I may have heard a passage a million times, I can still get something new out of it. I pray that as I read Your Word, You would give me an open mind and heart so that I can apply the passages to my life. May I learn something new every time I dive into Your Book.

Thank You,
Mark

2-26-12

Dear God,

First of all, thank You so much that I'm a pastor's son. When I have questions about the Bible or anything like that, Dad's always there for me. Thank You for him.

Lord, tonight I talked to Dad about service. I asked him why shouldn't we sell our comforts if we could save lives with the money we gain. He had two main points that stuck out to me: God doesn't call us to save the world; and it depends on what God's called me to do.

What are You calling me to do, God? I don't feel like You're calling me to live a life of poverty, selling all that I have to help the poor. God, I pray that whatever it is You're calling me to do, You would scream until the walls of my stubborn mind collapse. I will try to listen, but I often try to drown You out. However, my ignorance is no match for Your call, so show me what You want me to do. Put me where You can work through me.

Thank You,
Mark

3-13-12

Dear God,

You are so BIG. Bigger than I could imagine, infinitely bigger, stronger, more powerful than I am.

You speak, and searing balls of gas trillions of times the size of earth are formed. You opened Your mouth and light split the untouched darkness. You spoke, and life was made. But You didn't speak me into being. No, No, No. When man entered the world, You stretched out Your hand and FORMED him. You didn't watch the power of Your words in man's case; no, You breathed life into man.

You love me more than I could ever understand. You love me more than all the cosmos that dazzle me, than the music that entrances me, than the sunsets that floor me. I don't understand it. I really don't. But God, thank You. Thank You that You love the brokenness humanity is.

Thank You. Thank You. THANK YOU.

Mark

3-14-2012

Dear God,

Today I heard that I must throw off any sin that hinders my walk with You. However, I still gave in to temptations today. I still sinned.

God, sin is a tricky thing. It sneaks up on you, making you unsure of when to flee.

Lord, I pray that when the very beginning of temptation enters my head, I would flee. Give me strength to push the thought away, and if it pursues, give me the strength to flee. When I am tempted, remind me why that sin is wrong. Remind me why I don't want to do that sin.

Lord, I am not bound by sin. I have been crucified with Christ; sin's chains have been cast off. Help me, Father. Please pull me away from returning to those chains.

I will not, must not, put those chains back on. Take control, Father. Please stop the temptations that keep chasing me by screaming why they are bad.

Mark

3-14-12

Where is God in the wind?

Where is God in the earthquake?

Where is God in the fire?

These are not questions of doubt, but questions of faith. I must have faith that He is always there, in every situation I go through. In all the metaphorical winds, earthquakes and fires. All I have to do is search and He will reveal himself to me.

3-27-12

Lord Jesus,
tomorrow is the day I've been waiting for for so long: The day I actually play guitar in front of people. I guess you could call it my debut.
But I dont want it to be my debut.
I want it to be about YOU.

I WAS MADE TO WORSHIP

Lord, thank you that I get to play tomorrow. Please give me courage. May I play my best for you God. Thank You.

We are playing worship music. This isn't a talent show. ~~I am not~~ The focus shouldn't be on me, but on YOU.

Lord, give me the strength to keep my mind focused on you tomorrow. May every note I sing, every chord I hit, praise You. Keep the reason why I'm playing at the forefront of my mind.

4-4-12

Dear God,

In four days the world will celebrate Easter. They will wake up to baskets of candy, chocolate bunnies and Easter egg hunts. Some will go to church. Some will offer up a prayer of thanks. But then many of those people will go on with their days, their main focus being candy and fun.

Father, I do NOT want to be one of those people.

In the past, my Easters have always been focused on candy and treats and other things. Usually in the day there is some speck of guilt that my Easter is not more Christ-focused.

I want this year to be different.

This year, I want You to be my focus, with the candy being a little side pleasure. It's so stupid that something as worthless as candy can take the place of the Resurrection of the ***God of the Universe.*** This year, I dedicate my Easter to ***You***. It is You I celebrate, You I love. Easter is ***Your*** day, not some stupid egg-toting bunny's. I love You, Lord. You're worth so much more than the things of this world.

Amen

April 9, 2012

Mark turns fifteen years old

4-10-12

Dear God,

Thank you so much for these past couple days. Easter was AWESOME. I loved celebrating your Resurrection. It was honestly the best Easter yet and I think that's because my eyes were open to the real purpose of the holiday. Makes me excited for the Christ holidays in the future. The day after Easter was my birthday. Man, was that a fun day. I loved getting to spend nearly all the day at Busch Gardens with the Schancks. Thank You so much that the lines went well for us, God. And on a more important note, thank You for my family. They love me so much. My parents are AWESOME. They care so much for me and will do their best to always be there for me. Thank You for the Schancks. It's easy

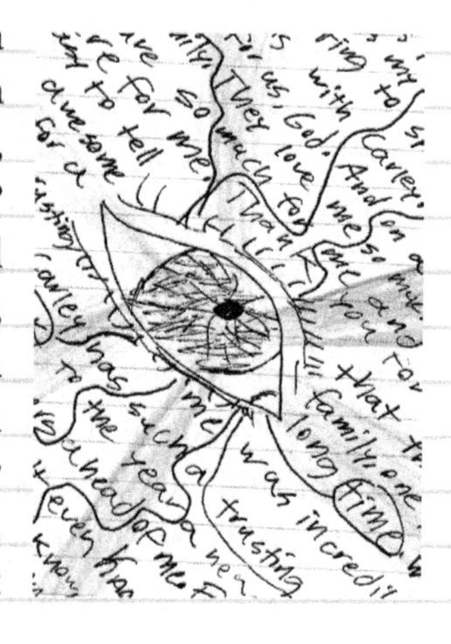

to tell that they care about me. They're an awesome family and one that I hope I'm connected to for a long time. Finally, Lord, I look to the year ahead of me. Excitement? Adventure? Heartbreak? I don't know if I'll make it through the year. But You know, Father. Lord, this year I want to know You more. I want to see Your beautiful love all around me. Keep my eyes wide open to your blessings, Father. I'm excited for what is in store. You will never leave me, and that gives me courage.

Thanks,
Mark

4-18-12

After all the lights go down, I'm just the words you are the sound...

Dear God,
E-man was talking in chapel today about how we will need new people to step up and lead music in chapel next year. Strangely enough, me and Logan were talking about the same thing yesterday. Are you trying to show me you want me to lead chapel? Lord God, part of me wants to, but part of me is scared to death of singing in front of people. Please Lord, force me in the right direction, I have come to understand that that is often uncomfortable, but it's also something I sometimes must confront. Lord Jesus, you are my King. I strive to obey your decrees. Please help me to have courage to carry out your will.

Love,
Mark

Lord,

I want to be so far gone in You, so far nothing else will ever do. I love You. You take the broken, sinful person I am and love me anyways. Thank You.

Mark

4-22-12

Dear Lord,

Tomorrow I'm giving a devotional in English on bitterness. Lord, bitterness is a sin that is so brutal, so secretive. It festers in our hearts and takes control. Lord, I pray that my message would reach my classmates tomorrow. I know it's just another project but it's one that has meaning, potential. Open people's eyes tomorrow to the bitterness in their own hears, and guide them along the path that leads to love.

I love You,
Mark

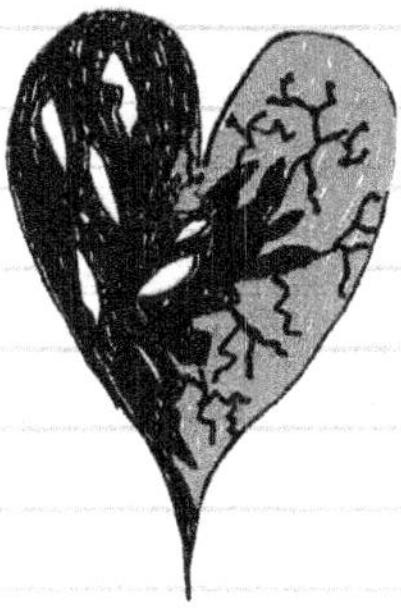

4-29-12

It would be right, fair, just of You to blow me to a million pieces. I have neglected You time and time again. I sin so much. So I have one question.

WHY DO YOU LOVE ME?

5-2-12

I can't wait for the day I see You. This world is so chaotic, so broken, so sinful. Things are not the way You built them to be, and

that is our fault. Sometimes, when I see a baby, I think to myself, "This poor kid is going to grow up someday. He is going to face pain, and sin will fight to make him succumb." I just wish that kid could be home, right now, with You. I wish it could all be over, that we could be up in Heaven happily ever after. That things could be how they were meant to be before we humans messed it up.

But the time isn't up. The story isn't finished yet. There are millions out there walking in darkness; not all of them will come into the light.

I just wish all this sorrow, all this sin, could be over with, You know? That I could go home.

But at the same time, I know there are things I want here. I want to grow up, get married, raise a family, start a job… and so much more. Also, I know I have a purpose here. This black world needs firelight, and in order for it to be carried, light needs a lantern. ***I am a lantern.***

I am Your megaphone. I'm just the words, but You're the sound. I want people to see through the glass walls of my lantern and be awed by Your fire. I want Your fire to eclipse me so completely that You're all they see. I am worthless if I fight that, because that is my purpose: to glorify You; to proclaim You.

Lord, eclipse my dark with Your light. I can't believe how much I downsize You. You are so much more than I could ever imagine. Open my eyes to the murk on my lantern that blocks people from seeing the fire. Without fire, a lantern is useless. It exists for one sole purpose, to proclaim light. To display the fire within for all to see.

Shine through me.

Burn past me.

Eclipse me.

Silence me so Your voice may ring.

You mustn't just become greater. I mustn't just become less. You must become ***everything***. I must proclaim that ***everything*** to ***everyone.***

Or my time here is ***nothing***.

Mark

5-10-12

Father, I have been so busy lately, I haven't been able to find much time in Your word. Thankfully, this mini-era of busy seems to be coming to an end. I'm really happy about that, not just because I can be more chill, but also because I am able to have time to speak with You once more.

You are amazing, God. You are so beautiful, and You've created so many beautiful things. I can't believe You love me even though I dishonor Your sacrifice all the time. I can't imagine what it would be like to be You, having to know that even though You gave it all for those You love, they reject that. Help me to recognize the sin that pollutes my life, God, so that I may fight to do away with it. I love You. I confess I have sinned.

Mark

5-19-12

Dear God,

Thanks so much that I get to lead worship with such awesome people. Lord, I just pray that You would give us strength and drive as we prepare. Help us to keep our minds firmly focused on You; may every chord we hit, note we sing, or drum we play be for Your glory.

Amen

Teach me. Sing to me.
Show me. Use me.
Change me. Burn past me.
Charge me. Form me.
Send me. Create me.
Free me. Know me.
Call me. Stand by me.
Eclipse me. Walk with me.
Transform me. Convict me.
Move me. Save me. Run to me.
Fight for me. Love me. Speak to me.
Draw me. Lead me. Forgive me.
Promise me. Empower me. Accept me.
Receive me. Help me. Redeem me.
Speak for me. Prune me.
Strengthen me. Guide me.
Replenish me. Place me.
Rebuild me. Surround me.
Remind me. Challenge me.
Fill me. Raise me.
Protect me. Complete me.
Mold me.
Own me.
Stand by me.

CONSUME ME

6-1-12

Father, become my life.

Influence my every action; show me You are greater than any other god. Fill me up with Your love, send me into the day consumed by You.

I am NOTHING without You.

You are Everything.

6-6-12

God, tonight I go back to Nicaragua for the first time in three years. Lord, Satan doesn't want us to make this trip. He will do whatever it takes to stop us from serving You. But You are with us, and You are stronger than he is. Give us peace and strength, Lord. Keep us unified so that we may be one force, not a divided one.

Thank You for this opportunity. I love You.

Mark

Note: There is a place in Nicaragua called Ruby's House of Prayer. Here, Christian Nicaraguans would pray for visitors. When Mark and his mission team visited, the people surrounded Mark and prayed a blessing on him. But he was also told in that prayer that his family would be divided because of his calling. He was very upset about this and didn't understand. I remember he got home from Nicaragua at around 4:00 a.m., and he was wide awake and wanting to talk. But he did not want to discuss what he had been warned about. I knew something was troubling him and pressed. He told me how upset he was and how worried he was that we might be divided. I told him that there was no way he would ever be separated from our love. No matter what he believed or what he did, he would always be our son. Inwardly, I was frustrated that someone had instilled such a fear into him because division was not something we considered an option in our family. Now, looking back, we see that the prayer warning that our family might be divided because of Mark's calling came true, just not in the way he feared. It came true not because of a conflict or situation in our family life, but rather because his calling involved his death at the age of seventeen.

6-12-12

I am a sword. In order to bring love and healing, I was told I may have to bring division and I have a feeling that I will. And apparently, this division may be within my own family. *MY OWN FAMILY.*

They told me, "Don't be afraid of leadership; bind spirit of doubt; YOU ARE READY; lead those who are older; embrace what He has given you; grab hold with both hands; God has removed fear; time to raise up; you are free don't be afraid; angels support you; It is not about you; God gives you power and authority; pray for the sick; God is anointing your life; speak through you; family sees new life in you and there may be division."

As much as I love unity, I may have to be the one to break that unity for Your love, Your healing, Your glory. And that's kinda scary. Division isn't some small event. It's big, thunderous, and messy. The thought of being the catalyst for that type of thing ... it's crazy. It's a job that's a lot bigger than me.

So thank goodness I'm not alone in that. Give me strength, Father. Thank You so much for choosing me for such an important job. Please continue to reveal to me what it means to not rely on my own strength. I love You Lord, and I thank You so much for speaking to me today.

Love,
Mark

6-14-12

"Gratitude is an attitude leading to peace."

Lord,

It's incredible how blessed we are, but it's astounding how easily we can ignore that. Your blessings are a part of Your grace. We have done nothing to deserve them. Yet somehow, we turn away from the beautiful things You hold out to us because of a love of ourselves. The product of this? Discontent, sorrow, longing, anger, murder, death, sexual immorality. We seek our own blessings that we build of broken darkness instead of Your blessings of perfect light. What are the results of Your blessings? Peace, joy, contentment, laughter, giving. "Our" blessings only result in evil, but Yours result in perfect good. And in that goodness we have peace. We go to sleep knowing You love us, we rise with excitement to see Your beauty in new ways. The product of this peace is joy, which is like water. It flows through our actions, our thoughts our lives. May that joy flow out of our team* today, Lord. May that joy give us hearts to serve and love others. Reveal to each member of the team Your blessings, so that we may live with a spirit of peace.

I love You,
Mark

*Nicaragua Missions Team

6-19-12 (Returning home from Nicaragua)

Right now, I'm staring at the most beautiful thing I've ever seen. I'm 40,000 feet above the ground, and it's 7:48 p.m. I'm on a flight from Miami to Washington DC, coming home from the two week Nicaragua trip.

It's a sunset. Rays of light fill my eyes and blast the sky and the Atlantic Ocean below with golden light. There is no land in sight, only water and sky. Puffy clouds of all shapes and sizes dot the scene far below, lit on fire by yellow beams. The ocean miles beneath me is laughing joyfully painted with the sun's reflection. Shadows are cast across the canvas by the sun exploding over the clouds. Next to me in the window seat, Mrs. Sandwell is sleeping. She's facing out over the ocean because when she was awake she was gazing at the real-life painting. She's one of the few people I've met that I can tell loves God's beauty as much as I do.

I'm caught in this moment. Right now I just feel God smiling at me and saying, "I love you so much." I told Mrs. Sandwell the most incredible thing about this is that we don't deserve it. I'm staring into that blinding light right now, while what I should be looking at is utter, crippling darkness. "The wages of sin is death, but the gift of God is eternal life through Christ Jesus our Lord."

What I'm talking about here is grace. I did not choose God, I chose me. I chose my way, so that I may have fleeting pleasures that have no worth.

But God chose me.

He looked at me and didn't find something about me that was better than other people. I was no more righteous than any other man, because we are not righteous in ourselves. God bestowed righteousness upon me, though He found no merit or love for him. God ripped me from the grasp of Satan and said to me that He is so much better, so much brighter than anything I could ever comprehend.

And He was so, so, so right.

My dreams can't rival this. My deepest thoughts cannot create anything as incredible as the scene that's bestowed up me.

I'm wondering right now: If this broken, fallen world can have this much of God's beauty in it, what will the New Earth be like? An earth purged of selfishness, of corruption, of pain? I'll definitely need a new body in order to stand before that because I'm pretty sure the one I'm in now would explode if I saw anything more beautiful than what I'm already looking at.

All I know is this: Trouble will come. I will cry, I will hurt, I will break. But the Lord of the sky will always, ALWAYS be by my side. He will always be amazing me beyond the boundaries I try to put Him in.

I just can't believe the Lord of the sunset loves ME. I mean, of course I believe it, but it's just so… so unfair. Fair equals me never seeing a sunset. But "the beauty of grace is that it makes life not fair." I am so, so thankful for that.

DEAR ONE, THIS IS ONLY A FRACTION OF WHAT'S TO COME. KEEP YOUR EYES OPEN.

MARK, I WANT YOU TO SEE ME.

NO MATTER HOW WELL YOU THINK YOU KNOW ME, I WILL ALWAYS BE ABLE TO AMAZE YOU EVEN FURTHER

"I want to be a freaking revolution. I want to ruffle feathers. I want to burn with holiness. I want to offend society by my existence. I want my hands to heal and cast out demons. I want to die a lover of God, going closer than anyone has ever dared."

—Ariel Bloomer, lead singer of Icon for Hire

7-3-12

Apathy.

It's one of the things I'm most afraid of, and one of the things I'm least understanding of.

My life is something others beg for, be they Ugandans or Nicaraguans or other Americans. There aren't riots on my streets. I am not being fiercely oppressed by my government. I'm not bullied at school. I'm not battered by a fierce social ladder in my grade.

I always have enough food in my pantry. I don't have any haters. I have a pretty girlfriend. I don't have to slave away to support my family. I've lived such a safe life it almost seems ridiculous to me sometimes. It's extraordinary for someone to be this protected in such a dangerous world. I sometimes feel like I live in a world of glass, a utopia. Don't get me wrong, I've cried a couple times in life, but mostly it's been because of petty, selfish things (I'm referring to when I was younger). The last time I've cried wasn't for a stupid reason, I was in a spiritual battle. But my wise, loving, awesome dad was there for me.

There are so many people who would consider their life complete if they had just one of the things I mentioned above. And that's where this whole apathy thing comes in. My idea of an apathetic me is a Mark who just lives in his utopia, soaking up the blessings, intentionally oblivious to any sadness or hurt outside his world. I'm not saying that enjoying blessings is wrong. They're meant to bring joy. It would be completely inconsiderate to reject blessings because there are people out there who lack them. That helps nobody. The reason I fear apathy is I fear I'll slip into a life of ignorance. I'm terrified of never leaving my comfort zone, yet I'm terrified of leaving it as well. There are opportunities to love, to help, to listen, to bless that I have passed up because of my utter <u>selfishness</u>. Opportunities I could have <u>seized</u>.

Carley is someone who I feel seizes those opportunities. She gets so much joy out of making someone feel important. I'm lying if I say I haven't had these opportunities because I <u>know</u> I have. I can think of them.

So how will tomorrow be different? Maybe I just passionately wrote out my feelings and tomorrow will check back in to my utopia of blissful ignorance. I sure pray that's not what happens. I think a way that I could start to move in a new direction would be if I'm a bit more open to people who aren't necessarily my core group of friends. If I'm more friendly, be it to acquaintances or strangers, maybe I can help them. There are people all around me whose lives are warzones, and they are <u>crying</u> for help. One thing's for sure, I can't let this be a checklist. Yay, someone confided in me, I'm not apathetic. Because it's not a checklist, it's a lifestyle. Tomorrow, when I wake up, I pray that it would be with eyes of love, with a relational, amicable attitude. Apathy can NOT own me.

Mark

7-9-12

I don't know how Nicaragua has changed my life, and I'm truly not sure it has.

First off, should Nicaragua have changed my life? There's nothing I think of that says so, but it seems almost… selfish, maybe, if I left it as the kid I was before.

Sure there are little things like noticing how inconsiderate I and others are sometimes. But I feel like my memories, at least my most prevalent ones, were of me having fun.

I just have this deep sense there should be more. Was the trip supposed to be a vacation? Heck no! It was a mission. A mission of light, designed and intended by God Himself!

So why aren't my main memories about others? Hold up… Okay, I guess some of them are. A friend forgiving her father wasn't exactly fun, and it sure as heck wasn't a "me" event.

I suppose what I feel is that those events should have impacted me more. And not just those events, but the entire trip.

I just don't know how to feel.

Lord God, help me. Give me the correct perspective. I just feel like I haven't changed in the way I should. What is that way? Enlighten me, speak to me Father!

Should things be different?

7-15-12

Dear God,

You are incredible. I see Your beauty all around me, in people, in places, in things. I can't believe some people believe that the intricate beauty of nature happened by accident.

It's so cool that I can know You personally. You created the entire universe, yet You want a relationship with me. That's just so incredible; please don't ever let me take that for granted.

Mark

8-1-12

She will provide for those who
Grieve in Zion—
To bestow on them a crown of beauty instead of ashes,
The oil of gladness instead of mourning,
And a garment of praise instead
Of a spirit of despair.

MARK, DON'T THINK YOU'RE ONLY HERE TO SUPPORT OTHERS, TO JUST SPEND YOUR LIFE WATCHING OTHER PEOPLE DO GREAT THINGS. I HAVE PLANS FOR YOU, GREAT PLANS. YOU HAVE NO IDEA HOW I CAN USE YOU. DON'T BE DISCOURAGED. BE FAITHFUL AND PATIENT. I HAVE NOT FORGOTTEN YOU.

8-4-12

Dear God,

Calling. I hate and love that word. What is my calling? Some people seem called to help the poor. I seem called to do... what? It's hard to hear them speak with such a focused passion when I don't have one. It makes me feel... almost inferior. Like I'm just here, moseying through life while their heart breaks for the broken.

When will my heart break for Your work? What will it before? I wish it would happen now, so I wouldn't feel like this passionless dude.

I'm impatient, I know. And I confess I'm jealous. I just... I want to be used. I'm searching, longing for whatever my calling may be. Please help me God. Tell me something, GUIDE me.

Mark

PSALM 27 NOTES

Vs4 I don't need to wait till Heaven to gaze upon the beauty of the Lord
Vs8 Even my own heart tells me to seek God
Vs14 My time will come

OH FATHER SHINE, MARK RODRIGUEZ

Chorus:
There is light within
It's burning bright
O Father, Shine

What a sight, my Father's might
You are so bright
O Father, Shine
Father, Shine

V1. I felt cold so I started a fire
Fueling it with my own desire
Couldn't keep it going, I needed more
But even the richest king is too poor

PC But then I was warm, because you were shining
Shining down on me

[Chorus]

V2. Thought I was blind but I covered my eyes
Stumbling into my own demise
In a pit of pleasures I let myself fall
But the deepest hole can't cover your call
PC And then, I could see, because you were shining, shining into me.

[Chorus]

Bridge: Oh my God
You are the rising sun
Oh my God
The revival has begun
Oh my God

Darkness turns and runs
Oh my God
The Battle has been won

Chorus: There is a light within this night
It's burning bright
O Father, Shine
[palm muted/acoustic]

There is light within this night
It's burning bright
O Father, Shine

What a sight, my Father's might
You are so bright
O Father, shine
Shine,
Shine,
Shine

THE PRODIGAL, BY MARK RODRIGUEZ

V1: You are majesty
I am poverty
Yet you want all of me
It's something powerful

I didn't bend my knee
Though it would make me free
Then you woke me up to see
You are so beautiful

Chorus:
I was the prodigal
Thought my chains, could set me free
I consumed but I was never full
Yet you want all of me, all of me

You chased me down, you picked me up
Won't thirst again, you filled my cup
And I was the prodigal
Yet you want all of me, all of me

V2: My iniquities
Fatal disease
But you can rescue me
You are all-powerful

Note: The following is written about a place in Nicaragua called La Chureca, or "The Dump." This was literally a trash dump that became occupied by a community of the homeless in Nicaragua. Fabiola was a young girl who was living in the dump and was abused repeatedly. Norfolk Christian was able to minister to her and her family over the years. When she was eight, she stopped eating and told her mother "NO MORE"—to the abuse by men in the dump—she gave up and told her mom that she wanted to die. This story haunted Mark and drove him to want to help victims of human trafficking. Casa Belen was a home set up to help such victims, and Fabiola temporarily lived there until she returned to her old life.

9-12-12

Sometimes, when I am walking, I unlock my mind and let memory take over. The tall, strong houses around me crumble down into huts, huts made of trash. The road beneath my feet crumbles away until there's nothing left but a dirt path rutted with potholes. Everything green: the grass, the trees, it all melts away. And then comes the garbage. It covers everything: the path, the houses, the lawns. And then the smell hits. The most pervasive, disgusting, rotten smell on earth, the smell of miles and miles of trash and human waste.

There's no doubt about it, I'm in the Chureca.

I climb up a ladder, pulling a tarp over the roof of one of the huts to help keep the family within dry. The tarp keeps slipping off, so in broken Spanish I ask a shirtless boy next to me if he can climb up and use rocks to weigh it down. And then breaks forth a smile, one of the most beautiful, innocent, joyful smiles I've ever seen. Like a squirrel, the boy climbs up onto the roof with ease and proceeds to help us.

As I try to position the roof right, I look over at the boy's mother, the owner of the house. She is smiling too, and though her teeth are dirty and yellow her smile is a thousand times more beautiful than any supermodel's. Her joy is contagious, and I find myself smiling too. I'll never forget her and her son's smiles. In the depths of poverty, in the heart of hell on earth there is joy, there is radiance. I wish I'd known more Spanish, I would have loved to speak with that woman, to tell her she's special, loved.

And then, the picture flickers as my foot catches on a tilted slab of sidewalk. And suddenly, I am back in the Land of the Free, the Home of the Brave. The land of perfectly set bricks, of water in abundance of full pantries but nothing to eat.

At school, it's sometimes hard to focus because while I'm getting my expensive, college-prep education, six-year-old girls are being forced into prostitution.

I just sit there wanting to scream, thinking how there's nothing I can do to save them, to save the families of the Chureca while I'm here. No matter how hard I want to, I have to remind myself that even if I was there, I wouldn't know how to save the Churecans. No, I must wait. While Fabiola, a twelve-year-old whose been forced into prostitution for six years, has mind and body destroyed. Her smiling, laughing face haunts me because I know that she is being destroyed, and even worse, that she's given up.

But God is not giving up. He does not turn a blind eye to the Fabis of the world. I have no idea what He has in store for her, for me. All I know is He wants me to go back, I'm just not sure when.

Until then, I must wait. I must wait knowing Fabi is being tortured. And there's no way to not think about it, no way to put it out of my mind. Which is probably a good thing, because if I were able to just forget about that, something would be wrong with me.

Until I am sent back, I will pray. I will pray without ceasing for Fabi, for Chureca, for Casa Belen.

There IS one thing I can do for them, and that's pray.

And I will wait in earnest, longing for my return.

Mark

9-17-12

I'm obsessed.

Obsessed with Nicaragua. With Fabi. With Casa Belen. With the injustice.

I can't, won't stop thinking about Nicaragua. My body is here while my heart is there.

WHEN, O Lord will You send me back? How long must I sit in school for hours on end while Fabi is destroyed, maimed, twisted? Her face won't leave my mind, I promise that.

God, she's given up. The forces of darkness wore her down and drew the fight out of her. She believes she's worthless, junk, ugly.

My God, save her. Free her. Show her that she is so much more than what these men, her mother say she is. Get her out of there, God. Wake her mother up. PLEASE. Show her light beats darkness. I pray a future for her, Lord, a life for herself. May she radiate joy so brightly that she becomes a weapon for You. Put the fight back in her God, show her she's worth something. Until then, as she suffers, I won't stop thinking about her, praying for her.

God, let me fight injustice. Let me proclaim freedom for the oppressed. Take me over, and proclaim light to the world. Please, tell me what to do about returning to Nicaragua.

Free Fabi.

Mark

10-21-12

Father,

There are times I feel inferior in relation to my friends. Times that I feel I act immaturely, or say the first joke that's in my mouth, even if it's not really that funny.

The liar tells me I am weak, impulsive, awkward, young, fake, scared, selfish, arrogant. When I tell a joke and no one laughs he whispers that I'm an annoyance. And he keeps whispering, ***ALWAYS*** in my ear.

He tells me Carley deserves better than me. Better than a dorky, dumb guy who thinks he's funny but really isn't. And it is so dang easy to believe him. That she could do so much better than me. It drives me INSANE. Little things that happen that make me feel like those I love are so much better than me.

THOSE WHISPERS, MARK, COME FROM THE FATHER OF LIES. THOSE THINGS HE SAYS TO YOU ARE OF HIS NATIVE LANGUAGE: LYING. HE MAY TELL YOU THAT YOU'RE WORTHLESS, BUT LISTEN TO ME.

I HAVE POWERFUL PLANS FOR YOU. IN MY NAME YOU WILL PERFORM WONDERS. I DID NOT CALL YOU A SWORD FOR NOTHING. YOU WILL STRIKE THE WORLD WITH LOVE AND JOY. YOUR ELDERS WILL LISTEN TO YOUR WORDS. YOU WILL LEAD MIGHTILY, MY SON. DO NOT LISTEN TO SATAN. HE ONLY WANTS TO CRITICIZE YOU AND MAKE YOU FEEL EXACTLY AS YOU SOMETIMES DO; INFERIOR. I TELL YOU I HAVE GIVEN YOU A SPIRIT OF POWER AND LOVE. NOW THOSE ARE THE WORDS YOU SHOULD REMEMBER. LIVE AS A MAN INSPIRED COURAGEOUSLY. I WILL NEVER, EVER LET YOU GO.

I PROMISE.

11-15-12

Then I heard the voice of the Lord saying, "Whom shall I send, and who will go for us?" And I said, "Here am I. Send me!" *Isaiah 6:8*

DEAR ONE,

I DID NOT CALL YOU TO BE A CREATURE CHASING FLEETING PLEASURES. NO, I CALLED YOU FROM THAT. I CALLED YOU TO BE A MAN OF LIGHT, WHO WALKS THROUGH LIFE LAUGHING IN AWE OF MY WONDERS.

WAKE UP, MY SON. I HAVE BLESSED YOU IN SO MANY WAYS. I PROMISE YOU JOY AND PEACE, THINGS THAT WILL

NOT BE GAINED IN FLEETING WANT BUT IN LOVE, IN FREEDOM, IN LIFE. I HAVE CALLED YOU TO LOVE FROM THE OUTPOUR OF JOY FROM YOUR HEART, SO THAT OTHERS MAY SEE MY GLORY AND TAKE PART IN MY BEAUTY. AWAKE, MY CHILD. THERE'S A WAR TO BE WON.

11-22-12 THANKSGIVING

Dear Lord,

You have given me so much to be thankful for. A loving family, great friends, an incredible girlfriend, and MANY other things. I feel like my eyes are opened to Your blessings more and more everyday filling me to the brim with joy and peace. I thank You so much that even by just walking outside, Your creation and world gives me joy. It's the best feeling in the world, knowing I am loved by the Creator of the Universe. Lord, today may I see Your blessings all the more. Thank You for dying for me, regardless of how messed up I was.

Thanks,
Mark

I know what it is to be in need,
and I know what it is to have plenty.
I have learned the secret
of being content in any and every situation,
whether well fed or hungry,
whether living in plenty or in want.
I can do everything through him
who gives me strength.
Philippians 4:12-13

Christmas 2012

12-25-12

Father,

It's terrible how much people have devalued this day. Though the holiday was created to celebrate Your Son's birth, the world has turned it into a day of getting and it seems that they are trying to suck the Christ out of Christmas.

Father, I pray that even though I'm going to get some cool stuff today, You would help me to remember the true meaning of Christmas. You gave up so much by becoming human, I don't want to disregard that sacrifice.

I love You,
Mark

12-27-12

Lord Jesus,

I'm sick of my vices. The sins that keep coming back and I *keep* giving in to them. Dear God, I want to be *free*. It seems impossible now, after failing so many times. How can I want to be free, yet repeatedly chain myself by my own will?

I'm SICK of it. Sin brings no joy. It brings fleeting pleasure but then deep pain. Pain that hurts ridiculously. For example, after failing time and time again, it's hard not to question my self-worth. To think of myself as weak. Although, truthfully, I am acting weak. I am not clinging to You in times of temptation. But I *want* myself to, Lord.

God, I don't know what to think. I don't know what to do. All I know is that when temptation rises up, I want it to be so absurd that I don't even think of giving in. I wanna be free, Jesus. I want to live a life of beauty and wonder, not of constantly giving in to sin.

I am a new Creation.

Mark

12-28-12

Praise be to God, who has not rejected my prayer
or withheld his love from me!
Psalm 66:20

Lord,

When I cry out to You, You listen. Even if sometimes it seems as though I'm just saying words, You ARE there and You DO hear what I say. Thank You, Lord that I can count on that.

Lord, You are incredible. Nature proclaims Your name to all the world, though many shut their ears. You've created such beautiful, complex things, some of which man will never understand. There's always something more to learn or discover.

Mark

NEW YEAR'S JANUARY 1, 2013

God,

Thank You so much for 2012. I feel like it was a huge year of growing and maturing for me. My relationship with Carley got even stronger and we love each other deeper. My relationship with my best friends solidified, and now we're trying to start a band. I became a more dedicated guitarist, a passionate photographer, and a more mature and confident boyfriend.

So, 2013. A whole year lies ahead of me, and for some reason I feel pretty good about it. One of my main goals is to get my band off the ground. Now this can honestly only be done with You on our side. We have a LOT of work to do, which can only be accomplished through dedication and sacrifice.

God, I have a New Year's resolution for once. I resolve to take risks in order to pursue my passions. To do things that get me way out of my comfort zone. People seem to almost hold part of my identity to excelling in school. I may have to sacrifice that in order to achieve what I'm passionate for. There is a sure road and an unsure road here. The sure road is me continuing to work hard in school, be sure of a good college and probably a well-paying job. The unsure road is just what it's called. Unsure. It could lead to success, it could lead to failure. However, I know that no matter what happens, You will be by my side. "I have learned the secret to being content in any and every situation. I can do all things through You who give me strength." Philippians 4:13 Here's to risks, fearlessness, and jumping off the diving board knowing my Father will catch me.

Mark

1-9-13

To Live is Christ, and to die is gain
Philippians 1:21

I love this verse so much, Lord. It makes me feel invincible, untouchable. If I'm alive, then I can serve and glorify Jesus, if I'm dead, I'm with Him. My enemies can't take that from me. Satan can't take that from me. No matter what, I will live forever, and I can have joy and peace every moment of that eternity. Now I know I'll block that joy and peace from myself sometimes, most likely in times of trouble. Which is kind of backwards, honestly. In a time of pain, why wouldn't I want joy and peace?

Anyways, Lord, I thank You that I have that assurance. That I'm untouchable, that I'm Yours. I am Your child. That's part of my identity as a new creation now. Give me the strength to remember that, to cling to it. No matter what troubles come, I am a child of God, and I will live forever.

Thank You,
Mark

1-12-13

Dear God,

You are incredible. I feel like in January there are so many gorgeous sunsets and sunrises; honestly they're what got me into photography. The skies really do proclaim the work of Your hands. God, there's a lot that I feel like I have to do today, and I confess that I'm allowing it to hinder my peacefulness. In fact, I've probably been doing that a lot lately. God, this time last year I was probably the most peaceful and joyful that I've ever been. And I still have peace and joy, but truthfully I've allowed my awe at Your blessings to somehow fade. That awe, that joy and peace, it increases my faith and decreases my self-indulgence because I know You're the best it gets. So Lord, I pray that You would give me the peace to not be stressed out all day. As I carry out the tasks I have to complete, fill me with a calm and peace that erases all worry. Help me not to waste time, to just sit around. I don't want to feel like I have to fill every scrap of time I have, but I certainly don't want to overindulge in Facebook and Instagram, which are honestly worth five minutes of my time a day.

Thank You for Your joy and peace, Lord.

Mark

Note: Sometime around the first of the year, Mark asked Carlos and I if he could go live in Nicaragua for the summer. My first reaction was "No Way!" after having lived there myself, but I didn't say that and agreed to pray about the decision. Carlos and I became more open to the idea and told Mark we would be comfortable with him going for a month if the conditions were ones we approved. This idea still seems crazy to me. He would only be sixteen years old, but he was so driven and passionate about it, we felt the least we could do would be entertain the idea. The more we talked to him, the more we became convinced it was right. Our dear family friends, Tim and Katie Adams, were going down for a month, so we timed Mark's trip with theirs, and he set up an internship at an orphanage. We missed him like crazy, but it is a decision we have never regretted. He grew in ways we could have never imagined, and his relationship with God was taken to a deeper level than ever before.

1-15-13

Lord,

You stun me. Even on a dreary, rainy day Your beauty is evident. In a Memphis May Fire song. In saying good morning to Carley. In playing guitar. It's everywhere Lord; there's nothing that can hide Your blessings from me but myself. Thank You for how plainly You show that You love me.

God, Carley and I were talking about an interesting concept the other day: *sleepwalking*, meaning living your life in ignorance of what we're called to do. I thought this was a very interesting concept because even though I am earnestly looking forward to my trip to Nicaragua in July, it's six months away. I'm not supposed to simply sit on my butt and hang out until July comes, I have a calling separate from Nicaragua that I need to fulfill here. There's nothing wrong with looking forward to Nicaragua, but I can't have my focus so far ahead that I don't see what's right in front of me. Lord, I could sleepwalk all the way to July but that's NOT what I want to do. Keep my eyes wide open Lord; show me what You want me to do in the here and now. I love You, thank You so much that I get to look forward to Nicaragua.

Mark

1-17-13

Your love never fails
Never gives up
Never gives up on me
And on and on and on it goes...

Adapted from "One Thing Remains" by Jesus Culture

Thank You, thank You, thank You, Jesus. You are limitless, boundless, endless. You paint the skies with love day and night. I swear I deserve none of it. But You surround me constantly with wonder, with newness, with sights and sounds that I've never known. Smile after smile escapes from my lips at the blessings in front of me. And Lord, these blessings are far from temporary. I'm going to live forever. With You. No person, no thing, can take that from me. "To live is Christ and to die is gain." (Philippians 1:21) "I have learned how to be content in any and every situation." (Philippians 4:11) You are with me in all I do, I need not be afraid. Write that on my heart Lord, let me never forget it.

Mark

1-22-13

Dear God,
You stun me. Set me on fire. Scare me. You heal me. You teach me. You speak to me. Lord, there's something I need. I am breaking down, losing joy under the weight of sin. I constantly say I want it

gone but it returns once again. And that's when the phrase "giving it to Jesus" comes to my mind. It's so cliché and I feel like I don't understand it at all. But God that's all I have left. I've failed time and time again and my only explanation for that is I've been trying to do this under my own power. But I am not strong enough. Oh my God, I'm not. So I don't know what this means, to let go and give this to You. I don't. But I'm giving it to You. And if I'm still somehow holding on take it from me. Please. I need You. I acknowledge that.

Create in me a clean heart,
O God, and renew a right spirit within me.
Psalm 51:10

Mark

1-23-13

God,

You are all that I'm made for. I'm not made to excel in school, to make music, or to take pictures. I'm made to worship You, to enjoy a relationship with You that surpasses all understanding. Right now, I'm stressed by the amount of work I have to do. Really stressed; I know I'm going to be up pretty late because of it. But Lord, I wanted to spend this time with You. I shouldn't have to find time for You in the midst of schoolwork. I should base my schoolwork around my time with You. Because I know my time with You is more rewarding and refreshing than anything. Yeah, I'm gonna be tired as mess when I wake up tomorrow. But Oh God, this is worth it. I can't live without time with You. I mean, I can survive but I can't *live, thrive*. I need You or my life is colorless. Your beauty penetrates my life and sets it aflame with Peace and Joy. Lord, I pray for that peace and joy right now. Strengthen me.

You're worth this ☺

Mark

1-25-12

MY CHILD,

I SEE SO MUCH POTENTIAL IN YOU. THE GIFTS, THE PASSIONS THAT YOU HAVE ARE MEANT TO OPEN PEOPLE'S EYES AND TO UNIFY THEM. YOU'VE BEEN PONDERING BEING IN A POSITION OF LEADERSHIP FOR A LONG TIME NOW, AND YOU'VE ALSO BEEN SADDENED BY THE LACK OF UNITY AMONG YOUR PEERS.

SON, IT IS TIME. UNITY WILL NOT SPONTANEOUSLY OCCUR, IT NEEDS A CATALYST. YOU ARE A CATALYST, MARK. YOUR PEERS, EVEN ADULTS LOOK UP TO YOU. YOU HAVE BEEN GIVEN WISDOM, PASSION, AND THIS SENSE OF JOY AND PEACE TO SHARE WITH THEM.

YOU ARE READY.

GRAB HOLD OF YOUR GIFTS WITH BOTH HANDS, MARK. UNLEASH THE LOVE FROM WITHIN YOU. YOU ARE FREE, DON'T BE AFRAID. IF YOU FALL I WILL CATCH YOU AND HELP YOU BACK TO YOUR FEET.

I PROMISE.

NOW, RISE UP.

1-29-13

God,

Thank You so much for these random warm winter days. There's nothing like a little slice of summer in the midst of January; thank You for giving me the chance to appreciate this. Lord, I've been pondering ways to start unifying my class, but the furthest I've gotten is being more friendly to people. Heck, maybe that'll have more effect than I think, but I know that's not all.

Lord, open my eyes. Guide me to ways to make my grade trust each other more, appreciate each other more, love each other more. You have put this unity in a special place in my heart: it is something I sincerely long for. I don't know how to accomplish this on my own,

I need Your strength and guidance.

Thank You,
Mark

1-30-13

Lord,

I'm extremely excited to worship You tomorrow. I feel like the songs I picked, "True Love" and "One Thing Remains" glorify You so simply, yet without clichés. Lord, I pray that people would be brought closer to You through worship tomorrow. May our passion and love for You be evident to all. There will be people, God, who look at us and think we're nuts. There always will be. But Lord, I pray that the unification we've been talking about would find a root in our worship. Let the songs be more than words, more than music. Let them be genuine, personal worship in which we draw close to You. When I pray and speak tomorrow, I pray that You would remove my faltering lips. Give me a strong tongue that speaks honesty and love. Thank You so much for this opportunity to worship You.

Mark

2-2-13

God,

You've created such beautiful sunrises lately. I love waking up at a natural time on the weekend and opening the window to Your beauty. You are truly incredible God. Lord, I want that fire from last January back in my heart. The fire that makes me marvel at every single little thing around me. There's so much I take for granted, Lord. Please give me the love for Your world, from the obvious things to the hidden.

Thank You,
Mark

2-6-13

God,

You are beautiful. You can bring me contentment through the simplest things, such as a light breeze on a warm day. I can literally feel You all around me, Lord. You've created and done so much more for me than I know. Thank You for loving me despite my failures.

God, I'm starting to give into anxiety and worry again. I'm very worried because Carley's birthday present still hasn't come in, and her birthday is less than a week away. Also, Lord, I still haven't been able to mail out my support letters for Nicaragua, which isn't urgent but I feel like needs to happen soon.

Lord, these worries are gnawing away at my joy, peace, and faith. Assure me, Father, that You have everything under control. I don't need to worry because that won't help anything. What happens, happens. Open my eyes to Your omnipotence, Father.

I love You,
Mark

Lord,

Thank You so much for the amazing time I had last night. Thank You for quelling my stress and making everything fall into place.

God, I confess I'm a little jealous. As all of my friends are starting to drive now, some of them are getting their cars for free, but I have to pay for half of mine and I'm not even near close enough. Or so I think.

God, drain me of my jealousy; fill me with joy for my friends instead. Help me to be content, knowing that if You want me to have a car You'll provide one. Help me to trust in You.

Mark

2-19-13

Dear God,

I see Your beauty in the stillness; I see Your beauty in the storm. It's impossible to escape. Some people claim You don't exist while the sky above and the earth beneath proclaim that You do merely by their existence. I am so blessed. Your work, Your beauty, Your love is EVERYWHERE, always in front of me no matter how I feel. Thank You for that. ☺

God, there's something gnawing at me inside me. It's like a mixture of jealousy, anger, shame... I don't even know. Whatever it is, I know it's a lie. Satan's trying to cover my eyes to Your blessings; trying to quench my joy and peace. I need You Father, I need You to silence those sneaky little thoughts of me not being good enough or me longing to be like someone else. My identity is founded in You. Not in school. Not in grades. Not in talent. Not in friends. YOU. If I didn't get into the college of my choice, so what? In the long run, in Your grand plan, that is not a failure.

Teach me to accept that You're in control. That all I need is You.

Mark

2-23-13

MY SON,
WHY THIS JEALOUSY? WHY DO YOU COMPARE YOURSELF TO OTHERS? WHY ARE YOU SO AFRAID?
OH MY CHILD, YOU ARE FEARFULLY AND WONDERFULLY MADE. YOU WERE MADE TO BE MARK RODRIGUEZ, CHILD OF GOD, NOT SOMEONE ELSE. STOP WORRYING ABOUT HOW THE WORLD VIEWS YOU. THE JUDGEMENT OF THE WORLD COMES FROM THE TONGUE OF SATAN. DON'T FORGET, MY LOVE, THAT SATAN IS THE FATHER OF LIES. HE WOULD LIKE NOTHING MORE THAN FOR YOU TO BELIEVE THAT YOU ARE FAILING, THAT YOU'RE NOT GOOD ENOUGH. LISTEN, YOU MUST UNDERSTAND THIS: I DON'T WANT GOOD ENOUGH. I WANT YOU IN ALL YOUR BROKENNESS, YOUR MORTALITY. I AM JEALOUS FOR YOU. I WANT NOTHING BUT ALL OF YOU. I DON'T CARE IF YOU DON'T GET INTO THE SAME COLLEGE AS CARLEY. I HAVE USED THE HOMELESS, THE DROPOUTS; I HAVE CHANGED THE WORLD WITH THOSE IT CONSIDERS FAILURES. STOP FINDING YOUR IDENTITY IN COMPARING YOURSELF TO THOSE CLOSEST TO YOU, THIS WILL ONLY MAKE YOU FEEL UNSATISFACTORY. FIND YOUR IDENTITY IN ME, AND I WILL SHOW YOU WONDERS BEYOND WHAT YOU CAN EVER DREAM.

2-25-13

WILL YOU NOT
REVIVE US AGAIN?
Psalm 85:6

2-27-13

Lord,

I seek You and I find You, for why would You hide Yourself from me? No, You are constantly seeking me; when I feel far from You it's my fault, not Yours. God, fill my cup. Open my eyes to the blessings around me. You have given me far, far more than I have ever deserved. Thank You that You forgive even though I sin time and time again. Remind me of Your beauty and grace that are far more fulfilling than any amount of earthly pleasure.

I love You,
Mark

3-5-13

Lord,

Every day that I wake up, there is a choice before me. I can go through my day being tossed between sadness and happiness due to circumstances and events, OR I can accept Your invitation to live with uncircumstantial, undeserved joy. Every day I wake up, there are THOUSANDS of blessings prepared for me. I'm realizing that I accept very few of them. I long for a life of joy that seems illogical to this circumstantial world. To live and to laugh and to enjoy every day to the fullest. This is not something that requires a long process. I can start living this life today. Help me to remember I can be content in any and every situation.

I love You Lord, ☺
Mark

I have learned in whatever situation I am to be content... I can do all things through him who strengthens me.

Philippians 4:11b, 13 (ESV)

"Be more concerned with your character than your reputation, because your character is what you really are, while your reputation is merely what others think you are."

John Wooden

YOU WILL GO OUT IN JOY
AND BE LED FORTH
IN PEACE.
THE MOUNTAINS AND HILLS
WILL BURST
INTO SONG BEFORE YOU,
AND ALL THE TREES OF THE
FIELD WILL CLAP THEIR HANDS.
ISAIAH 55:12

3-19-13

Dear Lord,

Open my eyes. Give me an understanding of Your grace, Your love, Your sacrifice. Remind me of the many blessings around me that I don't deserve.

I long to be filled with such joy that I proclaim Your glory from the rooftops. To be so amazed by Your glory and creation that I run from door to door, begging people to open their eyes so that they can too share in the joy that drives me crazy. I want to go crazy for You, Lord. I want to take risks and chances that others may see as wildly absurd. I want to DO things, to stop planning and analyzing and worrying and start doing. Too often I convince myself out of doing something because it might not work out. It's time to start doing those things because even if they don't work out I'll fall back into Your arms with no harm done.

Drive me, control me, amaze me.

Mark

3-20-13

O Lord my God, I cried to You for help, and
You have healed me.
Psalm 30:2

Lord,

I am crying to You for help. I'm sick of sin. Of failure. Time and time again I pray for strength, and still I give in to temptation. God, I want release. More than anything. My sins are blocking out Your beautiful light of blessing. I acknowledge that I've sinned, I'm sorry. I really, truly am. Every time I fall I feel as though my eyes grow darker and darker to Your joy. God, I am EMPTY. HEAL me, please. I see one light, and that is 1 Corinthians 15:57; "He gives us victory over sin and death through our Lord Jesus Christ." You WILL give me victory. I am not lost, I am not hopeless. But I'm tired. Lift me up and carry me to safety, to my solace where I can see nothing but Your brilliance.

Surely goodness and mercy
Shall follow me all the days of my life, and
I shall dwell in the house of the Lord
FOREVER.
Psalm 23:6

3-20-13 (EVENING)

Father,

Oh how I await the day I'm face to face with You. The day that I am no longer tempted, that I no longer sin. The day that I'm all I'm meant to be. But even though I long for that day, Lord, I pray for the understanding that I have a purpose here. And that purpose is to worship You and proclaim Your name to all the nations. God, I can do that now. I can do that tomorrow as I worship You in chapel. I pray that You would create me into the person who is out of their mind for You. You deserve all of me Lord, remind me of that.

Mark

3-21-13 (MORNING)

Dear Lord,

I am a new creation. Though I once embraced sinfulness I have been touched by Your goodness and seen Your love; therefore, I can never be the same again.

Though they may not come to fruition, my thoughts are where sin can often be found. Just casually, I let my mind wander to unrighteous things of the sinful nature. This ought not to be so. As a new creation, my actions shouldn't be the only thing transformed, so should my mind. Today, help me to set my mind on things above, not on earthly things.

I love You,
Mark

3-21-13 (EVENING)

Father,

Thank You so much for the opportunity to worship in chapel today. There are honestly few things I enjoy more than worshiping You unabashedly. I pray that You would work in me, Lord, to give me the confidence to worship You with all I have in front of my peers. This is one of the ways to unify the school: by showing them it's time to knock down our walls of self-consciousness and worship You together freely.

Thank You,
Mark

3-22-13 (MORNING)

Father,

This is the day that You have made. I will rejoice and be glad in it. Lord, I have nothing to complain about. Though I have sinned against

You time and time again You have not rejected me but embraced me. So often I complain, but I'm realizing that whenever I do it's about trivial matters. Not only have You told me not to complain, but it will get me absolutely nowhere; it will produce nothing but sadness and bitterness. Today, Father, remind me of Your grace. Open my eyes to see every blessing clear as day. You are all I need.

Mark

3-22-13 (AFTERNOON)

God,

You make beautiful things. All around me Your glory shines forth; be it in the complexity of anatomy or the simplicity of a hug from a friend. You shine forth in what You've blessed me with, and that is such a great deal that You shine forth constantly. Thank You for this beauty, Lord; I don't deserve any of it. Sometimes, I somehow close my eyes to all that You've given me. When that happens, wake me up from my stupidity to the wonders of Your grace.

Mark

3-23-13 (MORNING)

Lord,

You have put me in a position of leadership, both through position and socially at my school. My position gives me a great opportunity to share Your love and Your word to others. However, I need to be careful that I follow the Word I preach. I can't just spout truth and then have people find I don't really hold to it. Not only would that make me a liar but it would make my words seem unimportant and ungrounded. Humble me, Father, so that I might see where I am lacking, and then work to be faithful in that area.

Thank You for this beautiful day. ☺

Mark

3-23-13 (AFTERNOON)

Father,

I think I've discovered the reason I (and other Christians) still sin. I have not seen You in Your absolute fullness. If I or anyone else had, we'd be so grateful and amazed we wouldn't be able to bring ourselves to sin. However, the case is that You have not shown Yourself in Your fullness because our mortal bodies wouldn't be able to handle it. But to us Christians, You have revealed some of Your self, even putting Your Holy Spirit inside us. That Spirit does not stop us from sinning, but convicts us so that we yearn to do away with that sin. You know that's where I am now, Lord. I sin and I want to stop. Some sin can feel so deeply rooted within me and it takes a lot of strength and sweat to remove. I don't have that strength, Lord, but You do. I think if I understood who You are more, it would be easier to resist temptation. That is my desire, Lord, to know You more.

Open up my eyes.

Mark

3-23-13 (NIGHT)

Father,

You have sacrificed more than I'll ever understand. You gave up Your one and only son, who had only loved and never sinned, to be executed shamefully like a common criminal. I can't even fathom giving up my dog, let alone that.

Why do You love us so much? Why did You put Yourself through so much pain to free a sinful and vulgar people? I'm thankful, obviously, but I'm wondering.

This fact (Your sacrifice) is why I have nothing to complain about. Why I should cherish and appreciate each day. You gave up everything... for ME. That means I'm treasured, valued, LOVED, by You. You, what You've done, are incomprehensible. I will never be able to thank You fully as You deserve, but I offer You my music.

My photography. My mind. My running. Everything I do. It doesn't equal what You did for me, but it's all I have.

I love You,
Mark

3-24-13 (MORNING)

Father,

Thank You for the blessing of having Carley in my life. She earnestly pursues and seeks You and wants more out of life than just the status quo. We have that in common, Lord, and it's wonderful to build and strengthen each other in our journey for that.

Lord, her words have power. Her joy and love touch everyone she comes in contact with. Today, she is speaking before her church about Nicaragua, something dear to both our hearts. Father, take control of her tongue. Guide her words, give her the right ones that will click in people's minds. Give her confidence and courage to stand before Your people and proclaim all that You have done.

Remind her that You are always with her.

Mark

3-24-13 (AFTERNOON)

Father,

This time next week many will be celebrating Your wonderful resurrection that enabled us to live forever with You. However, much of this country will be counting that day merely as a day to eat candy. Once again, I'm baffled by how instead of praising You, people do that. How has an egg-giving bunny replaced Your triumph over death?

Lord, I pray that we as Your children would praise You so loudly that day that others may join in. Good Friday and Easter are what it's all about! You died and rose again, that's what we preach! Please, Lord, make that our focus that day. To glorify You, to proclaim You, to rejoice in You.

Mark

3-24-13 (EVENING)

Lord,

In four months I'll be on my way to Nicaragua. I don't know what to expect and, quite frankly, I kind of enjoy that. I enjoy the idea of needing to rely on You, to put my faith in You because it's too risky to put my faith in myself.

Father, prepare me. You know I regret the way I acted last trip. How self-centered I was and insecure. That, coupled with a poor perspective on my role in missions, made me realize months after I got home that that trip could've been so much more. I had two full weeks there and a lot of my "helping" was probably very fruitless. But, I'm going back. A lot has changed in me since last June's trip, Lord. I've grown to understand how to do missions well. I'm stronger, more determined, and have one intention: to learn while serving. I think someday I may like to live in Nicaragua, maybe even permanently, and if that's the case I want to learn how to truly help that country.

Father, I pray that You would continue to prepare my heart and soul for this trip. When I hit Managua soil I want to be filled to the brim with love, joy, and peace to infect everyone I come in contact with. Love, joy and peace are enough to change Nicaragua. They're enough to change the world.

I am Your instrument. I will sing Your song.

Mark

3-25-13 (MORNING)

Father,

So often I think of doing something cool or for Your glory, but then I think of everything that could go wrong and don't do it. The book Mr. Schanck gave me, *Love Does*, has shown me it's time to stop doing that. So much cool stuff could happen in my life if only I stopped worrying about the risks.

Father, You know how logical my mind works. I pray that You would start to show me the beauty of throwing down my fishing net and just following You. If I never take risks, I'll lead a very boring life. If I do take risks, I'll shine with joy like never before.

Mark

3-25-13 (EVENING)

Romans 6:20-23

Lord,

As glorious and beautiful as You are, somehow the things of this world still look better to me sometimes. However, as this passage says, those things produce absolutely no fruit. The only thing that comes from sin is death.

Lord, You are the best fruit there is. Following You produces joy unlike what anything else can give me. Remind me to look around, to take in the glorious things that You have given me.

Thank You,
Mark

3-26-13 (MORNING)

Lord,
You are due much more praise than I'll ever be able to give You. You are so grand and infinite that until perhaps when I die I won't come close to fully understanding You. However, You created me to give You praise in everything I say and do. I often forget that. In fact, I often seek ways to bring praise to myself rather than praising You. I pray, Father, that when the thought of glorifying myself pops into my head, You would remind me who deserves the praise.

I need to remember that my time here is too short for me to seek my own gain. Instead, I ought to seek ways to praise You and to lead others to praise You.

"Holy, Holy, Holy is the
Lord God Almighty,
Who was and is and is to come."

Mark

3-26-13 (AFTERNOON)

Romans 7

God, I love this passage so much because it shows how even though Paul was inspiring and loved You so much, he was human. He struggled with sin, just as I do, but he acknowledged something that I think is very important; just because you struggle with sin, doesn't mean you're not a Christian. In fact, acknowledging that means you're exactly who you should be. And that is someone who acknowledges they're a sinner but yearns for Your law. I pray that You would give me hope, Lord, when I fall into sin, that someday I will be free from the flesh.

Mark

3-28-13 (MORNING)

Father,

I have tasted and seen that You are beautiful. I have lived in wonder of every sunset sky, every bolt of lightning. I remember the days when I would stare in awe from the bus at the sunrise with my mind blown. But Lord, I think that amidst the struggles and the busyness of this year, I have lost track of that.

I want to feel that way again, Lord. So in touch with You that I'm constantly thanking You and admiring Your work. Those days were great because I constantly felt Your presence, constantly felt You at my side.

Those days don't have to be an era that is gone and past, Lord. They can start again today. I feel like that is me at my best, praising You every minute of every hour of every day. Today, Lord, instill in me that wonder again. Open my eyes to Your greatness.

Mark

3-28-13 (EVENING)

Father,

I pray that You would continue to give me Your eyes, to heal my perspective as I return to the man who doesn't complain because he's so stunned by Your glory. That is who I want to be, and that is who I feel I'm meant to be.

I love You,
Mark

3-29-13

Morning

Father,
I thank you for this beautiful world you've Created. Today I wanna go out and take some pictures, explore, adventure. I love that you've created such a world for that, with mysteries and surprises and wonders around every corner. I pray that you would surprise me today. Blow my mind, make me laugh. I pray that it wouldn't just be an adventure on my own, but that you'd come with me. Show me your world, your creation, your Majesty. Soften my heart to embrace every beautiful thing out there.

Thank you,
Mark

3-29-13 (EVENING)

Oh Lord,

What a sacrifice You gave 2,000 years ago. All for us, all for me. You felt the pain that I deserved so that I no longer had to pay the price for my sin. Lord, I will never be able to express fully the gratefulness a sacrifice like that is due. So I give You my life, Lord that You may use it to tell the world of what You've done for us. That I may be a beacon of light and hope to those seeking a Savior. Thank You for bearing the shame and blood that I deserved. I love You.

Mark

3-30-13 (MORNING)

Father,

2,000 years ago You died so that I may be free from sin as Your child. And that's what I am, a free child of You. You have given me strength, zeal, passion, joy, peace, love for the service of You. My sin is not failing, and does not make me a failure. It just means I've still got some human in me. The holiest, most righteous person still sins; I am not evil for sinning.

I live in a beautiful world. It is broken and permeated with sin, but it is also ablaze with Your beauty and glory. That doesn't mean it's a failure, it just means it needs to be cleansed. The same goes for me. I may have darkness in me (as a result of my mortality) but I am ablaze with Your Holy Spirit as well. Someday, all that darkness will be gone.

I can't let that hold me back, though. I may be mortal, but so is everyone around me, and they're longing for light. And I must show it to them.

Mark

3-31-13 (EASTER AFTERNOON)

Father,

Death has lost its sting. You, though You *died,* defeated death and rose so that I may relish in eternal life with You. I don't understand. How was my sin, my rebelliousness, my spite, my narcissism worth that? I know, Your death and resurrection brought You glory, but why would You want *me* to give You praise?

I think it may be because when I praise You, it's another victory. When I praise You, it shows Your triumph over darkness because that which was once sin has been made beautiful. Your light has pierced my darkness, I have become a new creation.

Thank You. Thank You for sacrificing so that I may have this. Walking with Carley yesterday, and feeling the gentle breeze of Your breath on my skin, reminded me how undeserving I am. How blessed I am! To experience so much joy, so much peace, and know that the best is yet to come.

Thank You. Thank You so much for giving air to my gasping mouth, blood to my empty heart, sight to my blind eyes. I may be undeserving, but You are deserving of whatever I have to offer.

Here is my heart. My soul. My voice. My arms, my feet, my eyes, my tongue.

I am Yours. Though my mortal body will fall and decay as the beasts of the field and the birds of the air, my soul has seen light.

And someday, my final chains and ties shall melt to ash, blown into oblivion.

No more fear, no more pain. Just eternal consuming love.

As it should be.

Mark

I think a lot of people go on missions trips to see the smiles on the faces of those in trial. But the point of missions is not our inspiration.

4-1-13 (MORNING)

Father,

You are light. This world is filled with darkness and negativity, but You have provided a way that I can be joyful, thankful, and content. However, the ignorance of our world really saddens me, especially the negative response to the Kony 2012 video. It is real; there ARE children being manipulated and mutilated, stolen and forced to do terrible acts. Why must people be so apathetic to decry a powerful cause so they don't actually have to get up and DO something in this world? It's awful Lord; the world is so lacking in compassion and brotherly love.

Help me to be someone who burns away the darkness of their negativity with light. We have so much to be thankful for. While some people devote their lives to hatred of something.

Darkness will not be my default.

Mark

4-2-13 (AFTERNOON)

Father,

How much I have learned and changed since Nicaragua! I feel like, though it hasn't been a complete transformation, I no longer dwell in self-centeredness and fear of the future. Though it's been a bit of a bumpy twisting road, I feel like I've arrived at a point of confidence, surety, and giving the reigns over to You.

My faith, my trust in You gives me strength. You have taught me that I have nothing to fear, nothing to worry about. It is better for me to give control over to You, for You're the only one who knows what I truly need.

Thank You for being my solid ground.

Mark

4-3-13 (MORNING)

Father,

You are magnificent. The stars and sky truly proclaim the works of Your hands. So many people take stuff like that for granted, but You have shown me how beautiful it is.

In Your wonders, in Your works, I find peace. I see Your glorious creation and it shows how much You truly care about me.

Open my eyes, Father. There's so much that I miss on a daily basis because of how I let myself get consumed with school and learning Spanish and guitar and photography, and so much more! Those things are not worth Your grace.

Thank You, Lord,
Mark

4-4-13 (EVENING)

Sing to him, sing praise to him;
Tell of all his wonderful acts.
1 Chronicles 16:9

Father,

This is kind of a scary time for me musically. Not with guitar, I know I have that down pretty well, but with my voice. I've always felt like I have so much to say, but I've never been sure how to say it. Lately, I've been thinking a lot about my voice. I worked hard to learn how to scream and I got it down, but it doesn't sound that great and I'm honestly not feeling like I'll really have an outlet for that. But recently, I've been experimenting with singing. I've always loved to sing, but I've never considered whether I might actually be good at it. And I'm starting to wonder if I might be.

God, this is something I definitely need Your guidance with. I want to have a way to personally tell the world about how great You are. And I wonder if singing is a way for me to do that. You've told me I could be a catalyst for unification. I've often thought that through worship, maybe that could be achieved. That as long as I demonstrated joy and love and honesty up there I could praise You. And I think that's definitely true, but maybe You have something more in store for me.

Dear God, if You do, show me. I want to tell the world about You. About how real You are. Show me how You want me to do that.

Mark

4-7-13

Father,

Thank You so much for the nice weather coming this week. Though I know I can be content with whatever weather, the forecast is literally my favorite. Thank You.

You have seriously given me so much to be thankful for, God. And it is such a glorious feeling to stop complaining and embrace those things. It feels like, suddenly, I have no fears, no anxiety. Just pure, undeserved joy. That's how I wanna spend every day, Lord. Caught up in Your beauty, drunk on it. Then, I will shout from the rooftops that there is so much more to live for.

Mark

4-8-13 (EVENING)

Father,

I think I just realized something! I went through that period where I struggled with jealousy about how some of my friends got their cars for free. I was so upset because I felt like I was the one with interests that needed serious financial backing, but I was gonna have to spend my summer working towards a car. However, I knew that jealousy was wrong Lord, and I fought hard to be happy for them instead of envious. And God, You rewarded me tonight for not dwelling in jealousy. My grandparents just gave me FIVE HUNDRED DOLLARS. I'm fully funded! Finally, I can start saving for a camera.

Father, You truly do reward Your faithful servant. Jealousy is a choice. It's <u>hard</u> to not be jealous, especially in the circumstances I'm in now, God. Strengthen me! Remind me of Your love for me. You are jealous for me, and I'm oh so thankful for that.

Mark

4-11-13 (MORNING)

Father,

You have taken the time to search and know me. You know me far better than I do, or even than my best friends do. You know who I am now and who I'll grow to be.

So there is no need to worry.

Something I've been working on lately is learning to give all I have to You. I used to worry so much about my future, thinking about how everything I do could help or hurt my plan for what I want to be. But I've learned not to have a plan for my life, Lord. Life is so complex that I wouldn't know how to get there and would end up angry and disappointed. But You, Lord, know the way, and You know the destination.

Help me to release any worry or stress I have, Lord. Part of Faith is believing ridiculously in You. Help me to let go of my plan and trust Yours, even if I don't know it.

Mark

4-13-13 (MORNING)

Father,

Thank You so much for the beautiful weather this week. It makes me really look forward to summer, all this warmth and clear skies. Thank You for this blessing.

God, today I'm shooting one of my friend's senior photos and I gotta say I'm pretty nervous. I know I'm talented, Lord, but I'm worried I won't get enough good pictures or find enough locations or something like that.

THE ONLY THING THAT CAN STIFLE CREATIVITY IS FEAR.

Father, give me peace. Remind me of why I love photography and what I want to accomplish. Display Yourself in new ways to both me and my friend today.

Mark

4-14-13

"It's really hard to be depressed around you."

—Carley

4-15-13 (EVENING)

Father,

My generation, at least much of it, is full of hopelessness, fear, negativity, and yearning. We cling to the shadows though they are the source of our blindness. We chain ourselves tighter as we search for liberation. Because of this seemingly endless cycle, the Color Life fades grayer and grayer.

Father, You've given me a gift; the gift to see. I get swept up in Your light and love to the point of giddiness. You have shown me the value of peace and joy, and taught me that I have nothing to complain about. This is a very, very powerful gift. I cannot be comfortable keeping it to myself, I must share it with the world.

May Your love and Your spirit be a fuel for my eyes that never goes out. Take over and touch the world through me.

Mark

4-20-13 (MORNING)

Father,

Thank You for giving me the gift of sight so necessary in photography. All around me I see potential for a good picture, or sweet locations. The cool thing is that finding those things brings me joy, just relishing in Your beauty and tasting and seeing. Father, something that will be essential as I start doing more senior pictures is the ability to talk to strangers. I feel like I've gotten a lot better at this over time, but now I'm gonna need to do stuff like going up to people's doors and asking if I can shoot in their backyards. I just pray that You would make me braver, Lord. Otherwise so much joy and beauty will be out of reach to me. Fear is the only thing that can stifle creativity.

Mark

4-21-13 (EVENING)

Father,

Thank You for the people around me who exhibit beautiful irrational faith. My neck had been hurting really bad today, and then the lady at PIN* prayed for it and boom, healed.

I strongly desire that type of faith, Lord. The belief of a child that doesn't think about what could go wrong.

Father, show me Your beauty. Teach me to believe. Show me that You are knocking on the door and all I need to do is open it.

Mark

*People in Need ministry to the homeless

4-23-13 (EVENING)

Father,

You have opened my eyes to Your glory. I can get wrapped up in joy merely by walking down a path at sunset. I have seen Your beauty, Your complexity, Your infiniteness.

What amazes me is that, despite how beautiful You are, You love me. While I am dirty and cursed and sick, You stoop down to cleanse, bless, and heal me. You have made me into one of the beautiful things I admire. Therefore, my sole purpose is to proclaim Your greatness and worship Your glory. Open my mouth and allow me not to keep my wonder for You in my eyes, but also in my voice.

You are beauty and grace.

Mark

4-24-13 (EVENING)

Father,

I think I've known that You want me to do a chapel for a long time. I have displayed You through my actions, but the time has come for me to proclaim You through my words. You have a message for me to share. You have given me an opportunity to speak to those around me about how beautiful You are. To show them that light pierces darkness everytime. I pray that You would inspire every word I speak. Give me words of joy and hope and love. Teach me Your message, perfectly designed to be proclaimed when I speak. Though it's a month away, stir in me, Oh God. I may know my peers better than most chapel speakers, but You know them even better.

You're the words, I'm the voice. Craft my sound into a word to change hearts and open eyes.

Mark

4-26-13 (EVENING)

Father,

What a glorious promise it is that if I seek You, I will find You. Life has become filled with joy since I started finding You all around me, in everything. I am never alone, I am always at home.

God, tomorrow I'm doing an engagement shoot with Alex and Marissa. I just pray that You would quell all nervousness and remind me why I love photography. May You give me a laid-back demeanor so that all three of us feel comfortable and can have a good time. May I get to know them better and learn from their love.

Mark

4-28-13 (EVENING)

Father,

I love that my gift of sight goes beyond when I'm just holding a camera. I see Your beauty and Your love all around me no matter where I am, because they really are everywhere. I pray, Father, that in the relationships I make in my photography You would give me the ability to share my knowledge of Your love with others as we relish in this beautiful world together. Make me not just a seer, but a teacher of sorts as well; teaching others about how much we have to live for.

Mark

4-30-13

Thoughts:

*My relationship with God isn't supposed to be casual, but intimate

*He is desperately in love with me and wants my love in return

*He has been beaten, spit upon, and crucified without a

word from me
*He won't stop coming after me until I give him everything
*I am an unfaithful lover, seeking pleasure rather than love
*He loves me anyway

5-1-13

I slept, but my heart was Awake.
A Sound!
My beloved is knocking.
"Open to me,
my sister, my love, my dove,
My PERFECT ONE
for my head is wet with dew
my locks with the drops of the night."
Song of Songs 5:2

It is time to let him IN.
Let passion overtake me
Like obsessed lovers
May my every word and move
Be out of love for my Savior.
Selah.

5-3-13 (EVENING)

Remember *Song of Songs 8:6-7*

Father,

I seek You in the Secret Place. Upon my bed, where there is no one to please with false piety and weighty words. Here it is just You and me.

YOU HAVE SLUMBERED LONG ENOUGH. THE TIME HAS COME TO WAKE UP!

The time is here, Father. The sword is set firmly in my grasp, I take it with both hands. The time has come to defend and divide. I will offend people, I will shock people with my boldness. But Jesus didn't hold back, Lord, He confronted the hypocritical, false generation firmly. He called them out and stood upon that call.

If I merely live a life of comfort zone Christianity, my faith is worthless and could be much better used by someone else. But no, I should be looked down upon, told off, scoffed at. For I will receive the richer prize, no matter the scorn I face.

I love You,
Mark

5-4-13 (MORNING)

Free, Father,

Today, just now, I cast out the demon that has been tempting me. My faith in You is increasing all the more. I ask and I receive. Thank You that I am starting to understand that prayer has power. I can speak directly to You. I can feel Your will. You tell me about people, about things that are going to happen in their lives.

Father, bring me closer to You in this intimate relationship. Actually, You have come as close to me as You can, it's time that I draw near to You.

Fill me up, Lord. With faith, with joy, with praise. Keep this demon away, give me a spirit of freedom and liberation.

Mark

5-4-13 (EVENING)

Shake yourself from
the dust and arise; be seated;
O Jerusalem; loose the bonds from your
neck, O captive daughter of Zion.
Isaiah 52:2

I am learning what it is to be Your lover, Lord. To relish seeing You in the morning and then receive gifts, signs of Your love throughout the day. Every opportunity I have to be alone with You becomes sacred. I dream of You, I tell others what You've done for me, I become obsessed with You.

You are my first love. My prize, my pearl, my crown. I burn with passion for You.

You have anointed me. You have made me into a sword to call out my peers and my elders. You have prepared me all year for this, I'm realizing.

Increase my faith. My child-like, simple belief in You is my greatest weapon. Remind me daily of Your grace and love for me.

Mark

5-5-13

For people will be lovers of self, lovers of money, proud, arrogant, abusive, disobedient to their parents, ungrateful, unholy, heartless, unappeasable, slanderous, without self-control, brutal, not loving good, treacherous, reckless, swollen with conceit, lovers of pleasure rather than lovers of God, having the appearance of godliness, but denying its power.

2 Timothy 3:2-5

Prayer:

—thanks for saving me from having to rely on myself
—Not about knowing the answers, it's about knowing the Savior
—I can feel You always with me
—opportunities for Kaitlin (missionary) to share her heart
—prayer for Carley to draw near to You and for her friendships to grow stronger
—prayer for gift of speaking in other languages
—increase in faith

5-6-13 (EVENING)

Draw me after you;
let us run.
The king has brought
me into his
chambers.
Song of Solomon 1:4

—He desires time with me in the secret place
—I am beautiful, He desires me to be His own
—He is jealous for me

Prayer:

—Thank You that I can be assured of my worth in You
—I've been unfaithful in my betrothal to You
—Thank You that no matter how unfaithful I am, we will still be joined, bride and bridegroom
—Show Kaitlin how much of an impact she has
—Strength and assurance of love and grace to Mr. N in whatever he's experiencing
—Make him a strong warrior and lover of You
—I pray for the power to speak the Spanish language
—Give me the words to speak in chapel, may I be a sword and lover of You openly before everyone

5-7-13 (EVENING)

The wicked flee when no one pursues,
but the righteous are bold as a lion.*
Proverbs 28:1

*This was the verse chosen to represent Officer Brian Jones' life at his gravesite.

—I am not meant to be afraid
—I am meant to be BOLD
—To boldly proclaim freedom for the prisoners

—Righteous anger is a fuel for justice
—To live is Christ, to die is gain
—There is nothing to fear
—I am meant to be bold NOW

Prayer:

—You want me to be a warrior no matter what holds me back
—I can be a warrior, but I need to have integrity and follow God's will (Proverbs 28:9)
—Thank You that You are beside me with the current task at hand
—I pray that my talk in chapel will go beyond just 1-on-group, that it will become 1-on-1 as well
—Can't find passion for learning Spanish, prayer for spiritual gift for learning languages as my calling requires

—Song 1:4
I HAVE CALLED YOU BUT YOU HAVE NOT RECOGNIZED MY CALL
—I AM CALLING YOU AT A YOUNG AGE
—SAY, "Speak, Lord, Your servant hears," AND I SHALL

5-8-13 (EVENING)

Go on up to a high mountain,
O Zion, herald of good news;
Lift up your voice with strength,
O Jerusalem, herald of good news;
Lift it up; fear not;
Say to the cities of Judah,
"Behold your God!"
Isaiah 40:9

—I have been called
—I am a herald of good news
—God has called me to speak boldly
—My message is for God's glory

Prayer:

—Thank You for calling me; thank You for giving me the power to fulfill my calling
—When I speak in chapel, give me the peace and the passion to move around, to be emotional, to be fueled by the Holy Spirit as opposed to caged by fear
—I'm in a period of life where You're giving me things to say
—Some of those things will be in other countries
—I pray for the spiritual gift of picking up languages with ease so that I may share Your word

5-9-13 (EVENING)

You keep him in perfect peace
whose mind is stayed on you,
because he trusts in you.
Isaiah 26:3

—Peace doesn't have to be temporary
—Faith produces peace
—We will not know peace if we try to keep hold of the reigns of our lives

Prayer:

—Thank You for leading me to these verses
—You are making Your word come alive by speaking to me through it

5-10-13 (MORNING)

Father,

Although the demon of my sin has been cast away, Satan is doing everything he can to tempt me. I need Your strength, Your assurance of grace. With You, I can overcome any temptation. Give me clarity of mind and give me faith to trust that that sin isn't worth it. A life of holiness is.

Mark

5-11-13 (EVENING)

Little children,
let us not love in word or talk
but in deed and in truth
1 John 3:18

—Mean what you say
—Be prepared to be held accountable for your declarations
—Life of worship

Prayer:

—I adore how You fill people with words of the Holy Spirit

5-12-13 (EVENING)

"And as for me, this is my covenant with them," says the Lord; "My spirit that is upon you, and my words that I have put in your mouth, shall not depart out of your mouth, or out of the mouth of your offspring, or out of the mouth of your children's offspring," says the Lord, "from this time forth and forevermore."
Isaiah 59:21

—God is calling me
—He will put the words in my mouth
—I will share these words in chapel
—My offspring will bear this message

Prayer:

—Thank You for anointing me even though I have been unfaithful
—Draw near to me, define the message You want me to share
—I am sometimes selfish even in my relationship with You
—My selfishness covers my ears from your call, I confess this

5-13-13 (EVENING)

Why are you cast down,
O my soul,
and why are you in turmoil
within me?
Hope in God;
For I shall again praise him,
my salvation and my God.
Psalm 42:11

—There is always hope
—I need not feel despair
—Despair is broken if I look on God

5-14-13 (EVENING)

You are altogether beautiful,
My love;
There is no flaw in you.
Song of Solomon 4:7

—Despite all my unfaithfulness, I am desired
—God goes so far as to call me flawless

Prayer:

—Thank You for making such a sacrifice, even though I'm unfaithful
—May I live a life proclaiming Your sacrifice as a bride would claim what her husband has done for her
—Help my unbelief
—If I ask, I will receive
—I want to share what You've done for me with the Nicaraguans
—I can't find the passion to learn Spanish
—Please give me the gift of naturally picking up languages
—Let me love You deeper

—Draw me closer to You, bring me into greater intimacy with You
—I love when You speak to me, when You move me, when You tell me Your ways

5-16-2013 (EVENING)

At night his song
is with me.
Psalm 42:8

Prayer:

—You have given me a song to sing, a message to share
—Don't want my idea of the message to be about me
—As I prepare, open my eyes to the people around me
—Show me what I need to share, don't need to worry about how I'll act
—Give me the words to share how much You desire an intimate relationship with us

5-18-2013 (MORNING)

I have blotted out your transgressions like a cloud
and your sins like mist;
Return to me, for I have redeemed you.
Sing, O heavens,
for the Lord has done it;
Shout, O depths of the earth;
Break forth into singing,
O mountains,
O forest, and every tree in it!
Isaiah 44:22-23

Prayer:

—Thank You for seeing my sins, forgiving me, and wanting

me anyway
—I love that You're so incredible that all Creation shouts Your name
—If the trees and the mountains do it, why aren't we??
—Trees can't even see, but all Your wonders are laid out in front of us and we still hide Your word
—We let embarrassment, persecution, and fear of losing our reputation silence our vision and our voice of an all-consuming God
—I pray for more than a revival, I pray for a revolution
—I pray we would cast off the chains of wanting to fit in and not offend anybody, and we would begin to proclaim Your name loudly.
—I pray for the strength and wisdom to start leading people in this revolution
—Put my focus off of me and onto You.
—I pray for the gift of learning languages quickly, so that I may share this revolution with other parts of the world.
—Thank You for my brother, Ryan

5-20-13 (EVENING)

But I have calmed and quieted my soul,
like a weaned child with its mother;
like a weaned child is my soul within me.
Psalm 131:2

—Calmed and quieted: at peace
—I don't need to be alone in a silent room to be at peace
—My soul can be near to God at all times

5-21-13 (EVENING)

—I'm sick of false religion!
—I want to fall deeper and deeper in love with You

—I want to live a life so transformed by love for You

Ezekiel 2, 3:1-15
—I will be filled with the Spirit
—Nicaraguans will be quick to listen to me, American teenagers can be stubborn and won't even listen to God
—Rebellious house
—I am a prophet
—You are speaking words into my heart (3:10)
—I need to speak His message whether or not they will listen (3:11)
—I want You to come into my heart and overflow my life, I want to live a life of evidence of transformation
—The veil is torn, I want to be close to You!
—More than anything, intimacy with You is my desire
—Until chapel next week, I fast of my bed
—When I wake because I am uncomfortable, find me
—All I want is You

5-22-13

When the veil broke, it wasn't just that we could now have a relationship with God. To Him, finally, He could have a relationship with us.

(EVENING):

I am my beloved's,
and his desire is for me
Song 7:10

—He loves me and longs for me
—I am a treasure to Him
—I want to have that beautiful connection with Him I see in people like Misty Edwards
—I want to be so caught up in His love that everyone can see it

—I desire a real, romantic, relationship with God

Prayer:

—I desire an intimate love with You
—I'm opening the door, please come in
—I am Your garden
—Come in, PLEASE
—Change me! Overwhelm me with Your love
—I want to live a life of passion for You

5-23-13 (EVENING):

Arise, shine, for your light has
come,
and the glory of the Lord has risen
upon you.
For behold, darkness shall
cover the earth, and thick
darkness the peoples;
But the Lord
will arise upon you,
and His glory will be seen
upon you.
Isaiah 60:1-2

—The world is dark
—Darkness has covered those around me
—God is light
—God is shining from within me
—I must arise, for my light has come

5-25-13 (EVENING):

It is too light a thing
that you should be my servant
to raise up the tribes of Jacob

and to bring back the
preserved of Israel;
I will make you as a light
for the nations,
that my salvation may reach
to the end of the earth.
Isaiah 49:6

Prayer:

—Thank You for not being a God who hides himself
—As You desire an intimate relationship, You reveal intimate things
—I praise You for letting me gaze upon Your beauty
—You have called me to minister to my homeland and beyond
—I pray for the tools and the passion to equip me for that purpose
—I pray for the ability to tell people about a revolutionary intimate relationship with You
—I pray for the gift of learning languages quickly so I may share the gospel with others

5-27-13 (EVENING):

Go on up to a high mountain,
O Zion, herald of good news;
Lift up your voice
With strength,
O Jerusalem, herald of good news;
Lift it up, fear not;
Say to the cities of Judah,
"Behold your God!"
Isaiah 40:9

Prayer:

—Thank You for being so direct and obvious with how You're calling me now
—Lord, I seriously pray that You would increase my desire for You

—Give me the longing of a passionate lover within me
—Remind me of Your faithfulness, Your sacrifice, and Your passion for me
—Father, inspire my words and writings for this chapel this Wednesday
—I pray for a message that would show the school how much You want intimacy with it, how desperate Your love is
—You tell me to lift up my voice. Fill it with words

5-28-13 (EVENING):

But I will sing
of your strength;
I will sing aloud
of your steadfast love
in the morning.
Psalm 59:16

Prayer:

—Father, thank You that You take over
—Thank You for giving me this song of "Relentless Love" to sing
—I pray that tomorrow You would eliminate my selfish thoughts
—Dissolve my reputation, free me from my inhibitions
—This is Your song, enter me and sing through me

5-30-13 (EVENING):

And though the Lord
give you the bread of adversity
And the water of affliction,
yet your Teacher will not
hide himself anymore, but
your eyes shall see your teacher.
Isaiah 30:20

5-31-13 (MORNING):

Behold, I am doing a new thing;
Now it springs forth, do you not
perceive it?
I will make a way in
the wilderness
and rivers in the desert.
Isaiah 43:19

—You are doing a new thing
—Souls that have been deserts are being renewed

Prayer:

—Thank You for how much You seek me
—Prayer for those touched by my message, that it would NOT fade away
—Prayer for "P", may You grow him into a warrior for You; sense of justice; may he desire You deeper
—Prayer for "L"; conflicting personalities; how powerful he would be as Your servant; You have chosen me to be a force for You in his life; give me the patience and tools to speak to him
—Prayer for me; make me into a man; maturity and growth
Give me a New Song: unprecedented Praise, fresh experience of God's glory that one has never known before

6-1-13 (EVENING):

I AM THE LORD,
I HAVE CALLED YOU IN
RIGHTEOUSNESS;
I WILL TAKE YOU BY THE
HAND AND KEEP YOU;
I WILL GIVE YOU AS A COVENANT
FOR THE PEOPLE;
A LIGHT FOR THE NATIONS,

TO OPEN THE EYES THAT ARE BLIND,
TO BRING OUT THE PRISONERS FROM
THE DUNGEON,
FROM THE PRISON THOSE WHO SIT
IN DARKNESS.
Isaiah 42:6-7

—This is my next calling
—*Isaiah 42:9*

Prayer

—Thank You for not being a hidden God, You are in my face and You are BLATANTLY moving
—Thank You that You have my WHOLE LIFE in the palms of Your hands, I am safe with You, to live is Christ and to die is gain.

6-3-13 (EVENING):

Let everything that
has breath praise the Lord!
Praise the Lord!
Psalm 150:6

Prayer:

—I seek You
—You are there

6-4-13 (MORNING):

Sing praises to the Lord,
who sits enthroned in Zion!
Tell among the peoples
his deeds!
Psalm 9:11

Prayer:

—Empower me, equip me for the task before me

6-5-13 (MORNING):

Isaiah 51:12-13

—"Who are you that you are afraid of man who dies?"
—Fear has blinded you to your Maker and His mighty works
—Why do we ignore the almighty, all-powerful God and fear the ways of the self-destructive oppressor?

Isaiah 51:9, 17

—We tell God to wake up, to move, to do something
—He IS moving, fear has blinded us
—"Wake yourself, wake yourself!"
—It is not God who needs to wake up, it's His people! We sit around out of fear and tell God to do all the work, while WE are His instruments, meant not only to fight for Him but praise Him as well
—Those in fearful apathy cannot truly praise

6-6-13 (MORNING):

Therefore justice is far from us,
and righteousness does not overtake us;
We hope for light, and behold darkness,
and for brightness, but we walk in gloom.
Isaiah 59:9

—We beg for Jesus to enter out hearts yet pursue other lovers
—Many people don't understand that that is why they can't grow close to God
—Intimacy with God gives us sight, a self-centered life leaves us blind

6-7-13 (MORNING):

For he satisfies the
longing soul,
and the hungry soul
he fills with
good things.
Psalm 107:9

Prayer:

—Praise the One who satisfies
—May I forever be a "longing soul"
—Prayer for Josh on the Nicaragua trip
—Prayer for Norfolk Christian's Nicaragua Team

6-10-13 (EVENING):

Rejoice not over me,
O my enemy;
When I fall, I shall rise;
When I sit in darkness,
The Lord will be a light to me.
Micah 7:8

—The Lord makes Himself known when I am sorrowful
—He raises me up
—My enemy will not have victory

Prayer:

—Thank You for being my light
—I pray that You would make me a man, not a boy
—A boy has no self-control, lacks respect, and is a hypocrite
—I want to be a "man of God"
—Give me strength

6-11-13 (EVENING):

—Time with God is essential to a life of faith and spiritual maturity.

I SEE YOU, I AM HERE WITH YOU. IT IS NOT A DIFFICULT TASK TO FIND ME BECAUSE I AM RIGHT BY YOUR SIDE. I WANT YOU, I LOVE YOU.

6-12-13 (MORNING):

For as the earth brings forth
its sprouts
and as a garden causes what is sown in it
to sprout up,
so the Lord God will cause righteousness
and praise
to sprout up before all nations.
Isaiah 61:11

—All nations shall bring forth praise
—A world worshipping together
—What is praise? Constant prayers of thankfulness

Prayer:

—Thank You for seeking me, alone, though You are perfect and I am not
—Thank You for Mrs. Mekkes's constant praise to You
—I pray that I would come that close to You, where I'm filled with joy and always thanking You
—Please Lord, keep teaching me to break down my own boundaries so that I can draw closer and closer to You
—I pray for opportunities to lead worship this Summer
—I pray earnestly for the ability to speak the tongue of the Nicaraguans
—Thank You for Kaitlin, please raise up wisdom to resist the devil and love for those around her
—Prayer for Josh, raise him as a man of God on this trip

6-13-13 (MORNING):

And it shall come to pass afterward,
that I will pour out my Spirit
on all flesh; your sons
and your daughters shall prophesy,
your old men shall dream dreams,
and your young men shall see visions.
Joel 2:28

Prayer:

—I am Your beloved
—For Ben's sister, Kaitlin, let faith and intimate love never leave her
—For "B", thank You for his gift with words, thank You for his honesty
—For "L", give me the opportunities to hang with him and build a friendship
—I pray earnestly for the gift of prophecy and the gift of speaking in the tongues of other nations
—Thank You for how obviously You are moving in my life

6-14-13 (EVENING):

Ruth 2:11-12
—The Lord is pleased when we leave behind what we love to follow him
—"Came to a people that you did not know before"
—"A full reward be given you by the Lord"

6-16-13 (MORNING):

—Matthew 16:23 "Get behind me Satan!" Satan hindering Jesus's ministry through Peter
—Satan is trying to hinder my relationship with the Lord, in the

name of Christ I command him out of the way
—I want more of You, God, show me what I have to sacrifice

The Lord will certainly make
my lord a sure house, because
my lord is fighting the
battles of the Lord, and evil shall
not be found in you so long as you live.
1 Samuel 25:28b

—As long as I fervently fight the battles of the Lord, evil will be far from me
—Show me the battles I am to fight
—I WILL

6-17-13 (MORNING):

For you have delivered
my soul from death, my
eyes from tears,
my feet from stumbling;
I will walk before
The Lord in the land of the living.
Psalm 116:8-9

Prayer:
—for a renewed mind
—I want to know You more
Beach Walk
—I have two options right now
—Walking on shore/shallow water or walking in deeper water
—Shallow water-easy, not dangerous, can see my feet, clear way (miles of beach, houses)
—Deep water-I have to work to move, could be knocked down, can't see my footing, unclear way (changing of tides, surging waves)

—On shallow water I've asked the deep water why it doesn't come up to me so I can experience it on solid ground.
—But I can't have the safety of the shallow water and the satisfaction of the deep
—In the shallow (easy) I may have a clear vision (I can see what's ahead) but it's monotonous
—Deep water--exciting, refreshing, strengthening
—The deep already exists (God's love), but it has already come for me
—I have to let go of the easy monotonous path to experience the exciting purposeful path.

6-18-13 (EVENING):

So we have come to know
and to believe
the love that God has for us.
God is love,
and whoever abides in love
abides in God, and God
abides in him.
1 John 4:16

—God will abide in me when I love those around me

—Who am I not loving?

Prayer:

—You are love, thank You for loving me
—Teach me to listen
—Prayer for gift of prophecy, I need often to be shown things plainly, guide me
—Prayer for speaking in tongue of Nicaraguan, help me love and communicate with them

6-19-13 (EVENING):

Because the poor are plundered
and the needy groan,
"I will now arise," says
The Lord.
"I will protect them from
those who malign them."
Psalm 12:5

Psalm 10:17-18

Prayer:

—Thank You that You are the Mighty Avenger, that those who abuse women and children will get what they deserve
—The trade of people affects everyone, I want to be a part in fighting it
—Be with me as I find my role
—Gift of prophecy, Gift of tongues

6-20-13 (MORNING):

O Lord,
You hear the desire of the
afflicted;
You will strengthen their heart;
You will incline Your ear

To do justice to the fatherless
and the oppressed, so that
man who is of the earth
may strike terror no more.
Psalm 10: 17-18

—Romans 12:19—"Vengeance is mine"

Prayer:

Father, I'm so thankful I worship a just God who does not turn his eyes from the innocent and the helpless. You say You will avenge them, those who harm them will receive the wages due such treatment. Lord, I want to rescue the prisoners, as You showed me. I pray for clarity of mind and courage as I find out how. Thank You that You are a just God.

Mark

6-22-13

Tonight I walked on the balcony, gazed over the ocean, and prayed for the people I love the most. For Carley, Kaitlin, Ben, Ryan, Ellen, Lauren, Mr. and Mrs. Mekkes, Mom, Dad, Will, Daniel, Rii. All of these people are family in some way, and I prayed earnestly and uniquely for each.

I cannot stand alone. These people inspire me, strengthen me, make me laugh, make me go deeper, and teach me about the Lord. They are all blessings to me.

Lastly, I prayed for myself. For courage. For guidance. For wisdom. That I would become a man. God has plans for me, crazy plans. He will, and He already is beginning to, prepare me.

God's not dead. Faith's not dead. I have a call, a mission. By God's grace I will fulfill it.

SELAH

I AM THE LORD, I HAVE CALLED YOU IN RIGHTEOUSNESS; I WILL TAKE YOU BY THE HAND AND KEEP YOU; I WILL GIVE YOU AS A COVENANT FOR THE PEOPLE; A LIGHT FOR THE

NATIONS, TO OPEN THE EYES THAT ARE BLIND, TO BRING OUT THE PRISONERS FROM THE DUNGEON, FROM THE PRISON THOSE WHO SIT IN DARKNESS.
ISAIAH 42:6-7

6-25-13 (EVENING):

For Zion's sake I will not keep silent, and for Jerusalem's sake I will not be quiet, until her righteousness goes forth as brightness and her salvation as a burning torch. The nations shall see your righteousness, and all the kings your glory, and you shall be called by a new name that the mouth of the Lord will give.
Isaiah 62:1-2

—my new name—kherer (sword)?
—I want to go to Ruby's House of Prayer again

6-26-13 (EVENING):

For they are a rebellious people, lying children, children unwilling to hear the instruction of the Lord; who say to the seers, "Do not see," and to the prophets, "Do not prophesy to us what is right; speak to us smooth things, prophesy illusions, leave the way, turn aside from the path, let us hear no more about the Holy One of Israel."
Isaiah 30: 9-11

—People don't want to hear the uncomfortable message I have to bring
—They will try to lead me off the path

6-27-13

We live in a world of changing and unchanging circumstances, but I believe that God has given each of us the ability to be joyful in everything. What areas of my life am I always complaining or grumbling about? I can change them.

(EVENING):

—Thank You for showing me what's had me so bummed
—Circumstance—my younger siblings need to be watched while my parents are at work
—I've been complaining and grumbling about this, but this is a circumstance I can't change and that You've put me in.
—Thank You for my parents trying to help me find time with friends
—I pray earnestly that I may see my friends before my trip
—prayer for Kaitlin's ministry
—for prophecy and tongues

Mark and Ben

6-28-13 (MORNING):

Give me neither poverty
nor riches; feed
me with the food that is needful

for me,
lest I be full and deny you,
and say, "Who is the Lord?"
Proverbs 30: 8b-9a

EVENING:

I found out today that Ben is leaving NCS. Though I was really bummed at first, God quickly revealed to me His plan.
—At school, I'm with Ben at nearly every social opportunity
—God has been making me more extroverted
—Mission of spiritual unification of grade from January
—With some of my best friends gone, I can now focus on forming relationships with guys from all over the place in my grade
—Timing: I'll also have my license to hang out with people
—I do pray Ben can continue to be a part of our worship ministry in chapel

6-30-13 (18 DAYS UNTIL NICARAGUA) EVENING:

Arise, shine, for your light has come, and the glory of the Lord has risen upon you. For behold, darkness shall cover the earth and thick darkness the peoples; but the Lord will arise upon you, and his glory will be seen upon you. And nations shall come to your light, and kings to the brightness of your rising.
Isaiah 60:1-3

—Saw this in church bulletin today, also shown by God in May!
—18 days, time to start preparing!

7-1-13 (17 DAYS) EVENING:

—Started and finished Ecclesiastes tonight
—Enjoy the fruits of your labor, they are gifts from God

—The endless patterns of life make it seem meaningless, but there is a greater calling.

7-2-13

SING! SING CHILD! OH HOW I LOVE THE SOUND OF YOUR VOICE! THE ROCKS, THE TREES, THE SKIES, EVEN THE ANGELS WILL SING WITH YOU!

I WILL SING WITH YOU!

ALL I WANT IS YOUR SONG! YOUR LOVE! YOUR WORSHIP! BOUNDLESS JOY AWAITS!

AWAKE, AWAKE O SLEEPER.

ARISE FROM THE DEAD.

I WILL SHINE ON YOU.

COME CLOSE.

7-3-13 (15 DAYS) EVENING:

Jeremiah 1
—I am only a youth
—I need not know what gifts He will give me
—All I need to know is that He has called me to proclaim His name (Isaiah 40:9)
—He will take care of the rest
—I need to remember that He loves me
—"His heart ripped out to show me He loved me" Flyleaf

7-4-13 (14 DAYS) EVENING:

Found out today that Ben actually is coming to NCS! I was a bit confused at first, because I felt like God was making Ben leave my school life for a reason. Then I realized something:

—By thinking Ben was gone, I gained a whole new idea and understanding how hanging with the same people can limit my mission of unification
—I still have the same calling but now I have Ben too!
—Answer to prayer—he can be a part of chapel

7-5-13 (13 DAYS) EVENING:

He will swallow up death forever;
And the Lord God will
wipe away tears from all faces,
and the reproach of his people he will take
away from all the earth,
for the Lord has spoken.
Isaiah 25:8

—Hallelujah! We worship a God whose victory is sure!
—To live is Christ and to die is gain!
—Death has lost its sting!

7-6-13 (12 DAYS)

"For the mountains may depart
and the hills be removed
but my steadfast love shall not depart from You,
and my covenant of peace shall not be removed,"
says the Lord, who has compassion on you.
Isaiah 54:10

7-7-13 (11 DAYS) EVENING:

But now, O Lord,
you are our Father;
We are the clay, and you are our potter;
we are the work of your hand.
Isaiah 64:8

—The work of one potter can be distinguished from another's
—Potter puts a bit of himself in his work
—I am being molded
—Am I being resistant to the potter's work?
—Nicaragua will be a huge time of molding
—Enseñame a amar……. "Teach me to love"

7-8-13 (10 DAYS) EVENING:

Read *Isaiah 65*

"But I do not account my life of any value nor as precious to myself, if only I may finish my course and the ministry that I received from the Lord Jesus, to testify to the gospel of the grace of God."
Acts 20:24

—If I neglect my calling, my life is worthless
—YOU WILL PRAY AND PEOPLE WILL BE HEALED

7-9-13 (9 DAYS) EVENING:

I am my beloved's
and his desire is for me.
Song 7:10

—I SWEAR I DESIRE YOU
—"Wanna look right at You, sing right to You"
—May I learn to worship and see God in new ways in Nicaragua
—Ask God for water, He will provide it in the rock
—DO NOT BE AFRAID TO ASK FOR POWERFUL MIRACULOUS THINGS

7-10-13 (8 DAYS) EVENING:

1 Chronicles 25:1—"who prophesied with lyres, with harps, and with cymbals."

The verb "to prophesy" (Hebrew. Naba) indicates that their songs were prompted or guided by the Spirit of God. This shows that "prophecy" is not always a direct announcement of God's plans; it indicated that the person is operating as God's authorized spokesman, here providing the right way from God's people to sing to him. (ESV footnote)

I want to be this
—People literally prophesied through music!

Psalm 130: 5-6 "I wait for the Lord, my soul waits, and in his word I hope; my soul waits for the Lord more than watchmen for the morning, more than watchmen for the morning."
—He's coming!

7-11-13 (7 DAYS) EVENING:

Psalm 34:1—"I will bless the Lord at all times; his praise shall continually be in my mouth."

Psalm 34:3—"Oh, magnify the Lord with me, and let us exalt his name together!"

Psalm 34:19—"Many are the afflictions of the righteous, but the Lord delivers him out of them all."
—Lots of verses about music and worship tonight
—Immediate worship opportunities—Tab youth Group,

Nicaragua, School
—I want my praise to be directed right to God
—I want my worship to be passionate and unashamed
—Thank You that I get to worship so much with my brother Ben!

7-13-13 (5 DAYS) EVENING:

—Talked to Carley about Nicaragua tonight
—She said that though I think it'll change (strengthen) certain characteristics of mine, she expects I may come back an entirely new person
—I'm scared of coming back broken and angry and confused again
—I wanna come back strong and fired up with mission and purpose

"Trust in the Lord and do good; dwell in the land and befriend faithfulness. Delight yourself in the Lord, and he will give you the desires of your heart. Commit your way to the Lord; trust in Him, and He will act. He will bring forth your righteousness as the light, and your justice as the noonday."
Psalm 37: 3-6

—If I trust in God, He will bring forth the light in me. Even if I hurt, He is bringing out the best in me
—Awesome verse on justice

"The wicked draw the sword and bend their bows and bring down the poor and needy, to slay those whose way is upright; their sword shall enter their own heart, and their bows shall be broken."
Psalm 37: 14-15

7-16-13 (2 DAYS!!) EVENING:

—Read both *Isaiah 6:9-10* and *Acts 28:26-27*

—People with hardened hearts, closed eyes and ears

Isaiah 6:8 "And I heard the voice of the Lord saying, 'Whom shall I send, and who will go for us?' Then I said, 'Here I am! Send me.' "

—*Acts 28:29*—If their hearts were to be opened, God would heal them

I think I will run into Nicaraguans like this

—HEARTS MUST BE OPENED

—Lord, I pray that You'd show me how!

7-17-13 (1 DAY!!!) EVENING:

—In Maryland with mom and dad

Pretty big connection!

—*1 Sam 25:28* showed up again (fighting the battles of the Lord)

—*Revelation 12:11*—"They triumphed over him (Satan) by the blood of the lamb and the word of their testimony; they did not love their lives so much as to shrink from death."

—*Revelation 15:2-4* Those that triumph over the beast are singing God's praises "All nations will come to worship you."

—BOLDNESS *Proverbs 28:1* "The wicked flee when no one pursues, but the righteous are bold as a lion."*

—VOICE WITH STRENGTH-*Isaiah 40:9* "Go on up to a high mountain, O Zion, herald of good news; lift up your voice with strength, O Jerusalem, herald of good news, lift it up, fear not; say to the cities of Judah, 'Behold your God!' "

—"What shall I cry?" Give me the words to shout and a voice to shout them with. Sustain the gospel in my mouth in happiness, hardship, joy, peace, sadness, sorrow, strength.

—Enseñame a amar

—Tomorrow night, I will sleep in Nicaragua

*Another reference to the verse that ended up being on Officer Jone's gravestone

Note: Letting Mark go to Nicaragua was difficult. It helped a lot to know that my trusted friend, Katie Adams, was a "Mom on the ground" and would be able to help him if he needed anything. We had talked to him a lot about going with a mission and that it was not a vacation. He took this seriously and raised enough money to help complete a greenhouse building that is still in operation today. He was able to help build it with his own hands and see how having sustainable farming would benefit the children living at the orphanage and provide potential income.

7-18-13
EVENING:(ON PLANE FROM ATLANTA TO MGA) NICARAGUA ☺

—"Happy am I to live a hungry life, blessed am I to thirst."
—I pray for constant hunger, to never be satisfied with how much I know You, but to always want to know and love You more.
—The "full" don't feel like they need You so they don't seek You (mediocre, predictable, lonely life)
Blessed are the hungry, for they are constantly being filled, constantly going deeper in You.
"Hunger is an escort to the deeper things of You."
Nicaragua!
—Just drove in the dark with Josh to Bernabe
—Talked about music, his past struggles, and effectiveness of teams
—"It's kinda rude for Americans to think they need to give our kids love for a day, when that's exactly what their caretakers are sacrificing time, energy and money to do."
—Have to admit Nicaragua's a little scary on my own
—Stories of how kids misbehave—running away, making out with girls, even having sex with them
—Revolution holiday tomorrow, we'll see what's up

Give me neither poverty nor riches; feed me with the food that is needful for me, lest I be full and deny you, and say "who is the Lord?"
Proverbs 30:8b-9a

Things I wanna be able to teach the kids:
—They are meant for more than just having fun
—A steady girlfriend is so much better than just making out with random girls
—Armondo—LEADERSHIP
—How much their leaders love them
Los ñinos de la pesada:

Yader	Bayardo
Chepe	Armondo
Julio	Cairo
Marcos	Norbin
Ricardo	Julian
Brayan	

7-19-13 (NICARAGUA DÍA UNO)

Salvo o valiente?
(Safe or Brave?)

MORNING:

Sin palabras, sin lenguaje,
sin una voz perceptible, por
toda la tierra resuena su eco,
sus palabras llegan hasta los confines
del mundo.
Salmo 19:3-4a

Salmo 19:8—Los preceptos del Senor son rectos, traen alegríaal corazon. El mandamiento del señores claro: da luz a los ojos.
—Enseñame a amar.....
"Teach me to love"
—Show me what You want me to do
—I WANT YOU TO BEFRIEND THESE KIDS. SHOW THAT YOU ARE MAKING AN EFFORT TO CONNECT. SIMPLY LOVE THEM AND KEEP LISTENING TO WHAT I WANT YOU TO DO.

—You've led me this far.
—Of course this is gonna be a challenge
—I pray for realness, transparency. I pray that I would not let my love for You be limited by anything.
—THIS PLACE MAY LOOK LIKE I'VE ABANDONED IT TO HOPELESSNESS. BUT I SENT YOU HERE, DIDN'T I?
—It is hard to feel like I'm doing anything worthwhile when I and the kids are sitting around. I need to remember that although that may be true, I was called here for a reason.
—It's time for me to put the principles I preach in practice. Bravery over safety, Blind Faith, Uncircumstantial Joy

What I did Today:
—Woke up, met boys, told Armondo "hi" from Carley and Mr. Schanck
—Helped Armondo tie up some tomato plants, each boy has their own set of plants
—Tried teaching Armondo some guitar chords (GDCF)
—Painted auditorium floor (drank coke out of plastic bags)
—Card games, soccer (got beaned in the face)
—Devotions at auditorium (William talked about the free will of the soul)
—Going to bed

7-20-13 NICARAGUA DÍA DOS

Marcos—has parents (sees sometimes) and siblings at Casa Bernabe
—I felt really bummed out this morning
—Was still feeling like I'm not doing anything, not making an impact
—While helping build greenhouse (mixing cement), the idea of speaking at Friday night devotions popped into my head. Asked God for someone else to ask me about it if He wants me to do it.

—At the guys/girls youth group, I thought they were talking about abstinence but then a bunch of kids (none from Bernabe) got up and accepted Christ.
—Seeing the tears and sincere love for God kinda brought me back to life
—Still had my doubts, was wondering if God really sent me
—The group played a video with a ton of verses, one stuck out to me
—It was *Isaiah 6:8* which showed up before the trip too.
—"Whom shall I send?"—God
—"Lord, send me." Isaiah
—The music came on and I felt stoked on God and sure of my calling again.

Tú me quieres a ayudarte aprender la guitarra? —Do you want me to teach you guitar?

Solamente Sorprendiendo—Just Wondering

Today:

—Poured concrete for greenhouse (I loved getting to help)
—A ton of Jesus Culture (Band)
—Solid game of fútbol Americano in the storm
—One of the guys showed up with an iguana
—Youth group at Verbo Church
—Mario Kart! The kids were in awe of my gringo powers
—Shaved the beard…Wasn't as great as I thought
—Talked to Ben on phone, left Carley a message

Yader—sister Kimberly at Casa Bernabe, parents in Veracruz

I AM SO HERE. YOU ASK WHAT DO YOU TEACH A PEOPLE WHO SEEM OKAY WITH THEIR SITUATION? YOU TEACH THEM JOY AND OF MY GOODNESS. THAT'S WHY I SENT YOU.

Since I don't have many ways to relate with these people, joy is my greatest weapon.

7-21-13 (NICARAGUA DÍA TRES)

Today:
—Taught Bayardo, Armondo and Chepe chords, scales and strum patterns
—Armondo is getting really good
—Threw football in living/common room (or whatever) with Chepe and William. Chepe imitating dives by jumping on the couch
—Church—Incredible worship team, a ton of dancing
—Waited outside church for the Adams, going to El Cañyon (Maria's Orphanage)
—Met Guillermo, Nicaraguan guy who asked what I was doing in Nicaragua short but cool conversation in Spanish
—Woman (short, older) came up to me and asked me for medicine or money because she has cancer, I didn't have any, asked her if I could pray for her but she said she didn't understand English. I told God I'd pray for her if she showed up again but she didn't
—Went to Adams and chilled (no El Cañyon)
—Met James Belt, cool talk
—Need to give those in poverty spiritual and tangible hope

NICA Church
—God is not mumbling, He wants to speak with you!
—The worship is so dang real here, like a party, people dancing around…pretty much a mosh pit
—SEE THESE PEOPLE AROUND YOU? SEE THEIR JOY, THEIR ALL-OUT LOVE FOR ME? YOU DON'T SEE THIS EVERYWHERE. I CALLED YOU TO SHARE IN THIS LOVE AT CHURCH AND TO SHOW IT TO THE NICARAGUANS WHO DON'T HAVE IT.
—It is truly a blessing to get to speak with leaders (Tim, James, Josh, William) about their visions for Nicaragua
—William—loves miracles and seeing God at work, just like me!

"You are my witnesses."
declares the Lord,
"and my servant who I have chosen,
that you may know and believe me
and understand that I am he.
Before me no god was formed,
nor shall there be any after me."
Isaiah 43:10

—God wants me to know Him!
—Americans not spending money for guilt of those with less—
Are you being called to (and will you) give that money to those in poverty?
—Guilt is a terrible motivator.
—Only creates more poverty if you're just giving stuff away randomly (need to support a solid cause)
—Dice game with Tucker and Mr. Adams
—met Steph, sort of Mr. Adam's intern
—Tip Top with the Adams, James and Steph
—Talking to Mr. Adams about job at Orphan Network and after
—He says he thinks he could set up going to Ruby's House of Prayer
—Got home, almost straight to skype with mom and dad
—Skyped Carley for almost an hour, so good to see her face and talk to her!
—Came back and had an awesome talk with William
—The boys have heard a lot about God, but it's pretty easy to tell they're not on fire
—The goal is that in the end (through our teaching) we will leave them with something and see a change.
—William—didn't grow up with a father, but knows God is his father
—want to get boys involved with devotions, reading their Bibles
—A tarantula came in la posada.........aye, aye, aye

MONDAY DEVOTION NOTES:

TOPIC—As men, It is our duty to protect and care for women and children

—Though we're young now, someday you may have a wife and children
—A family is like one of the tomatoes Armondo is planting
—As men, we are like farmers
—If we don't care for our families, they will be weak and fall apart
—Like a good farmer, we need to support the plant so it can live and grow healthy
—This is like our wives and children because we will need to protect them and work to provide for them
—It is a man's job to defend those who aren't as strong (women and children)
—There are a lot of men who like to hurt women and children and those who aren't as strong as them
—These are the weakest men on earth, because they need to use their strength against others to feel happy
—Men like that end up alone
—It proves you are strong if you take a stand for those you are responsible for
—Protecting someone is one of the best feelings in all the world
—verse on widows and orphans (*James 1:27*)

7-22-2013

Today:
—Woke up at 5:50, gave devotion, expression on the boy's faces was like middle school youth group (indifference/disinterest)
—Boys left for school
—The sun finally came out, (beautiful outside), had an awesome devotion outside
—Thought Samuel's (Isaac's son) nanny was his wife and talked

to her like that…finally figured it out
—Went into Managua with Josh and Andrea, dropped Andrew off somewhere went in mall to get flip flops
—Andrew and Stanley (former Bernabe) showed up, had a chai latte (first time I've liked something coffee-ish)
—Came home, kids finishing school, lunch
—Music teacher enlisted me for guitar lessons, taught Bayardo, Armondo and Chepe
—Armondo and Bayardo—switching chords and scale, Chepe—working hard on strums (he's left-handed)
—Worked in field with Armondo, talked about his family
—"Do you want to be a good man?" "Yes. Someday"
—Made sure Chepe was working, climbing a tree like a monkey and cutting branches, came down when storm hit (actually not that bad)
—Cairn, Jeremy (not sure where he lives), and I threw football, lots of fun
—Showered, dinner, worked on strums with Chepe a little more

7-22-13 (NICARAGUA DÍA CUATRO)

Morning prayer

—Teach me to worship You in new ways
You won't relent…

Set me as a seal upon your heart
as a seal upon your arm,
for love is strong as death,
jealousy is fierce as the grave.
Its flashes are flashes of fire,
the very flame of the Lord.
Many waters cannot quench love,
neither can floods drown it.
Song 8:6-7a

—Nothing quenches God's love for me
—True love—patient, kind, selfless, enduring
—My love for God is meant to be constant, strong in the storm
—Lord, give me the faith to follow this calling wherever it may lead
—I've seen a lot of youth groups where no one cares (devotions)
—Show me how to teach them in a way that will interest them
—Thank You for Your faithfulness

DAILY NOTES:
—Armondo wants to learn to play and sing a toast to the future kids
—Taught him a little bit
—Left for "meeting" with Josh, Andrew and William about Friday nights (Herberto wants us to take over Friday nights)
—Ended up going to dinner (I already ate, just got a coke) with two gringas who know Katie Beasley (went on Carley's March trip)
—Awesome, hilarious night
—Found out more about Norbin, though he smiles like he's up to something, he's actually really nice
—Also, it's not that insulting that the boys call Marcos gordo (fat), in Nicaragua people tell it like it is
—Went back to Josh's (and Andrew's) house (still with gringas)
—Kinda practiced "One Thing Remains" and "Enseñame a amar", turned into random acoustic jamming with screams
—Came home with William, everyone in bed
—The last two days have really been a break, I wanna be around the kids more
—Also, Bryan came back today (ran away, and because he ran away he was kicked out for a while), seems like a nice kid.
—At dinner Josh asked me to speak at one of the Friday night

devotionals, direct response to my prayer for someone to ask me if me speaking is in God's will.

Prayer/Devo

—So awesome how Josh asked me to speak without me saying anything about it, I love when You speak to me like that!
—I wanna talk on relentless love
—Thank You for the breaks, I feel like I need to get back in it with the kids
—Gonna pray tomorrow about whether God wants me to speak this Friday or later

7-23-13

Today:
—William gave devotional, impressive ability to use humor to get the guys interested (I think the language barrier limits me in that area)
—Two little Bluefields girls ran up and said hello to William and I at breakfast
—Pastor William from Mayasa (or Masaya...eh) talked to male leaders after kids left for school, I couldn't understand much but it made me think that I wanna talk to the leaders more
—Awesome sunrise-ish devotional (again!)
—VNDF Quarterly meeting (James, Mr. Adams, Josh, Herberto, Bob Trolese, others) kinda boring but cool to get an inside look
—VNDF—focusing on four specific areas
—self-sufficient model agribusiness
—spiritual and moral instruction
—career-oriented education
—sustainable vo-tech programs
—Ran various errands (and grabbed lunch with) Josh and Herberto. Talked about how busy Josh's job is, I told him it may be time to take one step back and entrust certain people with responsibilities to find a good person to share his huge workload with.

—Herberto asked me if I'd be interested in speaking to the girls, I think I am, need to pray about it
—Dead tired, finally got home and helped Marcos and Norvin with some farming stuff

7-23-13 (TUESDAY, NICARAGUA DÍA CINCO) MORNING:

Hallelujah
I'm cavin' in
Hallelujah
I'm in love again
Hallelujah
I'm a wretched man
Hallelujah
Every breath is a second chance

"Always" by Switchfoot

—*James 1:27* has showed up twice in the past two days
—"Religion that is pure and undefiled before God, the Father, is this; to visit orphans and widows in their affliction, and to keep oneself unstained from the world."
—Where am I? Surrounded by orphans and widows
—Interesting that I challenged the Posada boys with this, and now it's my challenge as well
—Lord, I think I'll be in many situations like the woman with cancer
—I pray that You would give me the wisdom and the faith to deal with those

7-24-13

—Worked on frame of greenhouse, first time working with Bryan, he seems like a funny/nice guy

—Started teaching Armondo how to play "How He loves"
—Finally Chepe mastered a new strum pattern, I strumming with him, and as he watched my finger he got the hang of it
—Quick soccer game, two teams shooting on Harry's (caretaker of younger boys) brother
—Dinner, Bryan apologized for running away in front of everybody
—Arm wrestled Julio, Norvin, and Bryan (who actually won, ridiculously strong)
—Headed off to worship practice with Josh
—Enseñame a amar, One thing Remains, Take it all, Spanish Hosanna (not a cover, it's its "own thing"
—Awesome U2 "with or without you" intro to take it all
—So stoked to sing these, perfect keys
—At end of "One thing remains", sweet "Enseñame a amar" chorus repeat (Switchfoot style)
—Practicing with Andrew tomorrow
—A fan sent in one of Josh's band's tracks, they won a Battle of the Bands! Playing that song this weekend, haven't practiced it in like three years
—Came home, guys asleep, Julian jumping rope in the dark

WEDNESDAY DEVOTIONAL NOTES

Isaiah 64:8
—God is the potter, we are the work of His hand
—If a potter is good, his work stands out from others
—A potter puts a bit of himself in his work
—Like William said Friday, we are the only creation God made by hand.
—The potter (Jesus)
—drove out demons, He has given us power over evil
—Brave, He walked to His death without a word
—Leader, people like the twelve disciples gave everything to follow Him
—Faithful, believed God's promise that He would rise from the dead

—Self-sacrificing—died for people who didn't even deserve it

Today:
—Another beautiful morning, had devotions
—felt like going to meet some of the staff
—helped a man named Obaldo with some welding
—He said something crazy in Spanish, turned out all he said was he wanted Coca-cola
—Helped me with some Spanish (empujar, jalar, deslizar, girar)
—Wants to learn English
—Said something about "Playboy", got kinda a weird vibe on him
—Helped cook lift a big pot of soup, I couldn't lift it because it was burning through the rag I was holding, then the cook (a woman) lifted it easily and everyone kinda looked at me…ah
—Lunch, then worked on greenhouse for like four hours
—moving cinder blocks
—Attached more perlin (steel bars) to frame, this took most of the time
—Dinner, then started blog post
—Skyped Mom, Carley, and Ben
—Homesickness kinda hit right there
—Music practice with full band, pretty stoked
—Also, some soccer before and after dinner

7-24-13 WEDNESDAY (NICARAGUA DÍA SEIS)

—*James 1:27* just showed up for the THIRD time in "Notes from home"*
—AND *Isaiah 6:8* for the fourth time in *Matthew 13:14-15*

In spite of all this,
they still sinned;
Despite his wonders,
they did not believe.
Psalm 78:43

—The Israelites, though they had seen so much of His glory, still didn't have faith and tested God
—It's easy to ignore the awesomeness of the miracles around me in want of more or "bigger" ones
Talk with Carley (skype)
—We often mentally turn things into time periods and make them matters of success and failure
—The fear of failure closes our ears to God's will and takes away our joy
—I've been trying to get to know the boys so I can minister to them, but I need to be trying to get to know them to get to know them
—No motive, just friendship

7-25-13

Today:
—Breakfast, then straight to music practice
-singing in Spanish is TOUGH
-Spanish Hosanna—Making this essentially the most metal worship song ever
-Attic is so stinking hot
—Waited for Andrew to be done with computer so I could post blog, awesome talk/sharing of music between the three of us
—Finished blog, headed home at nearly midday
—Lunch, then went to work on greenhouse
-Mainly just mixed concrete
—Helped Norvin string up tomatoes, some of my favorite conversations are happening in that field
-Parents live together in Panama
-Sister, a year older (14) at Casa
-Gets to see his parents next year...long time
—Tried to peg a mango out of a tree with Julian, Bayardo, Yader, and Norvin
—Surprised how much I liked it
—Chepe and Armando practiced a bit of guitar, tried to teach

Ricky some, not really happening
—Gorgeous sunset on the way to dinner
—Played Uno with Marcos, Bryan, Chepe, and Julio…two plus fourteens…
—Kids had world view class, I checked out my care package
—More UNO
—A bat flew in La Posada before bed…yay
—Also worked out with William and the guys

7-25-13 THURSDAY (NICA DÍA SIETE)

—Wondering about how calling works
  -Does God always send you with a defined purpose?
  -Is every missions trip a calling?

EVENING:
—That talk with Carley is really resonating with me
—If I were to keep thinking of this trip as success and failure, life would grow dark very quickly
—The goal of this trip should not be success
—When I get home, what matters is this: Did I worship God with all my heart and soul? Did I shamelessly proclaim the Gospel with my life?
—Mom sent me a letter saying a lot of what I've been thinking: Don't try to "complete God's sentences"—God sent me to Nicaragua to ________________? I have no idea why He sent me here. I just need to follow the Spirit.

STORY OF SAUL/PAUL
—Saul was not given specific orders of how exactly to minister
—All that happened was this: He saw God's awesomeness, so he preached His name
—God may call us to certain places, but we are meant to be constantly preaching the gospel wherever we are
—"I will show him how much he must suffer for the sake of my name." *Acts 9:16*

7-26-13

Today:
—Kids off to school, went straight to greenhouse
—Lunch then Uno
—Messaged Dorothy to try to get together at some point
—Back to Greenhouse
—Before lunch—James, Adams, Steph, and Savannah came by to check out Greenhouse with Josh
—At four, dropped off laundry with Josh and started setting up for our worship band
—Setlist: Música del cielos (sing, sing, sing), Tómalo (Take it all) Hosanna, Una Cosa Permanere (One thing Remains), and Enseñamea amar
—Awesome set, pretty much the heaviest but most passionate worship I've ever played
—William spoke about how you can't blame anything for your future because you have right now.
—Tómalo again during offering, they told me to just sit since I didn't have the strap on so Josh had to sing…went interestingly.
—Hosanna one more time, I talked quickly before to Spring Branch about uncircumstantial worship
—Josh screamed!
—Porch time with Spring Branch—Devotional and games
—Evil cicadas

7-26-13 FRIDAY (NICA DÍA OCHO)
MORNING:

I'm in Nicaragua, but I haven't seen the sorrow, the hurt I expected to find yet. I remember Fabio, I remember her brokenness how far she's retreated into herself. I remember hearing about the hell she's lived in. How violated her soul has been. And I remember that though she smiled for a second while were with her, soon after she was pulled from Casa Belen back into the darkness.

I have no idea what the Posada boys have been through. But they all laugh, they all get along (for the most part) and they all seem to be doing well. I don't see them struggling. Yeah, they're disobedient sometimes. Well duh, they're teenagers.

God told me He wants me to bring from the prison those who sit in darkness. In my mind, that's Fabi. That's the sex slaves, the child laborers, the abused.

MARK, ISN'T THE WHOLE IDEA OF DARKNESS THAT YOU CAN'T SEE?

Then show me their pain! Show me the mourning of the people around me. You say my salvation goes forth as a burning torch, illuminate the dungeon around me. Show me the hurting; give me the understanding, the empathy to mourn with them. Take my pride, take my fear, and show me them.

Please.

7-27-13

Today:
—Sound of kids woke me up, straight to breakfast
—Everyone but Brayon and Julio went…somewhere
—Went for a thirty minute run
—Showered, then helped Herberto
 -moved bags of cement
 -painted parts of greenhouse with Julio
 -tried to bend parts of framing back into place
—Josh picked me up to take me to the Adams
—On the way, we talked about his new music, (#1 song on only Rock station in Nica second day in a row)
—Went home with Adams, had lunch
—James Belt came over, in a wacky mood, said something I didn't really get, then left
—Went to pool, played shark and bulldog
—Off to Catarina with everyone, including James's parents
—Gorgeous overlook of Laguna de Apoyo

—Pelirojo gringo selling legit stuff made of plastic bags.
—Checked out random shops
—Back to Bernabe with Tim
    -Tip Top
    -Amazing sunset, God showing off
    -Talked about calling/sharing gospel
—Uno with some guys, threw football with Chepe and Brayan
—Julio wanted me to help him with some English to speak to a girl who had come down on a trip and written him a letter that said God had "put them together for a reason"
—He wanted to tell her "I love you with all my heart and my soul."
—It honestly hurt to help him translate, because this girl who "knew" him for a week will never be able to be what he wants her to be. He will hurt because of this
—Boys chased me around with cicadas and a humungous moth that definitely could've been a bat (bombitos)
—Went to Team Center, met Caleb
    -Came here in March with Nicaraguan Orphan Fund (college thing)
    -Not really with Spring Branch, came back to get to know the country better
    -When helping hurts—not necessarily about the product but the process
    -Matt Damon
—Signs with Spring Branch
—Found out from Piper the girl who wrote Julio isn't coming back to Casa
    -she wants me to tell him to write to her anyways

7-27-13 (MORNING):

BREAK MY HEART FOR
WHAT BREAKS
YOURS
Acts 14:8-23

—Paul prays and a man is healed
—The people STONE him, yet he gets back up and goes to preach somewhere else
—And then he comes BACK to the city that stoned him and keeps preaching!
"I will show him how much he must suffer for the sake of my name."
"To live is Christ and to die is gain."

What's incredible to me about this story is that the next city Paul went to could've stoned him too. But life and death literally don't seem to matter to him because he has Christ no matter what. The only reason for him to be on earth is to preach the gospel.

I want to be like this!!!

7-28-13 SUNDAY (NICA DÍA DIEZ)

Today:
—Woke up, breakfast
—Some guitar with Armando and Chepe
—Off to church, on Felix's bus! But no Felix ☹
—Awesome Verbo Church Worship
—Looked at the people dancing and praying during worship, thought how much I want to be like that
—God told me that becoming that begins now
—Why let what people may think stop me? Realized there's something attractive to me about being looked down upon for going crazy for Jesus
—Raised my hands and it felt so good, some Nicaraguan lady came up and prayed something in Spanish for me
—Went home with Adams, headed off to El Canyon
—So weird to be there after fiveish years, some of the girls I played with (we were all like fourth graders) are teenagers now
—Recognized some of them (Leyla and Arlen), Leyla is apparently really serious about her faith and in love with Jesus
—Checked out some El Cañyon houses where Adams' teams will be teaching families to grow their own food

—Everyone left, but I stayed and played soccer with James and some local young guys
—pouring rain, basically turned into water polo
—came home and changed
—went to dinner at Galerías at Hippo's, incredible wings
—Grabbed some ice cream
—Came back home, skyped whole family
—skyped Carley, long talk with Julio and "When Helping Hurts" book type stuff
—updated blog, "Necesitando a amar" about how we need to be careful about how we treat orphans
—Actually checked FB for the first time, went to bed way too late.

JULY 28, 2013 (FROM ENSENAME A AMAR BLOG)

Hey everybody, I know I just posted recently but a lot has happened the past couple of days and I thought I'd share it with you. P.S. This may be a pretty long post

On Friday, I led one of my favorite worship experiences of my life. Our band consisted of Josh (guitar and some vox), his brother Andrew (drums), me (vox and guitar), and Marysol (killer harmonies), one of the caretakers for the girls. All the Bernabe kids and the Spring Branch Nicaragua team came out to the auditorium to worship with us.

Though it was in Spanish, I've never enjoyed singing live this much. It was definitely the most rock & roll (verging on heavy!) set I've played, which I think was a product of playing with an incredibly passionate, on fire team. At one point, I played Enseñame a Amar on acoustic guitar, and after I explained the lyrics to Spring Branch, it was a beautiful thing to hear Nicaraguan and American voices begging God to teach them to love like He does.

Anyways, I can't wait to lead again this Friday night, and I'm so blessed to get to praise God with such a talented group of people.

Now, I need to say something that may be a little uncomfortable to hear. Last year, with my school, I met six kids from a home for girls, Casa Belen. I have a little sister (that I love very much) who was once an orphan in Nicaragua, and due to the similarities of the cases, I quickly became protective and what I guess you could call paternal to the Belen girls. I looked at it like this: they didn't have a male figure in their life, so wasn't it my duty to become that for them?

Before I left for the States, I was overwhelmed by the crying of these girls I thought I'd developed such a bond with. "I'll be back," I promised. When I got home, I wrote them a note from their "Uncle" (that's what they called me), telling them how much I loved them and how I looked forward to seeing them again.

You may be surprised, but there are few decisions I regret as much as those above. I promise to explain.

Last night, one of the younger kids in La Posada asked me to help him learn some English. Naturally, I jumped at the chance. It started out with some basic words, like "goodbye" and "I love you." He told me they were from a girl from a team that had come for a week; she'd sent him a letter.

I suddenly realized this may be a lot more than some translating. Something God has been teaching me since my experiences with the Belen girls is about attachment issues and boundaries with the kids we minister to. Many missions trips focus on spending time with kids from various orphanages and refuge homes.

The reason I regret my actions with the Belen girls is that I never came back. I never saw them again. I was with them for two weeks, in which they began to treat me like a big brother/fatherly figure. I'm very protective and loving to my little sister, and these girls were in a very similar situation to what my sister had been in. So I was protective and loving to these six girls.

I promised them I'd come back to them. I never did. I want you to think about something. Think about your typical (if that term can be used) kid in an orphanage. Obviously, they don't live with their parents. Most likely, it's because they weren't wanted or couldn't be taken care of. I'm very blessed to have two awesome parents who provide for me, love me, and teach me a ton about everything. Kids are born with the need for that affection and that teaching. And these kids have been abandoned, for whatever reason.

This is the tricky part. When you come on a missions trip and play with some kids, you may feel like you're developing a bond with a couple of them. Because of the amount of time you spend with them, they may begin to look to you for affection, as they used to with their parents. So while you're with them, you take on this responsibility of being around them and looking out for them. And then, even though you may have hugged them countless times, told them you love them, made them laugh, you leave them. And it hurts you. Because you may be gone forever. And even though you may return, you will have to leave them again.

I assure you that when you leave them, it hurts them more than it hurts you. Not because they love you, but because you left. Just like their parents.

That's what I did to six little girls who had already been through hell.

This kid I'm telling you about, I read the letter that was sent to him. The girl told him God had put them in each other's lives for a reason (which is honestly quite possible), but then took it further by talking about their relationship as if there was a bond. Though she knew him for a week, she spoke to him like they had a very, very close relationship. Like I thought I did with the Belen girls.

He told me she was coming back August 9th. And he wanted me to help him translate some stuff to say to her. He wrote a sentence down, and as I translated it, my heart seized up.

"I want to be with you forever and never leave you." *Wow.*

I stared as he wrote again. I could hardly bring myself to lift the pen this time.

"I love you with all of my heart and my soul."

Before this trip, I regretted my actions with the Belen girls because I broke a promise. But I never expected how firmly kids may cling to our words. This boy is practically counting down the days till the girl returns. The one person who has showed this much interest in him; though he knew her only for a week, she treated him like a mother. Now, in his mind, he *needs* her. I found out something that night, from a friend of the girl's. The boy has his information mixed up. The girl is coming back to Nicaragua August 9th. But not to Casa Bernabe. Not to him.

The person he loves with all his heart and soul isn't coming. I don't blame her for this, because if she did come, she'd have to leave again. Which honestly makes perfect sense, missions teams come and leave.

The girl's friend told me to tell the boy to write a letter back to her. If he did, I could give it to her and she could take it with her. All I'd have to do is get it to her before tomorrow morning, when she leaves for the States.

That night, yesterday, I made a decision. I didn't tell the boy to write back a letter. I'm not telling him his friend isn't coming until her friend leaves, so I guess tomorrow or Tuesday afternoon. Because I know that this girl, who seems like an awesome, well-meaning person, will never be what he expects her to be. He wants her to never leave him; even if she came, she would have to.

And I know that though it may break his heart when I tell him she's not coming, I can't let him keep this "relationship" going. Because even worse than hopelessness is false hope. And that is what he has. False hope that this girl, who spoke to him in such an intimate way, will fill the gap of the provider that he needs. Unless she were to adopt him (and she won't, she knew him for a week), she will NOT fill that gap.

And I will NOT let him keep thinking she will.

Why am I sharing this with you? Because for those of you who have been on missions trips, you probably can relate to how I felt to the Belen girls. But it is NOT our job to act like these children's providers. Josh told me something interesting: "It's kind of rude for Americans to think they need to love on these kids, because that's what their caretakers are already sacrificing everything to do."

Before you go on your next missions trip, think of something. Why am I going? And will what I'm doing really help?

What's going on with this boy is crazy to me. I think a lot of us feel like we have this bond with the kids we're ministering to. But look at this case! And look at what you can offer! We can't fill the hole in the kids' hearts for parenting; what's scary is we may make it larger.

My words may seem offensive. They probably do, they did to me as I was first understanding this. But this is something we need to understand. When you are going on a missions trip, why are you going? Be careful. Be so so careful that you're actually helping, not hurting.

This kid's story is not a rare one. He's not just a special case.

So how should we act to these kids? Honestly, the way many trips are run throw you into constant situations of playing with them. I'm not the biggest fan of these, because that kind of confuses me about the "mission" part of the missions trip. I suppose there are many reasons for missions trips to poor countries, but I think that at the core the mission should be to come alongside the impoverished and empower them to escape their poverty. To give them what my friend James Belt calls "spiritual and tangible hope".

To avoid this attachment issue, choose your trip wisely. When choosing, focus strongly on your reason/what you want to accomplish. If your situation still puts you in constant contact with orphans, remember *who you are.* You're there a limited period of time. you're not their parent, their uncle/aunt, their big brother/sister. If you want to help these kids, don't give them temporary happiness. Give them joy. Share the gospel. In reality, that is what changes lives, communities, countries.

Yes, these kids need love. No, we can't fill that. But I know someone who can. I have a Father who can. Point these kids to Him. Then, they will never have to be empty again.

Enseñame a amar.

MARK RODRIGUEZ

7-29-13 MONDAY (NICA DÍA ONCE)

Today:
—Got up, took a shower
—Cleaned out soda bottles for a project Mrs. Adams was doing at Bethel school
—Off to El Canyon

-Tried to stop at Casa del Café but the dude was on the phone
-Stopped by Quinta-something to pick up the team
—Tuck and I made lunches for the team in El Canyon's kitchen, picture of Rii on the fridge
—Mrs. Adams brought us donuts for breakfast
—watched part of the agriculture class, then went to pick up Tip Top with James for Mr. Adams team at Bethel
—Talked more about tangible and spiritual hope
—"Security guard" with AK grabbed James's arm when he asked for directions, wanted my Fanta, James nearly krav-maga'd him in the throat.
—Dropped off food, went back to El Canyon and spoke to Maria Jose in Spanish
—Went with team to Bernabe, left the team and played guitar with some kids
—Three Spring Branchers came over, played soccer with the posada boys.
—Tie game, off to dinner
-Bluefields girl came up and asked if I like bombitos…seems like everyone knows this joke now
—Headed to Josh's after dinner to talk this week's set
—Spring Branch porch time, just caught the worship and the talk

NOTE: 7-30-13

Today:
—Woke up early to music again…Agh
—Breakfast, then dude leader meeting with Masaya pastor again
—Grabbed team center breakfast with Josh before music practice
—practice was alright, the usual early uneasiness
—fantastic devo by the field, then kind of napped on a bag of humus
—Read some Harry Potter (en Espanol), off to lunch
—Music teacher enlisted me to teach Armondo and a teenage

girl Spanish Hosanna. It went alright
—worked on greenhouse
—came back and played Uno with Bryan, Armondo, Cairo, and a couple other dudes
—Dinner, then read a bit more HP and practiced my own guitar
—Josh came and talked to guys for awhile, I called Carley but ran out of minutes right in the middle of the call
—Spring Branch Porch Time
-signs
-Talk on living intentionally
-Came home
—Josh and Andrew found kittens in the attic

7-30-13 TUESDAY (NICA DÍA DOCE)
MORNING:

1 Corinthians 13:1-8
—Love bears all things, all good things stem from it
—You can be a martyr, you can be a prophet, you can be a healer, but if you don't have love it is all worthless
—Love with the Lord—relationship
-A God that has always loved me
-The world is a product of God's love
-Beauty is a product of God's love
—I want to speak on relentless love on Friday
-I don't know these kids well enough, I will need Your eyes, Your mind
-Guide me and prepare me as I get ready
-I pray the language barrier wouldn't stop my message from reaching these kids
—I need to talk to Julio about the American girl today
—God show me how to point him to You, how to tell him that people will always disappoint you at some point
—Didn't get a chance to talk to Julio, waiting until we're either alone or I have a good opportunity.
—I used to think it was my calling to love people in Nicaragua,

but now I know my calling is to love people wherever I am
—Guilt is a terrible motivator
—For most of my life I've let other's perceptions of me control my behavior
—If you pray for God to break you, He will
—Suffering earns you faith
—Blessed are the hungry, for they shall be filled
—I can be hungry and content at the same time
—My love for others (family, friends, whoever) has been blocked by a love of myself
—Poverty doesn't mean hell
—I'm skilled with my words and I've been using them to build myself up. That needs to change
—If I love others more than myself, I'm gonna find I don't talk as much
—I will never stop learning to love
—Love does
—Beauty is a product of God's love
—I'd rather live a life of love for the oppressed than of hatred for the oppressor
—I shouldn't divide things into time periods and make them matters of success or failure
—A friendship built on a motive isn't a friendship
—My parents are super-wise and I seriously take them for granted.
—I'm so good with people that I can conduct myself in just the right way to look awesome to them. I wonder if there are ways to use those skills to glorify God
—"Teach me to give without counting the costs."
—I wanted to teach these people about faith, but they taught me more about it than I already knew.
—I wanted to learn to love others, but I realized that first I need to examine my own heart condition
—It's good to learn from mistakes but not to dwell on them
—I used to try to show who I am by talking about myself, but now I know I'd rather just be myself
—Love and joy go hand in hand. Love begets joy, joy begets love.

—I used to try to be like the people I admire, but now I know God made me unique
—Convenience is never an excuse for sin
—I've seen some marriages filled with stress and arguments. When I'm married, I want my love, joy and peace (and my wife's!) to help us just roll with the punches and stay smiling
—Even though some team trips may not have a huge "impact" on the country, the exposure counts for something
—If a team wants to leave an impact on the country, the best way to do that is to hook up with a good organization
—I came here to bless others, but they blessed me the most.

NOTE: 7-31-13

Today:
—Left with Mrs. Katie at about three
—Talked more about her family's history with Nicaragua, talked about Eddie's talk
—Went to the Quinta for dinner
—Came home and skyped, everyone else went back out for porch time
—Adams brought me Pops, put it in the freezer and totally forgot about it
—Gave Savannah journal for Carley

7-31-13 WEDNESDAY (NICA DÍA TRECE)
MORNING:

1 Samuel 14
—Jonathan and his armor bearer defeat the Philistines
—"God has delivered them into our hand."
—Asks for a sign whether or not to attack, and God sends him forward
—kills twenty Philistines, the rest are thrown into a panic and start slaying each other

—I love the faith and all-out confidence Jonathan has here
—When God tells you what's gonna happen, it will.

8-1-13 THURSDAY (TWO WEEKS)

Today:
—Woke up, grabbed some coffee, Mrs. Adams made delicious bacon, eggs, and toast
—Met up with the team and headed off to grab some Gallinas(live chickens) from the market. (Wembays)
—Never been to this one before
—Like a filthy, crowded labyrinth
—Classic pirated DVDs like Man of Steel and Lone Ranger
—One dude (big smile) tried to sell some DVDs to Mr. Tim, but Tim told him he'd bought from him before and he had poor quality. The dude's smile dropped.
—Ridiculously bad-smelling meat section, found the chickens just tied under a table
—Barely got out of market alive, poor Mrs. Belt stepped in a puddle of…something
—Guy tried to sell us fo-bans for 8 bucks, I've gotten them for five
—Went to El Canyon and dropped off chickens in lady's chicken coop
—Victor's son Elias fell like four or five times down the hill
—Ate in cafeteria
—Headed off to Laguna de Apoya, SUPER long drive
—Mr. Tim got a ticket and had to give up his license, saw his car pulled over (hehehe)
—Beautiful, beautiful rural town of El Crucero up in the mountains
—At a couple points I'd look out the window and see gorgeous green mountains stopped only by the Pacific.
—Got into jungleish area near Apoya, a couple of beautiful wrong turns
—Got down to the Laguna at a beautiful (everything's beautiful

here) cottage called Abuela's
—15/20 ft jump into the water with two sketchy ladders leading back up
—Swam out a bit into the Laguna, "Lord of all creation, of water, earth and sky."
—10x10 block of wood anchored in Laguna, we jumped off of it and "skim-boarded" with our feet
—Delicious grilled chicken for dinner
—Headed back up steep entrance of Abuela's to Mr. Tim's car, others in their cars behind.
—I decided to jog up. Once I reached the top I went to give the valet-ish dude a high-five and fell a pit.
—One leg out, one in, if both had gone in I wouldn't have fallen five feet or more.
—Nica problems
—Drove back, talked about trying to make Ruby's work
—Power out at Bernabe, hung out at team center and met Caroline, gringa intern for ONET
—nice girl, seems to have a good vision for missions
—Passed out at home, BEAT

RIGHT AFTER 8-1-13

Talk with Julio
—Told him the American girl not coming to Casa
—Told him a lot of teams come to the team center, but they have to come home eventually
—He asked if she's coming next year, I told him it's possible, but it's also possible she won't
—I told him everyone will fail him because we are human and imperfect
—God is the only one who is perfect and will never leave
—I was shocked, because he didn't cry or seem fazed or anything
—Super confused, but I was so tired I just went to bed
—Called Mom in the morning
—Mom said the fact he didn't react was the saddest part

—He wrote those words, but to him the girl was just another hope
—He's used to being abandoned, to being lied to
—He's actually becoming dulled to love
—It'll be harder for him to trust people in the future
—Those words, which are meant to be passionate, are just desperate shots now that he's not even confident in
—He'd say them to anyone who shows interest in him

8-2-13

Today:
—Got like 8 ½ hours of sleep
—Caroline wanted to finish our conversation on missions this morning, didn't work out
—Journaled yesterday's stuff at team center to give Josh and Andrew more time to sleep before music practice
—Cook practically shoved coffee and delicious toast in my face, such a nice woman
—Music practice, a lot more stoked now (as usual)
—Hung with Josh, Andrew, and William on the porch until lunch
—Worked on Greenhouse, with the plastic on it looks really official now
—Set up for worship
—Wasn't too stoked on my singing this time, I think mixing was a little weird
—Gave my talk
—Came home, somehow out of minutes again
—Watched Nacho Libre, much funnier with Nicaraguans

MORNING:
—I want to talk to Bernabe tonight on being disappointed and the only one who never disappoints
—Thank You that Your word is legit alive, You speak through it in amazing ways Paul and Silas praising in jail
—IMPORTANT: They were not praying for freedom or to be set free, they were simply praising God for who He is

—Most missionaries, when thrown in jail, would probably be confused with God
—Paul and Silas, however, have faith. They have done God's will, and have ended up in jail. They can have confidence His Will will still be done, because they have been faithful and right in the middle of it up to that point.
—Because of this, they need not worry about anything, but can praise God and wait for whatever He has next
—Earlier in Acts—Peter and disciples tell the authorities no matter what they do, they can't stop them from proclaiming what they've seen and heard
—Why would we hide our thankfulness for what Jesus has done for us from anyone?

RELENTLESS LOVE NICA (notes from Mark's Friday Night Talk)
—Thank you for accepting me so quickly here
—I've loved hanging with you, having fun with you, and working with you
—Even though I live here, there's an obvious difference between us
—I'm white, from America, not a Nicaraguan
—Discovering a lot of similarities
—Main: We've all been disappointed by people. People have made promises and broken them. Parents, friends, whoever
—Even though I love these people, it still hurts when they let me down
—I don't know who has disappointed you, but I know that it's hurt you too
—Gonna come back to that
—Another similarity with many, I've heard about Jesus since I was very little
—Kinda got used to hearing the same message of how He died for us over and over and over again
—And I heard this term "relationship" over and over too.
—Didn't really begin to get that until a couple of months before I came here.

—Something about America I'm not proud of is that a lot of worship there is safe. Everyone wants to look like a Christian, but nobody wants to look too crazy.
—I was raised in this kind of church, and for a long time was scared of standing out. Just wanted to come every Sunday, sing quietly, look normal.
—At home, I was sincerely thankful God had taken away my sins
—But still, I didn't want to be defined by that
—This year, I began to realize something
—faithful v unfaithful lover
—Analogies with having a girlfriend: cheating or being faithful and how You would feel, and how that would impact the relationship
—How does that make sense?!
—I had a God that loved me. But I didn't want to let go of my other lovers—reputation, pride
—So, I didn't fully give myself over to God
—Then, He saw how those other things were hurting me. My concern for my reputation made me insecure and feel like a failure
—And He saw that if I kept ignoring Him, if I kept sinning, I would die and have to be apart from Him forever
—He loved me so much that He got beat up. Stabbed, punched, and spit on, and finally killed, because He didn't want me to hurt anymore. He wanted me to know Him and love Him forever. He wanted to know me and love me forever.
—So even though He is the God of the Universe, He let humans tear Him to pieces. And He didn't fight back. Because He knew it was the only way He could get me to let go of everything and see all the amazing things He has for me.
—When they nailed Him to the cross, He could've turned off the pain. But He felt all of it. Because the punishment we were supposed to receive for disobeying God was eternal pain. But He died so we can have eternal life. With Him. (Romans 6:23)
—You know what's scary? I have known that He did all this all my life. But I still thought my reputation was worth more than

fully embracing Him and looking crazy
—This year, I started to meet these amazing people who are so openly in love with God and have this awesome faith
—One of the things I noticed about them is how much they smile, even if nothing great's going on
—They don't seem worried about anything
—Kaitlin—Bulgaria
—Some have been disappointed, have been abandoned, have been called crazy
—But they are the most content, satisfied people
—why? Because they have one person who has never hurt them. Who has always loved them. Who has been begging to know them, and laugh with them, and bless them since before they were born.
—And they left everything for Him
—Their prize is not wealth. Or fame. Or friends.
—Their prize is that they are never alone, they can be content no matter what, and they get to talk with the God of the Universe.
—This year, I discovered that. Jesus has been banging on the door of my heart this whole time, even when I was blatantly disobeying Him
—No one has ever done that for me
—This year, I fell in love with Christ. And suddenly I understood how much He has done for me
—and now, when people disappoint me, it hurts, but it doesn't destroy me. Because the God of everything beautiful will never leave me.
—Since then, I've heard God talk so clearly. Sometimes, He makes stuff clear through other people. Most of the time, He shows me Bible verses that answer questions and unveil parts of His plan for me.
—Scary one He showed me recently *Hechos 9:16* "Yo le mostrare cuanto tendrá que padecer por mi nombre."
—In that moment, I felt God telling me that if I follow Him with all my heart, people will hurt me.
—It's not safe to follow Jesus. I'm not exaggerating when I say

you could die.
—But there's a passage I love in *Acts 16*
—Paul and his friend are beaten and thrown in jail
—But they're sitting there singing praise to God
—God's love for them feels so good that they just ignore the pain and the prison
—So I can tell you, if you take this dangerous step, stop caring what others think, and worship God with all your heart, all the pain you receive for that will be worth it
—Because you will understand that the God of all Creation loves you and will never disappoint you.
—Prayer

POST-TALK
— I guess I expected a similar reaction to when I spoke in chapel, but the reaction seemed like just another talk
—Trying to remember that what matters isn't if my message was accepted, but whether or not it glorified Jesus
—Paul, was rejected by a lot of regions, and though I'm sure he was bummed about that, he got right back to work
—My purpose is to love God and praise Him for what He's done

AUGUST 3, 2013 NECESITANDO A AMAR (SEGUNDA PARTE)

(from Mark's Enseñame a Amar blog)

You need to hear the end of this story (it isn't what you think).

A couple of nights ago, I was walking home and found myself alone with the boy from my last post. As soon as he asked me if I could help him translate more stuff for the girl who wrote to him, I suddenly felt God tugging at my heart and realized it was time to break the news.

Watching for his reaction, I told him she wasn't coming back. He looked at me in surprise and recited the date he thought she was coming. I shook my head.

"Next year?" he asked.

"I have no idea, man. It's possible, but it's possible she won't."

I told him I was sorry she wasn't coming back. I told him that even if she did, people like her and I have our own homes in the States and have to return eventually. I told him about me and the Casa Belen girls, and about how even though I had wanted to go back to them, God had different plans. I told him it wasn't right for me to make a promise like that because I'd had no idea whether or not I'd actually be able to come back.

Reaching the porch of La Posada, we sat down in the rocking chairs. He said nothing, just listening quietly.

I told him that a lot of people have disappointed me too. But I told him that there was one person who has never left me, has never let me down, and that's God.

I kept pausing, feeling like I was talking a lot and hoping to hear something from him. But still, nothing. I even asked him at the end if he wanted to ask me anything, but he said no.

And then, calmly, he walked inside.

I was stunned. Of course I was happy he wasn't hurt, but I couldn't believe it. He had wanted to tell her that he loved her with all his heart and soul. And now, without a tear, he shrugged it off that she wasn't coming back.

Confused and dead tired, I went to bed and decided to call my super-wise mom in the morning. I explained the whole conversation with her and asked her why in the world the boy didn't show any reaction.

"Honey, there are two possibilities here," she said. "Either he truly believes that God will never leave and he's holding on to Him, or he's used to being abandoned and is just pushing it down with all the other times this has happened."

The first case was doubtful. Though he's fourteen, his attitude reminds me of a mischievous ten year old. I examined the second case, and realized that was even sadder than him crying about it. Despite the passionate words he'd written on paper, they were just another desperate plea he wasn't confident in. Words he'd say over and over again until someone took them. But they didn't hold any actual significance, as he'd say them to anyone, so that meant that he's essentially being dulled to love. I've heard of many kids who've been like this, and it killed me to see that it was happening to him too. Mom also said all this abandonment he was pushing down would make it hard for him to trust and hold onto people in the future. All we could do now was pray that that wouldn't happen.

Mom also mentioned that I should ask him why he wasn't sad, but I kind of disregarded that in my head. As far as I understood, the story was over.

Then, tonight, while washing dishes next to the boy, I felt that tug on my heart again, and I decided to ask him about his reaction.

"Why weren't you sad?" I asked him. "The words you wanted me to translate, they were pretty serious."

"I was, a little bit," he said.

"A little bit?" The words I'd translated didn't justify just being "a little" sad.

"I thought you would be a lot more upset," I told him. "How were you just a little sad?"

And then he said something that cut straight to my heart.

"Because in my room that night, I prayed."

He.....prayed?

Not really knowing what else to ask, I just asked why.

"I always pray. I believe in God."

He smiled up at me, and I felt tears welling up in my eyes as I smiled back.

"That's *awesome*, dude," I said.

He went inside as I turned away and walked off to the table where I do my prayer time. And I began to weep. Because I'm amazed that a kid who has been abandoned and put down over and over can keep from breaking because he truly believes that God will make everything okay. That he can love God and have faith enough to be joyful through even another broken hope.

I called my parents and told them the whole thing. Once more, my mom said something typical of her super-wiseness.

"Think of how much suffering it's taken for him to earn that kind of faith."

This kid has suffered a lot. I don't know his story, but I do know he's in an orphanage. I do know he's not being raised by his parents. I can't imagine being in that situation. He inspires me, because he is a true example of loving God despite whatever circumstance. I love God and am convinced that if I really want to get to know Him and be in the center of His will, then there's gonna have to be some suffering.

I haven't gone through suffering. Not yet. I've hurt, of course, we all have. But I have not had life-shaking stuff happen to me like he has. I have a nice house, awesome parents, an incredible girlfriend, and a great education. I haven't had to suffer that much. But still, I doubt God sometimes. I get angry at Him. I second-think promises He's made me.

And then here's this boy in an orphanage with faith like a child that shakes my heart.

I realize that many children in Nicaragua have been abandoned like him. And I know many of them are becoming dulled to love or are having their hearts broken over and over again to the point of depression. And that's what I expected to find with this guy.

But instead, I found life. Instead, I found vibrant, infectious joy. Because he trusts in Jesus.

I think we all can learn from that. I know I can.

Enseñame a amar.

MARK RODRIGUEZ

8-3-13 (MORNING):

—Breakfast, then filled up some water containers and delivered them with William

—Went into town, Andrew and William switching between English, Spanish, and Creole is quite confusing

—Nearly hit a stupid pig chilling in the road

—Came back, kids built a trench around the greenhouse, back to Posada for chilling (UNO)

—William went out, Josh and two Canadian guys with a water filter organization came over and chilled

—Talked to one of them about how I feel like many youth missions are ineffective, he brought up a good point that though that may be true, the exposure is worth something
—Lunch, more chilling
-taught Armando Open the Eyes of my Heart
-More Uno
-Read Harry Potter
-Shot on varying goalies (soccer) with Julio, Brayan, and Jeremiah
—Dinner, Posada boys served it cause girls had a thing
—talk with Julio, then prayed by workbench
—posted blog, put salt in my coffee and nearly drank it
—tried to shower, but water smelled gross so I'm just waiting til tomorrow

8-3-13 SATURDAY (NICA DÍA DIECISEIS) AFTERNOON:

—If I'm always trying to figure out if there's more to life, I won't find joy in what God has given me

If you pour yourself out for the hungry, and satisfy the desire of the afflicted, then shall your light rise in the darkness and your gloom be as the noonday. And the Lord will guide you continually and satisfy your desire in scorched places and make your bones strong; and you shall be like a watered garden, like a spring of water, whose waters do not fail.
Isaiah 58: 10-11

—I like the first part of this, pouring myself out will give me joy
—Jesus, refill me. Satisfy me with Your living water
I'm good at sounding like an awesome Christian. I don't want to use that "skill" to my advantage.

8-4-13 SUNDAY (NICA DÍA DIECISIETE) MORNING:

God, I know You're real. And I know You're there. And I know You want so badly for me to get to know You better.

I know that if there's anything that's stopping that from happening, it's me.

I'm at a low point right now, God. I'm worn out, I'm homesick, I'm lonely, and I'm realizing just how little my faith is.

Somehow, I've tricked myself. At home, I was convinced I'd reached a point of huge faith. Convinced that I knew You better than ever. And though that part may be true, I hardly know You at all. I'm still selfish, still prideful, still a hypocrite.

And right now, I'm broken.

Dear God, I need You. That verse about suffering, I don't know if I didn't believe it before or what, but I am now convinced that suffering produces faith. All I want is to feel You here with me. All I want is to feel that beautiful joy You give. I want to know You more.

Break me to pieces so I can see that You are the perfect Creator, the perfect builder, the perfect healer. Do whatever it takes, God Just don't leave me.

For it has been granted to you that for the sake of Christ you should not only believe in him but also suffer for his sake, engaged in the same conflict that you saw I had and now hear that I still have.
Philippians 1:29-30

—I'll forever be in awe of Paul's faith enduring through suffering
—I need to talk less and listen more, not only because I lie to myself, but also because it feeds my pride to speak of my faith
—"And I am sure of this, that he who began a good work in you will bring it to completion at the day of Jesus Christ." *Phil 1:6*
—"Behold, I am doing a new thing; now it springs forth, do you not perceive it? I will make a way in the wilderness and rivers in the desert." Isaiah 43:19
—"Blessed are those who hunger and thirst for righteousness, for they shall be satisfied." *Matt 9:6*
—Prayer for Kaitlin—peace, blind faith

—Prayer for Carley—That she would know You better

CHURCH AND AFTER:

—In worship today I thought about how awful it is that I still regulate whether or not my worship is too crazy. So I praised with all I had and prayed that I'd stop caring how other people see me, whether good or bad.

—I have been such a hypocrite, even to myself. Collecting compliments on my faith and piety and storing them up. Saying, posting, writing just the right things to look like an awesome Christian in the eyes of others. This is terrible. Why don't I always feel like God's with me? Because our relationship is meant for two and I'm making it into something to earn me praise.

—I prayed God would take all of me. Not only do I not want to let negative remarks get me but positive remarks as well. It needs to be all for Him.

—I'm tired of thinking how I look in the eyes of others while worshipping.

—If I want to fall in love with Christ, I will have to care only about what He thinks then I will see His will for me more clearly.

—No more falsities. I pray that I'd catch myself when I am doing something for my glory.

—At the end of the day, even though they fight, cuss, play loud music at 5 AM, steal, run away, take advantage of our language barrier, flirt with the girls, make annoying sounds, strum open on a guitar for hours and yell their heads off, there are some awesome kids here who are full of life and have a lot of potential. I want to think of my siblings like this.

Mark and his littlest brother, Daniel.

BEFORE 8-5-13

Today:
—Went to bed early last night, woke up feeling good, did in-bed pull-ups on my bunk frame
—Breakfast, had like six pieces of pico
—Prayer, then joined William and cooks in team center for coffee (these cooks are some super awesome women)
—William and I read some of Josh and Andrew's books while Andrew slept, I read some of Head's devotional
—Read *Love Does*, HP, and made up songs on acoustic (popped a string)
—Lunch, then finally found football and threw it with Armando
—Agriculture, pulled weeds around our prized tomatoes
—Emailed Mr. Buzbee, then helped Josh in moving from his old house to new, found some of his kittens and put them back up with their mom
—Went home with everyone, played UNO till dinner, ate two meal's worth (super hungry)

8-5-13 MONDAY (NICA DÍA DIECIOCHO) MORNING:

I, I am he who comforts you;
who are you that you are afraid of a man who dies,
of the son of man who is made like grass,
and have forgotten the Lord, your Maker,
who stretched out the heavens
and laid the foundations of the earth,
and you fear continually all the day
because of the wrath

of the oppressor, when
he sets himself to destroy?
And where is the wrath of the
oppressor?
Isaiah 51:12-13

And do not fear those who kill the body
but cannot kill the soul.
Matthew 10:28a

What I tell you in the dark,
say in the light,
and what you hear whispered,
proclaim on the housetops.
Matthew 10:27

—Posada boys and leaders went to auditorium to clean up chairs
—Came back and hung with Isaac and William on porch, maybe the most Spanish I've tried to speak at one time.
  -Isaac asked about my opinion on Casa's rules with dating
  -Hilarious Dude
—Back to Josh's to check email, stopped by his new place (looking really good)
  -The cooks/maids were there too, helped him all day without losing their joy, seriously some solid ladies
—Beat all the kids in UNO before bed
—Maybe what we need to worry about isn't giving all we own away but not letting material things rule our lives.
—Glorifying God among the accepting and the unaccepting is worth any pain
—I don't think I'll begin to understand this until I have to suffer for the gospel

I am suffering
bound with chains as a criminal.
But the word of God is not bound!
2 Timothy 2:9

—*2 Timothy 3:16-17* talks about scripture as means for training and equipping God's people

—I want to find out who I really am as opposed to who I think I am.

—I've spent so much time thinking about what my actions and I look like from the outside that I haven't done much looking at my heart/soul condition.

—I want to bless people in simple ways

—Also, when I'm so focused on myself, I can't see the awesome stuff God is doing around me.

8-6-13 TUESDAY (NICA DÍA DIECINIEVE)

Went for a hot morning run, then as I was coming towards the Posada to shower and pray, one of the Bluefields guys asked if I could help Josh move into his new house. I was about to say I couldn't, because I didn't want to miss prayer and I smelled awful, but then I remember love throws down its nets and just does. And I had an awesome time working with Josh and Jordan where I really experienced God's peace and ended up with enough time to pray and shower. When we make time to love others, God will show us love.

—Love doesn't always talk about what it's gonna do, Love just does

Love is patient and kind; love does not envy or boast; it is not arrogant or rude. It does not insist on its own way; it is not irritable or resentful; it does not rejoice at wrong doing but rejoices with the truth. Love bears all things, believes all things, hopes all things, endures all things. Love never ends.

1 Corinthians 13:4-8a

Love doesn't finish the chapter, take its scheduled coffee break, do one more lap, or get to a stopping point. When it's time to love, love does.

Love doesn't mope. It doesn't ask, "are we done yet?" It doesn't complain or argue. It just does.

Love sacrifices. It says, "I'm with you to the end." It delights in service. It sees the beauty in people. It perseveres relentlessly. It does.

—Jesus called us/calls us to love people

—When you're in love with yourself, you can't rightly love God and others.

8-7-13 WED (NICA DÍA VEINTE) MORNING:

—skipped normal breakfast so I could eat with Trinity, had a prayer time.

—Delicious breakfast (pancakes with nutella, bacon, fruit) with Trinity

—bus ride to airport, fun game of mafia

—Said goodbyes, then hung with Ellen and J Lo for the morning

-Gas station (got a khoas)

-Mechanic for bus, went to a store so the girls could get some clothes

-Papa John's with Josh, Ellen, and J Lo (nicest Papa John's I've been to)

—Came back to a team from Texas doing VBS songs in Comedor, surprisingly not even the little kids were into it (I've heard Casa kids are hard, but that was even kinda weird)

—Really liked what this team was doing

-abstinence talk for the girls (that was apparently successful at the other orphanage)

-skit and art for the little guys

-baseball for guys (Julian is a crazy good pitcher)

-Also, really nice group of people

—Girl who completely looked like a YWAM-ER turned out to actually be one (did it in India)

—Talked about YWAM and her desire to do long-term stuff

Love doesn't always wait for an opportunity, often makes one.

Paul to the Corinthians-- "For I decided to know nothing among you except Jesus Christ and him crucified." (*1 Cor 2:2*)

—No lofty words, no complex theology, no condemnation, just the gospel

—v. 5 "so that your faith might not rest in the wisdom of men but in the power of God."

"For the Spirit searches everything, even the depths of God."
1 Cor 2:10

—And we have this spirit within us!

I feel like I'm learning a lot about how to love people, but more than that, I want to learn to love You.

I should be careful to keep my eyes open to the simple joys and beauties around me. In the little things I can find great joy.

Genesis 2—God formed man personally

I need not worry about "how intimate" or "how developed" my relationship with God is. I just need to know how much He loves me and worship Him.

—skyped Carley, guest-featuring Josh

—dinner at team center with William and Victor

—UNO with a couple guys

—Played guitar on porch with kids listening

—Just because I've learned a lot doesn't mean I'm done learning. And it doesn't mean I should stop praying for God to break my heart for what breaks His

—Something I witnessed in Ellen Jones (old babysitter of Carley) today, endless joy and love for people

—walking through streets of Managua with Ellen and J lo and hearing dudes catcall and whistle made me so unsettled and protective. And scared, honestly. But God reminded me that He sees all and not to fear men who can only kill the body.

—It's good to learn from mistakes but not to dwell on them. I've been looking back at things I did and going, "Did I do that because of who was watching?" and then I beat myself up about that. Instead, I should focus on what I'm doing at the moment and check my current motive for whatever I'm doing.

8-8-13 THURSDAY (NICA DÍA VEINTIUNO) MORNING:

Love doesn't make fallbacks. When the disciples threw down their nets, they didn't first examine the things that could go wrong and make a plan of action in case they did. They just followed Jesus.

Today:
—coffee, prayer time
—Learned about joy today. I woke up and thanked God for what He'd given me and asked Him to show Himself to me. And He did.
—I think joy and love go hand in hand. Love begets joy, joy begets love.
—James gave a tour of the farm to Cedar Run and Crossroads
—Had a medical clinic at the school, served 183 people.

8-10-13 SATURDAY (NICA DÍA VEINTITRES) MORNING:

Today:
—Got up, Mrs. Adams brought home some muffins for breakfast
—Stopped by the Quinta and then headed off to Bethel
—Medical day, I helped at the glasses station and with basic translating
—We only had adult sizes, so when the little kids came through their eyes looked huge through the lenses
—Our van driver Freddy accepted Christ!!!
—Doctor Dan (young, from Bluefields) had a patient who had a cockroach stuck in her ear, he did what he could but in the end she had to come to the hospital
—One patient was a girl about my age who was cutting and being beaten by her brother at home

-They're trying to send her to El Canyon
-As she left, I smiled at her and she smiled back through her tears. So awesome
—Served around 80 people, 400 in total over our three days
—Went to the VIP lounge and saw Red 2, all the seats were Lazy boys
—Came home and went pretty much straight to bed

I don't want to love because I want to love. I want to love because the Spirit within me causes me to abound in love for God and others.
Just read Matthew's account of Jesus's death and resurrection

Matt 28:20 "And behold, I am with you always, to the end of the age."
John 13:35 "By this all people will know you are my disciples, if you have love for one another."

I don't want to be known as spiritual, or religious, or someone with awesome prayers. I want to be known as someone who loves.

8-11-13 SUNDAY (NICA DÍA VEINTICUATRO) MORNING:

Today:
—Woke up to a gorgeous morning sky
—Coffee, zucaritas, and Harry Potter—killer combo
—Church at the Cañyon—Youth band worship
-Pastor Josué talked about echoing for Jesus no matter where you are
—Met Amanda, on second day of a year-long stay by herself, seems like a cool girl
—Saw William!
—Off to Granada with "family team" –3 moms, 2 with one daughter each, 1 with two sons
-Mainly gonna play with the kids
—I kinda struggle with getting stressed and paranoid as random

guys whistle and leer at our girls

-mentioned it to James, he said good to be alert but not really a point in being scared, if something were to happen, we'd do something

—Granada was beautiful though it was kinda a giant drunk party

—Drunk horseman nearly ran us over

—Ate at a pretty nice pizza place

—drove home with Mr. Adams for men of the community at the auditorium

—Ran back to Posada, boys watching some movie of a white girl at a black club or something...good to be back ☺

Psalm 107 talks about people in chains and in darkness because they've rejected God and His word. And then, when they cry out to Him, He "delivers them from their distress." Then, verse 22 says: "And let them offer sacrifices of thanksgiving and tell of His deeds in songs of joy."

I was the prisoner in chains, but God freed me. Today is Sunday. I want to thank Him with all I've got!

The only praise I can offer that is worthy of what He's done is all my life.

Teach me to love You!

Prayer for Freddy:

—reveal how good and real You are to him

—may he feel released from his sins

—may he love and seek a personal relationship with You

For some reason I didn't really expect to feel this way, but getting back to the Posada I realized I really missed the guys and it feels really good to be back.

8-12-13 MONDAY (NICA DÍA VEINTICINCO) MORNING:

Today:

—Got up, good to get back to the rice and beans breakfast

—Logan, young ONET dude chilled at Posada for a bit.

-Coffee with Josh and Cedar Run team, glad I got to say goodbye

—Prayer

—Read on porch

—Went with William to U-shaped courtyard at front of Bernabe and cleaned out room for bikes, some superweird looking skunks were crawling around

—Caught a ride on back of Herberto's truck to Posada

—Chilled on porch with Isaac and William, William talked about how he saw a man with a ravaged arm get healed on the spot by prayer

—Rice and beans lunch, baby

—Ridiculous down pour while Armando and I worked on some guitar, so proud of this dude

—Played UNO in Music Room introduced the boys to Sent by Ravens

—Went to Team Center, two guys from Eaglebrook met with the boys about an ongoing table project they're working on

—Tried to Skype (kinda all afternoon) but it couldn't happen

—Helped unload the shipment of 300 bikes

—Grabbed a soda at TC and met Natalie, another rad ONET person

—Chilled in Josh's with a tall red-headed guy, talked about how he's noticed poverty looks pretty similar all over the world

—Got to call mom and dad and Carley, really looking forward to seeing them soon

—UNO with Posada boys, guy with most cards in end gets slapped on arm

—Bayardo gave me pico…dude's officially a saint

I think loving the Lord produces a natural response to love others.

Father, I think there are times when a verse comes up and I incorrectly discern Your will from it. I don't know how to combat that, but I pray that You'd show me so I stop twisting Your will for my own pleasure.

"Do not be conformed to this world, but be transformed by the renewal of your mind, that by testing you may discern what is the will of God, what is good and acceptable and perfect."
Romans 12:2

—Renewed Mind video from Kaitlin
-A renewed mind is pure and full of godly, holy thoughts
-not the "religious" or "super-spiritual"
-*2 Cor 10:5* The renewed mind pulls down demonic perspectives and replaces them with heavenly thinking
-Taps into the perspective of God

That's how I'll know the Lord's will, by studying His word and learning how He thinks.

"Wondrously show your steadfast love, O Savior of those who seek refuge from their adversaries at your right hand." Psalm 17:7

In order to love God, we gotta first understand that He is great.

Revelation 22: Beautiful picture of Heaven
—"We will see His face" –of course I love when people look at me with love and pride (Dad), but I can't wait to see God's expression
—verse 7—Behold, I am coming soon!
—verse 17—The Spirit and the Bride say "come" –I and the Holy Spirit within me beg for the coming of the Lord
"The Spirit and the Bride say, 'Come' "
And let the one who hears say, 'Come' "
And let the one who is thirsty come;
Let the one who desires take the
water of life without price." *Rev 22:17*

NOTES ON 8-13-13:

Today:
—Breakfast, then Leader's group (good coffee and pico) (pico's always good)

—Prayer time
—Read a bit, then helped William organize some bikes
—Took a break with William, Isaac, and Harry at little tienda/ shack by school, got "Big Limón,"(essentially Nica Sprite)
—Organized a little more, than headed to lunch
—worked on more guitar with Armando, he's got Hosanna and we're working hard on Open the Eyes of my Heart
—Helped him put more tomatoes upright
—Realized I was getting annoyed at some basic stuff, remembered that love isn't irritable
—I think a basic 1 Cor 13 tat on my forearm would be sweet
—Checked on William at bike shop already we're getting customers, made over 600 bucks today!
—Norvin and Armando gave me this gorgeous pink fruit, delicious stuff
—Some fun soccer before dinner
—Dinner (eggs with salsa!) and then some Posada grown/ cooked corn.
—UNO, more arm slapping
—Small group thing, Isaac wants each of us to memorize ten verses by Thursday, this'll be interesting
—Earlier I asked Ricardo what he thought about Jesus, he answered Sunday School fashion with a bored look

8-13-13 TUESDAY (NICA DÍA VEINTISEIS)

Leader's Group:
—The Pastor of Masaya opened it up focusing on the story of Joseph
—Herberto asked me how my life is similar to Joseph's
-I told him Joseph had to suffer to get where God wanted him to be, and I know I will too. I also said Joseph had the courage to endure that suffering, and I'd like to have that as well.
—At the end, the pastor and all the other men in the group stood

and laid hands on me and prayed for me. They prayed that I would have heavenly perspective (which, ironically, I prayed about yesterday) for my future wife, and proclaimed God's name in my life. This was one of the best parts of the trip because I came to bless others. But few times have I felt more blessed than right then.

—I feel like this was kinda my Ruby's House of Prayer

MORNING:

Jesus said to her, "Everyone who drinks of this water will be thirsty again, but whoever drinks of the water that I will give him will never be thirsty again. The water that I will give him will become in him a spring of water welling up to eternal life."
John 4:13-14

"Blessed are those who hunger and thirst for righteousness, for they will be filled."

Make me hungry, Lord!

8-14-13

Today:

—Eaglebrook guys gave a devotion on fruits of spirit, for the guys, they're gonna take them on a spiritual retreat (really liking this team)

—Breakfast, then a straight up killer cup of coffee at the Team Center

—Devo, talked with crop guy

—read Harry Potter (Spanish) till I finished it

—Hung out with Chepe on porch until lunch

—Lunch, practiced juggling soccer ball a bit

—Taught English with William, lots of fun

—Went with Julian to buy pico, 24 pes for 24 dv

-talked to him in English about Puerto Cabezas, he says

he likes Bernabe but is looking forward to spending December at home
—Mind-blowing sunset
—Helped Josh with some water, then dinner and chilling at TC
—worked more guitar with Armando, doing so good

8-14-13 WEDNESDAY (NICA DÍA VEINTISIETE) MORNING:

One of the crop dudes just came up and we just randomly started talking music! Talked about Blink, Linkin Park, P.O.D…It's so cool how music can connect people.

Before I came here, I started that blog, calling it Enseñame a Amar. What I didn't know was that God's plan seriously was to break apart my heart and tear down my perception of love so that He could begin to make me understand how to love as I was made to. What was originally a motto quickly and suddenly changed my life. The thing that guided my every thought and action, my love for myself, was taken away, leaving me empty. But God had to empty me so He could fill me with His perspective. Now, I'm realizing that I was missing out on so much joy, so much peace, and of course so much love. So many relationships, probably all of them, honestly, will look different now. My drive will no longer be for my glory, but for loving and uplifting others. I'm excited to love Carley, my parents, Ben, and everyone else in new ways.

8-15-13 THURSDAY (NICA DÍA VEINTIOCHO) LAST DAY!

Today:
—woke up, played "Open the Eyes" and "You Never Let Go" before devotional, so fun to worship just with acoustic and voices.
—Gringos talked on how God uses bad things for good
—Breakfast, then went to work bikes with William

—walked a girl living down here (named Jocelynn) back to team center, seemed cool
—Did a ton of bikes, then took a break with William, Harry, and his brother to grab glass Pepsi
—Grabbed lunch, then went to teach English
-one group of just three teenage girls, but what was sweet was they weren't flirty at all
—Level 3&4 students did a shopping/job fair thing with the gringos, ridiculous storm hit
—Dinner, got to get up and say goodbye and thanks to Casa
—The girl from Carley's profile pic (Joselynn) showed me somewhere in her journal where Carley had written, then wrote Carley and I letters
—Isaac cooked corn and chicken for a going away party
—Awesome to just get some last chill in
—Isaac and the boys prayed for me
—Essentially prayed for my future, for bravery, thanked God I was doing this at a young age
—Isaac said they'll remember me in the story of the Posada, remembering the month I shared with them
—The boys said thanks for being a good friend, for teaching guitar, and for sacrificing to be with them
—Last games of UNO, then hit the sack
—Also, I got to pray for them. Prayed they'd be brave rather than safe and that God would raise up leaders among them

8-16-13

Today:
—woke up at about five
—Said goodbye to William and the boys, didn't/doesn't feel real
—Josh grabbed me and took me to the airport, gorgeous golden sun
-asked prayer for Linda who sometimes randomly stops eating and gets a little aggressive

-Thanked me. Said it was an incredible thing to live with the boys, and not to lessen the value of that in my mind
-Prayed for me and blessed me at the airport.
—Said goodbye, walked in to grab boarding pass, met a friendly returning American family
—Security, then up to gate, saw and said hey to an American/ Asian family that had visited the Posada
—Headed on the first flight
-met José, carpenter who has to leave his wife and one-year-old daughter for a couple of months
—Arrived in Atlanta, grabbed Qdoba for lunch and chowed hard
—Next flight, gorgeous blue sky
—Met Debbie, woman form Alabama going to visit her daughter-in-law in Va. Beach since her son will be gone during the couple's 1 year anniversary
—Arrived in ORF randomly saw Marsh
—Family arrived with awesome signs, then Ben and Frech randomly showed up too
—drove home, then delicious dinner of strombolis, Dr. P, and Dr P cake
—Called Carley
—Looked at videos of Rii dancing and Kids at Bounce House thing, then Nica photos
—Game of lie, then quick FB check
—Devo

Thoughts:
Love isn't manipulative.
America:
One of the biggest lies that Satan wants me to believe right now is that I won't feel God the same way here.
Don't let me forget the things I learned. Don't let me forget how I was taught to love. Don't let me forget how I loved people.
Before I left America, there were a lot of things that annoyed me. But Lord, I pray that You'd help me remember that love isn't irritable.
Think I'm gonna step back from social media a bit. It distracts me

from loving the people around me.

It was easy to see God in Nicaragua, with all the beauty around me. But it should be just as easy to see Him here. I need to keep an open mind.

Let me love You more, deeper than ever.
Light is sown for the righteous,
and joy for the upright in heart.
Rejoice in the Lord, O you righteous,
And give thanks to his holy name!
Psalm 97:11-12

8-17-13 SATURDAY (MORNING):

I'm in a land where it's easy to be typical, but now that I'm back I want to abound in love for others. I want to take chances through love.

Rev 4 :God, You're worthy of praise. You are the only perfect being. Teach me to give You the praise You are due.

"Hallelujah! For the Lord our God, the Almighty reigns. Let us rejoice and exult and give him the glory. For the marriage of the Lamb has come, and His Bride has made herself ready; it was granted her to clothe herself with fine linen, bright and pure. " Revelation 19

Before I left, my love for You was blocked by a love of myself. Now, You have crushed my pride. I'm excited to know You in new ways.

No matter what country I'm in, God's the same.

8-18-13

When I look at your heavens,
the work of your fingers,
the moon and the stars, which you have set in place.
What is man that you are

mindful of him,
and the son of man that you are
for him?
Psalm 8:3-4

Who am I, that You choose to give me such joy?

Father, I can't give You all the praise due Your name. But I can give You what You seek from me. And that's all I have to give.

8-18-13

I've noticed that when I get all theological, what I believe is constantly being reevaluated and changed. It's never done. And there's no satisfaction in it. No, it's when I love without caring about being correct about every little thing Christians believe, that's when I feel joy, that's when I feel closest to God. In the end, God will not judge us based on how right our creed was.

What I learned in Nicaragua was that we are called to love. Not religion, not theology. To love. Theology makes me feel alone. Love makes me feel alive. Yes, it's good to know what I believe. But I'm called to love, that's what He wants me to do.

I asked Dad why it's important to be a member of a church. He pointed out that it's Biblical. In the New Testament, Paul talks to people who are accountable to authorities in the church. Yes, all Christians are part of a body. But it's valuable to have a set family of believers holding to a set of beliefs together.

I think I'm a little turned off to caring about theology because a lot of the people I've seen who care about it don't look like they're in love with God. But the Bible shows it's important to know what you believe. And that doesn't mean when I sit down and pray in the morning I should be ecstatic over infant baptism. All infant baptism means to me is whether I believe it's scriptural for my kid to be baptized as a baby. But love, and grace, and beauty, those are things to praise God for. I can know what I believe and still glorify and love God the same way I do now. Sure, a lot of theology-minded people I know don't seem in love, but that's the same with many non-theology-minded people. I don't have to choose theology or love. I can have both. I just need to be careful that first and foremost I love God and remember what He's done in a way it deserves to be remembered.

8-19-13 MONDAY

I feel like one difference between my return from Nicaragua this year and last year is I can feel the change now. Last year, I was questioning whether the trip changed me. This year there's no question. I feel like in that moment of brokenness in Nicaragua God really did take my pride, He really did empty me. And I feel like He really has begun to fill me.

Now that I'm back in America, and I feel these changes, I'm realizing that I feel strangely disconnected from life. Not even necessarily in a negative way, I think. I'm just still trying to process the sudden transition between Nicaragua and here. And part of that is that I want to feel and talk to God the same way I did in Nicaragua. The way that worked there gave me this constant joy and awe and seeking for God. I became so dependent on Him praying once in the morning wasn't enough, I had to pray continuously.

I firmly believe I can have that now. Living with love as my only mission and motive brings forth passion and adoration for God. I pray that as I return from my disconnect, I'd settle into this new, unsettling life of dangerous, bold, real love. Thank You Jesus that You have so much in store for me, and so much love for me as well.

8-21-13 WEDNESDAY (MORNING):

I want to know His will and I want to know Him more.

"Let us not grow weary of doing good. Let us do good to everyone, and especially to those who are of the household of faith."
Galatians 6:9-10

When I was in Nicaragua, I woke up everyday to a life I knew I was called to. It is a little weird to not have that in the exact same way, but I guess I'm still waking up everyday to the life I'm called to. My mission in Nicaragua was love, and honestly, it's the same here.

In Nicaragua, I learned love doesn't complain or even ask if it's done yet. As the verse above says, it doesn't grow weary. It loves hard, and does good to everyone. That is something Jesus wants me to do here and to everybody around me.

Let me know Your love for me and feel that intimacy You desire.

8-22-13 THURSDAY MORNING: (FIRST DAY OF SCHOOL)

No one has ever seen God
if we love one another,
God abides in us and his love is
perfected in us.
1 John 4:12

In verse 13 we know He abides in us by His Spirit
Father You abide in me. Teach me to love.
Help me be myself. I am Yours.

EVENING:

Father, I don't know who I am. I'm realizing that I spent so much time trying to make myself something that I forgot who I am. But Father, I know who You are and I know how You view me, who You say I am.

I long for the point in my life when I don't have to worry about who I am. Right now, there are certain things, relationships, environments my body wants to act one way in but then my soul remembers what You've taught me.

Bring me to the place where I am constantly worshipping You and living, acting, being out of love.

8-23-13 FRIDAY (MORNING):

"But as for you, O man of God, flee these things. Pursue righteousness, godliness, faith, love, steadfastness, gentleness. Fight the good fight of the faith." *1 Timothy 6:11-12a*

"We who are strong have an obligation to bear with the failings of the weak, and not to please ourselves." *Romans 15:1*

God says straight up right here how He wants me to live: a life of seeking those things listed. And He tells us to come alongside the weak and their trials.

Had a good talk with Carley on the way home about what's been going on in my heart since Nicaragua. For some reason, I kind of want to keep a lot of that to myself, but it was nice to talk to her about it. I still don't exactly know who I really am, and I know that as I seek this life of love my relationships will look a little different.

8-24-13 SATURDAY

You don't need to know who you are to love people.

And I will give you a new heart,
and a new spirit I will
put within you. And I will
remove the heart of stone from your flesh
and give you a heart of flesh.
Ezekiel 36:26

Ezekiel 37:4-6 Dry Bones
—The Lord tells Ezekiel to prophesy over the bones that they will live and will know the Lord
—Ezekiel does so and the bones rise up
—"A great army"

We who were dead now live. We can know the Lord! And as His army, we will fight for Him.

8-25-13 SUNDAY (MORNING):

Love doesn't milk it.

Come, everyone who thirsts,
come to the waters; and
he who has no money,
come, buy and eat! Come,
buy wine and milk
without money
and without price.
Isaiah 55:1

Joel 2:28-29 The Lord has poured out His spirit on people of every age.

I want to know You more! I want my Spirit to fade away, my old heart. And I want them to be replaced by the heart of flesh and the Holy Spirit. I feel them within me, I know I'm made new. But Lord, what I want is to know You more! I love You and I thank You that You let me talk to You at all parts of the day.

8-26-13 MONDAY (MORNING):

"Whom have I in heaven but you? And there is nothing on earth that I desire besides you. My flesh and my heart may fail, but God is the strength of my heart and my portion forever."
Psalm 73:25-26

Just because I'm back from Nicaragua doesn't mean God's done teaching me. Not at all, actually He's always teaching, always molding. I just need to listen.

You emptied me in Nicaragua, but I pray that You'd continually be emptying me of anything bad I'm filled with. Take envy, jealousy, arrogance, take them all. Fill me with Your Spirit! With love, with joy, with peace.

Father, like in Nicaragua, let me learn from You today. I'm open to Your will, to Your voice. Let me see You and hear You anew today.

1 Corinthians 2—You have no idea what I've prepared for you

8-27-13 (MORNING):

Heavenly Father, don't let me go monotone in my life. I spent a lot of last year going through the motions and not listening to You. Let me be constantly hungry for You, and I pray that You'd make Your will clearer to me. Make me listen so I can hear what You want me to do.

Break my heart for what breaks Yours.

Revelation 5:13—Every creature proclaims God's holiness and seeks to worship Him forever.

This is what I'm here for!

God's on the inside of me now, but for some reason I still try to find Him on the outside.

Father, do you want me to speak in chapel again? Please show me.

8-28-13 (MORNING):

Might be time for me to start praying for what to do next in terms of loving another country.

I think I may be subconsciously trying to build another identity for myself. I think it's my automatic reaction to life because I'm scared I and others won't like who I really am. But God taught me not to be concerned with the eyes of others, and I know He made me to be unique.

Replace my pride with love!

Isaiah 49:6 was the verse that rung with me before this year's trip to Nicaragua. And reading it, I don't feel it was just intended for this trip. So I do think God has somewhere else for me to go. I just don't know where or when yet.

8-29-13 (MORNING):

One thing that makes me feel close to God is praying continuously. With school and homework and Cross Country, I'm usually pretty busy and it's easy to lose focus. But Father, I pray that I would see Your glory throughout the day, so that I'll be reminded of who You are and what You've done, and praise You for it not matter where I am.

Isaiah 40
The poor spend money to make idols that can do nothing, but God is right here! He keeps watch over His sheep and brings them back.

You say I will seek You and find You when I seek You with all my heart, so if I'm not finding You I must not have my whole heart in it.

8-30-13 FRIDAY (MORNING):

Two weeks ago today, I left Nicaragua.

For I consider that the
sufferings
of this present time
are not worth comparing with
the glory
that is to be revealed to us.
Romans 8:18

God is excited, like a lover with a secret, elaborate plan for His love, to reveal the glory and beauty of His plan and His wonders to me.

Have I forgotten how in love with me God is?

8-31-13 SATURDAY

You are beautiful! What a beautiful thing to watch You start the day off by shining the sun through the trees.

Job 40-41 Who are we to question God? He is great, He is powerful, and He is the Creator of all things.

> Then the eyes of the blind shall be opened, and the ears of the deaf unstopped; then shall the lame man leap like a deer, and the tongue of the mute sing for joy. For waters break forth in the wilderness, and streams in the desert....
>
> *Isaiah 35:5-6*

I love this image of the mute singing!

When they know of God's glory, the sick can be healed.

I think Jesus is going to use me as an instrument to miraculously heal people.

9-1-13 SUNDAY (EVENING):

Jesus, let me understand as much as possible how much You love me and what You are doing for me.

I think it's time to start thinking and praying about where God wants me to go next.

Father, I would absolutely love to go camping with the Mekkeses in a couple weeks. I feel like it would be a time of strengthening in joy and faith and drawing closer to You. The only problem is that I have a cross country meet. Father, I absolutely believe that if Your will is for me to go camping, something will happen with the meet and I'll be able to go. But I also know that might not happen. Whatever,

Your will is, I will accept it joyfully and without complaint. Thank You for putting the Mekkes family in my life ☺

9-2-13 MONDAY (MORNING):

I'm very thankful that God taught me how to love my family in Nicaragua. And a big part of that is not complaining or arguing.

"Do all things without grumbling or disputing, that you may be blameless and innocent, children of God without blemish in the midst of a crooked and twisted generation among whom you shine as lights of the world." *Philippians 2:14-15*

This is sweet because it means there is so much complaining and arguing around us, that if we simply don't do that people will see the light in us.

Idea: What if I have one day a week where I sit in the Hinshaw chapel with an acoustic guitar and worship and pray? I can have a general invitation on Facebook and just do it whether or not people show up. Something to pray about.

9-3-13 TUESDAY (MORNING):

Love is strong as death,
jealousy as fierce as the grave.

Go on up to a high mountain,
O Zion, herald of good news;
Lift up your voice with strength,
O Jerusalem; herald of good news;
Lift it up; fear not;
Say to the cities of Judah,
"Behold your God!"
Isaiah 40: 9

This popped up again, is this God saying He wants me to go through with the Hinshaw worship idea?

9-4-13 WEDNESDAY (MORNING):

Jesus, let not a single prideful thing be on my mind! Don't let me think of myself, Father, how I appear or how people view me; being careful to act in a way that people would like me. Lord, You are the only one that I seek to please! You are the only one worthy of my heart! Let not my mind wander from glorifying You.

Today marks a month since Jesus broke me and began to rebuild me!

I wanna be more aware of the times my parents are trying to make family times. They sincerely value that time, and I have plenty of other opportunities to be with friends or do my own thing. I wanna love my family by seeking time with them.

Love <u>definitely</u> isn't belligerent.

God, ever since I fell in love with You I have lived with the same cry of my heart: to know You more and to fall deeper in love with You. But God, there are days where for some reason I don't feel Your Spirit, I don't feel Your joy carrying with me through the day. And that bugs me Lord, because they're just random days. But that's not how love works; love lights up the face of one seeing his lover. And You are <u>always</u> right by me, God. So I pray that You would show me what's wrong, Lord. I don't want to feel You most of the time, I want to feel You <u>all</u> the time. You have done and are doing so much, Lord. You are moving, and my heart jumps at the knowledge of that.

Let me love You more.

9-5-13 THURSDAY (MORNING):

Whoever closes his ear to
the cry of the poor
will himself call out
and not be answered.
Proverbs 21:13

I am AMAZED at the way You put people in certain parts of my life to grow me.

Whoever pursues righteousness
and kindness will find life, righteousness,
and honor.
Proverbs 21:21

Ecclesiastes 4:1— "Again I saw all the oppressions that are done under the sun. And behold, the tears of the oppressed, and they had no one to comfort them! On the side of their oppressors there was power, and there was no one to comfort them.

The oppressed are still all around me. Show me how to love them." —Through prayer!!!

My soul cries out
These dry bones shout

My heart is a turbulent, raging mess. I am confused, lost, in pieces. I am sick and tired of feeling close to Jesus one day and not the next. My natural instincts are to believe it is Jesus who is leaving me and making me feel this way, and to just stop seeking him. But I am met with a promise: "You will seek me and you will find me, when you seek me with all your heart." I have known and am aware of how beautiful and mind-blowing it is to be in love with the God of the Universe. I believe that I can be crazy in love with him for the rest of my life. But I have got to keep seeking Him. And He promises it is the most rewarding pursuit, and oh my gosh I know it is.

Lord, I pray that you would break me, smite me, shatter me to the point of emptiness and then heal and fill me in Your beautiful way. Forever, God, I want to rest and thrive in passionate love for You. Become my purpose.

9-6-13 FRIDAY (MORNING):

You keep him in perfect peace
whose mind is stayed on you,

because he trusts in you.
Isaiah 26:3

"Your name and remembrance are the desire of our soul. My soul yearns for you in the night; my spirit within me earnestly seeks you."
Isaiah 26:8b-9a

"Your dead shall live; their bodies shall rise. You who dwell in the dust, awake and sing for joy! For your dew is a dew of light, and the earth will give birth to the dead."
Isaiah 26:19

9-7-13 SATURDAY

Even though I'm a Christian, I'm not immune to feeling negative or depressed. However, with the Holy Spirit in me, I'm able to kill those feelings. Love isn't negative. And it isn't naively positive; it's just real. And what's real is that God has done and is doing so many beautiful things for me.

If I feel "far away from God," I should check my heart. Am I angry? Scared? Negative? These are feelings that can't block me from the beautiful love of my Savior, but can make me hide my eyes from Him. I want to be forever growing in love and appreciation for Jesus, and in order to do that, I must keep my eyes open to the glorious things He's doing.

I love You Lord ☺

9-8-13 SUNDAY (MORNING):

Wondrously show your steadfast
love, O Savior of those who seek refuge
from their adversaries
at your right hand.
Psalm 17:7

"And me? I plan on looking you full in the face. When I get up, I'll see your full stature and live heaven on earth." *Psalm 17:15* (MSG)

1 Corinthians 2: I absolutely love how this passage talks about how we can't even comprehend what God has prepared for us. I imagine Him as a lover with a wonderful gift He has worked so hard on, eager to give it to His beloved but waiting for the right time ☺

There is nothing rewarding about jealousy, but there is everything rewarding about being stoked for someone. So thankful that God taught me that!

9-9-13 MONDAY (MORNING):

Love isn't stressed!

I love when God makes different people and ministries show up multiple times in my life to show me I need to pray for them!

Talk with Mrs. Wetzel

—She told me about her trip, said Mr. Shoaf has a very open-hand way of giving that she liked

—I told her about my trip, told her about how I want to talk less and be a better listener

—She called my pride thing "being a social chameleon"

—Said though it's good to be a good listener, it's one of those spectrum things where you may find out you know a lot about everyone but nobody knows a thing about you and that can result in an untrue friendship.

9-10-13 TUESDAY (MORNING):

God sometimes doesn't act til the last minute.

He brought me out into a broad place;
He rescued me, because he delighted in me.
2 Samuel 22:20

"And he said, 'Naked I came from my mother's womb, and naked shall I return. The Lord gave, and the Lord has taken away; blessed be the name of the Lord.' In all this Job did not sin or charge God with wrong."
Job 1: 21-22

"As a deer pants for flowing streams, so pants my soul for you, O God. My soul thirsts for God, for the living God. When shall I come and appear before God."
Psalm 42: 1-2

Psalm 42-43: Psalm 42 talks about how the singer used to lead people in worship but now feels far from God. But then He says, "Why are you cast down, O my soul, and why are you in turmoil within me? Hope in God; for I shall praise Him, my salvation and my God."

I was about to pray that God would start speaking to me through Scripture again, but before I could He showed me a verse. Before we ask, He knows our question ☺

This is exactly how I was feeling last week. It shows an important response to that inner turbulence: Hoping in God. When I feel far from Him, I should give Him glory and praise. Then I will see Him and His beauty again.

It's said three times...emphasized confirmation.

9-11-13 WEDNESDAY (MORNING):

"Search me, O God, and know my heart! Try me and know my thoughts! And see if there be any grievous way in me, and lead me in the way everlasting!" *Psalm 139:23-24*

Let me know the things that I am holding too tightly to.

Love rejoices with the truth.

What a life it is to be in love with You! What most would see as little things give me fantastic joy and peace. When you recognize who a gift is from, it changes how you think about it. And knowing what God went through to give me these gifts...MAN!

By day the Lord commands his steadfast love, and at night his song is with me, a prayer to the God of my life. *Psalm 42:8*

9-12-13 THURSDAY (MORNING):

Isaiah 42: 1-17

Verse 1: “Behold, my servant, whom I uphold, my chosen, in whom my soul delights; I have put my spirit upon him; he will bring forth justice to the nations.”

I truly feel a connection to this verse and the others in this passage. This is my calling!

I didn’t get to go camping with the Mekkeses, but God still answered prayer. A couple months ago, finding out that the trip couldn’t happen would’ve made me complain and be bummed and probably take it out on my parents. But God has shown me to take joy in everything, for if I’m inside His will and I’m not going camping, that means He has other stuff in store.

9-13-13 FRIDAY (MORNING):

I’m in love with the Creator ☺

"Whom have I in heaven but you? And there is nothing on earth that I desire besides you. My flesh and my heart may fail, but God is the strength of my heart and my portion forever." *Psalm 73: 25-26*

"My soul longs, yes, faints, for the courts of the Lord; my heart and flesh sing for joy to the living God." *Psalm 84:2*

He surprises me with beauty ☺ I look down, then back up and there’s a glorious sunrise in front of me. Oh what it is to be in love!

9-14-13 SATURDAY (MORNING):

"If any of you lacks wisdom, let him ask God, who gives generously to all without reproach, and it will be given him."
James 1:5

A lot of verses about seeking wisdom have popped up lately. Wisdom gives insight into the mind of God, and therefore lets me know and understand His love more.

Kathy:

—Ms Kathy drove up again today

—I love that she always drives up and tells me about these little miracles

—She was praying for pizza, friend drives up with pizza

—Really cool one: Sydney (her first dog) had a seizure and died, but Kathy prayed and said she wasn't ready for him to go and he came back

—"People think I'm crazy, but they just don't get faith!"

9-15-13 SUNDAY (MORNING):

I've had a lot of stuff about Africa pop up lately, and it's honestly been on my mind since Nicaragua. I need to pray a good bit more about it, but I honestly wonder if that's where God wants me to go? *The Final Quest* talks about seeing and dwelling in the glory and the love of the Lord. It warns that what we see with our eyes may be different than what we see in our hearts. In our hearts, we can always see the glory of the Lord. But with our eyes, though He's moving all around us, we can be confused and distracted.

Kaitlin:

—Got to Skype with Kaitlin today

—She is such a blessing, her joy and love for the Lord are infectious and powerful

—Talked about our trips, what God's been teaching us

9-16-13 MONDAY (MORNING):

Psalm 16:11

"You make known to me the path of life; in your presence there is fullness of joy; at your right hand are pleasures forevermore."

I've been back a month now.

I'm praying about where God wants me to go next, and if He wants me to go next year. After I asked Him, this verse showed up:

Declare his glory
among the nations,
his marvelous works
among all the peoples.
Psalm 86: 3

Don't know if this is straight-up confirmation yet, I need to keep praying.

Now *Isaiah 6:8* showed up…still don't know for sure

I've had points in my faith where I've felt sad and dark and far away from God. But His love is not a dark path. It is a path of radiant love and joy and peace.

It's nice to wake up and lie down to a worship song. This, and everyday, is the Lord's ☺

9-17-13 TUESDAY (MORNING):

Whoever mocks the poor insults his maker; he who is
glad at calamity will not go unpunished.
Proverbs 17:15

John 14:15-31 The world can't see Jesus, but we can because His Holy Spirit is within us. The Spirit teaches us and reminds us of the things Jesus said. Also, in the Spirit we find peace.

Today, a group of armed men got into Casa Bernabe Orphanage, went to Herberto's house and robbed him*. They took his computer and beat him up, sending him to the hospital. I can only imagine the kind of darkness that would lead someone to attack an orphanage. Praying that God would bring light and glory out of this.

*Casa Bernabe Orphanage was where Mark lived and worked for part of the summer of 2013. He had barely been home a month when the gunman attacked the orphanage. They opened fire on the staff at the orphanage and were said to ask for the "gringos." Had Mark still been there, he would have been in serious danger.

NOTE: 9-18-13
MY CALLING

Today, Ben (piano) and I (guitar and vocals) led worship for the High School. I absolutely love worship because no matter my current feelings my mouth has to give God praise, and I instantly feel the presence of the Lord. We played "Grace Like Rain", "Like an Avalanche", and "All I need is You", and after "All I Need is You" I opened my mouth to pray and I felt like my words were legit being heard by God (as opposed to the brickwall thing). I prayed for God's light to shine in powerful ways, acknowledging my faults and seeking His light. After the chapel, Mrs. Wetzel came up to me and told me that as I sang, she received a word from the Lord. I shivered with joy. "Oh boy," I said expectantly.

She told me that she'd flipped open to two passages. *Psalm 149* was one, which talks about rejoicing in the king and singing a new song, but at the same time bearing a double-edged sword. The other was *2 Chronicles 20*, in which God calls forth worship leaders to stand and worship in front of Jehosophat's army, and the opposing army falls to pieces.

Mrs. Wetzel told me I was made to be a worship leader. But not just that, a warrior as well. My music is to be brought into battle. I am so, so excited to pursue this, and beyond thankful for Mrs. Wetzel.

One of the most important things for me to remember is that at the end of the battle Jehosophat gave the Lord all the glory. I've found a talent of mine, and pride is eager to rule it. But I am nothing without Christ, and only He is worth praising.

9-18-13 WEDNESDAY (MORNING):

Two months ago today I prayed for hunger for Jesus, and it was given to me.

Isaiah 58:6-11

I don't know if this is my "life verse" but I feel like my call is within it. It says that this is true worship: to release the prisoners, to pour myself out for the hurting. Then the verse says that I will call to God and He will answer me. And it says the Lord will make my bones strong and make me like a well-watered garden.

My prayer from Ruby's tells me God is giving me authority and that I should pray for the sick. Up to this point I haven't prayed for Dr. Sandwell's, Kathy's, Mrs. D's, or anyone else's healing because I'm scared they won't be healed. And, subconsciously, I want to see it happen miraculously right in front of my eyes. But today, I'm gonna start praying for them earnestly until they're healed or God calls them home.

9-19-13 THURSDAY (MORNING):

I have been given my life's calling. And it's confusing as mess. But I'm excited that it involves straight-up worshipping the God of the universe.

Worship today was so fun. But this talent is gonna literally bring me up against my greatest struggle—pride. I'm gifted at something, and people tell me that, and instantly there's a war between my renewing mind and my ego. There is a very visible line here—if I'm a worship leader and every word I sing and move I make is directed at God, then that is so awesome and I'll be blessed for it. But if I'm a worship leader and what I do I do for my own glory, then I am the most wretched of men because while my mouth praises the Lord, inside I praise myself. When I came back from Nicaragua I wanted to avoid being put in positions where I will struggle against pride. But now, I'm called to one of those positions.

I have a feeling this will be one of the most rewarding struggles of my life.

9-20-13 FRIDAY (MORNING):

Jesus, cut open my heart and drain me of pride and jealousy and bitterness as many times as You have to.

My verse (*Psalm 149*) says I will execute the sentence God has set against the kings. I'll need to keep praying for wisdom and a renewed mind, cause I sure as heck don't know how to do that.

9-21-13 SATURDAY (MORNING):

Reflecting on my calling, I realized something very interesting. It is dangerous, wrong, and false to put your surety and worth in a calling. Surety and worth can only be found in the Caller, who has been gracious to give my wretched self gifts for His glory. I don't want to feel confident about my voice and my talents, I want to be confident in the love of the Father who gave me them. This is humility.

Final Quest—The greatest in the kingdom of Heaven are those who were devoted to the first and greatest commandment - loving the Lord.

Nahum 1—The Lord is jealous and avenging. He is jealous for his Bride and wants to be her only lover, and He enacts vengeance upon those who hurt her.

9-22-13 SUNDAY (MORNING):

Do not rob the poor, because he is poor,
or crush the afflicted at the gate,
for the Lord will plead
their cause
and rob of life those who rob them.
Proverbs 22:22-23

Life Passage

Let the godly exult
in glory;
Let them sing for joy on their beds.
Psalm 149

Wherever, whenever I am, God is glorious and worth praising.

God, You are so good! So beautiful! Oh, how You have blessed me again and again. I love Your master plan, Your intricate design. I love that You spin, You dance, You rejoice over me! What a love this is!

9-23-13 MONDAY (MORNING):

My inmost being will exult
when your lips speak
what is right.
Proverbs 23:16

It's kind of interesting to me that I didn't really think I was able to sing until I fell in love with God in May.

9-24-13 TUESDAY (MORNING):

Isaiah 61:10 "I will greatly rejoice in the Lord; my soul shall exult in my God, for he has clothed me with the garments of salvation; he has covered me with the robe of righteousness as a bridegroom decks himself like a priest with a beautiful headdress, and as a bride adorns herself with jewels."

I love the way I feel God's joy even when I'm just thanking Him for simple things.

9-25-13 WEDNESDAY (MORNING):

I have seriously seen so many things having to do with wisdom lately. Even license plates that start WSE; I see them everywhere. I'm gonna start praying earnestly for wisdom.

If any of you lacks wisdom,
let him ask God
who gives generously to all without
reproach, and it will be given him.
James 1:5

9-26-13 THURSDAY (MORNING):

God, there is so much more to learn about You. So many more ways to know You and fall more in love with You. Right now, Lord, I feel like I'm on the verge of sleepwalking. I need Your powerful love and glory to burn within me and give me purpose. I am meant to glorify You, and I am to love others. What I seek, Lord, is to fall deeper and deeper in love with You until I'm giddy with joy at the things You're doing. I know You want this too, Father. Break me as much as it takes for me to fall passionately in love with You.

NOTE: 9-27-13

Wisdom:

I wrote a few days ago about seeing references to wisdom all around me. Then, as I'm reading through James, I turn the page and see the caption "Wisdom from Above." This is also right after reading in *The Final Quest* wisdom is imparted to the author, who has sought it for years.

The passage in James talks about how jealousy and selfish ambition do not lead to wisdom. I know that to be true firsthand! Then, it gives the wisdom version of *1 Corinthians 13*:

But the wisdom from above is first
pure, then peaceable, gentle, open to reason,
full of mercy and good fruits, impartial, and sincere.
James 3:17

I'm on a quest for wisdom now. So many stinking references to it, and now my daily reading leads me here. I'm so excited to learn from my awesome God!

9-27-13 FRIDAY (MORNING):

I feel like, in some relationships, I'm on the verge of being a "social chameleon" again. And sadly, some of those are with the people I'm closest to.

Jesus, before Nicaragua, I found much of my "worth" in people's praise of me. And that's what a social chameleon seeks. But Jesus, in Nicaragua You painfully tore me from that idol and brought me into the paradise of knowing how You think of me. And in turn, I began to love others and feel joy like never before.

Father, I refuse to accept pride as a viable way of life. Help me recognize when I'm compromising myself to increase someone else's view of me. I now know how painful it is to live a life of self, and how glorious it is to live a life of love.

Enseñame a amar.

9-28-13 SATURDAY (MORNING):

Because your steadfast love is
better than life,

my lips will praise you.
So I will bless you as long
as I live;
In your name I will lift
up my hands.
Psalm 63:3-4

This is what I was made for!

Send out your light and
your truth; let them lead me; let them
bring me to your holy hill
and to your dwelling!
Psalm 43:3

James is absolutely blowing my mind lately. He writes in such straight up language that applies so well to my life. James 4 talks about how God is so jealous for us, and friendship with the world is adultery towards Him. And worse, we still ask for things from Him when we mean to spend them on our lovers.

9-29-13 SUNDAY(MORNING):

James 3:17 is the Bible App's verse of the day…I'm seriously wondering about all these things about wisdom that keep popping up.

Do you see a man who is hasty
in his words?
There is more hope for a fool
than for him.
Proverbs 29:20

I want to keep reins on my tongue.

9-30-13 MONDAY (MORNING):

Final Quest: Angelo

Am I faithful with all I've been given? Do I enjoy and see the Lord everywhere that He really is? Am I using all of my skills and talents for His glory?

Jesus, I love the touch of Your hand on my soul when I worship You. Let me know You more, know Your glory more, so that I can give You praise You deserve.

10-1-13 TUESDAY (MORNING):

God, I want to know You better!

I want to fall more and more in love with You.

So whether we are at
home or away (heaven, earth).
We make it our aim to
please him.
2 Corinthians 5:9

I love reading the last chapter of Revelation. Jesus is coming in all His glory, and His Spirit within me cries out for that.

God let me know Your glory and love more. Amaze me, fill me with awe, so I may fall more in love with You.

I will know Him and love Him more the more I love others.

10-2-13 WEDNESDAY (MORNING):

Show me where there is a need for You in the course of my daily life.

Break my heart for what breaks Yours!

"And this is my prayer; that your love may abound more and more in knowledge and depth of insight, so that you may be able to discern what is best and may be pure and blameless for the day of Christ, filled with the fruit of righteousness that comes through Jesus Christ—to the glory and praise of God." *Phillippians 1:9-11*

Jesus, show me how to advance Your gospel from where I am right now.

Proverbs 2:1-6 "If you seek for wisdom like silver, you will understand the fear of the Lord and find the knowledge of God."

We will see as He sees!

As painful as it was, the most beautiful and joyful moment of my life was when God burned my pride from me in Nicaragua. ☺

NOTE: 10-3-13

Do nothing from selfish ambition or conceit, but in humility count others more significant than yourselves. Let each of you look not only to his own interests, but also to the interests of others.
Phillippians 2:3-4

Love isn't deceptive
Love isn't selfish
Love isn't manipulative
Love isn't prideful

Love is true
Love is compassionate
Love is honest
Love builds others up

I love what Aaron Gillespie says about not worshipping God just because we're prospering or because we're hurting and need something from Him, but worshiping Him because He is God. Worshiping Him because He is Love, He is Power, He is Glorious. God is SO good.

10-3-13 THURSDAY (MORNING):

Yesterday, I was at the lake with Ben, and after biking back to the car I realized I'd left the keys hanging on my bike and they were no longer there. We biked back to the part of the lake we'd been at, but couldn't find the key. I started to feel something I gave up in Nicaragua: stress. But I quickly reminded myself of how good God is and how much He's done for me. I prayed for serenity and decided that on our ride back, I'd praise Him in prayer and glorify Him. I told Him I knew He could show me those keys, but if He didn't I could still be at peace and not feel stress.

At one point, I stopped at a spot where I'd slipped off my bike earlier. And there they were. A ridiculously long distance from the lake, these keys had somehow hung on. I smiled and recognized what had just happened: God is faithful to those who are faithful to Him.

I love that He listens to the littlest things. He actually cares about what we care about, because He loves us!

10-4-13 FRIDAY (MORNING):

I'm not called to judge people, but I'm not to hold back in my music. My music isn't necessarily for calling people out, but I shouldn't sugarcoat stuff. My words should be words of war.

Jesus, You are worth worshiping no matter if something great is happening or we feel that we need You. Uncircumstantial praise is what I want to give You. I love You because of who You are, not because of where I am.

For the Lord comforts Zion;
He comforts all her waste places
and makes her wilderness like Eden,
her desert like the garden
of the Lord;
joy and gladness will be found in her,
thanksgiving and the voice
of song.
Isaiah 51:3

He comforts my waste places and turns my darkness to light.

10-5-13 SATURDAY (MORNING):

Keep me aware, Jesus, of Your glory around me. I know it's there, but knock on my head and remind me of just how good and awesome You are.

Philippians 4:6-7 Don't be anxious, but present to God your requests with prayer and thankfulness. Then, He will fill you with this incredible peace.

I've loved experiencing this lately. No stress, just trusting and faith.

I want to be aware and acknowledge how sinful and dirty I am. But I don't want that to be something that makes me depressed and turns me from God. I want that knowledge to make me more and more grateful and stoked on God's mercy and grace. I am so undeserving, but He passionately loves and pursues me.

10-6-13 SUNDAY (MORNING):

I know the ways to make myself look righteous. That's one of my biggest vices. While my Spirit yearns to give glory to God when I worship Him, the flesh is always looking for my own glory.

For I have derived much joy and
comfort from your love,
my brother,
because the hearts of the
saints have been refreshed
through you.
Philemon 7

Philemon loved people so much that they felt refreshed, and joyful, and comforted. I want to be someone who loves people to that degree.

The Lord takes pleasure
in those who fear him,
in those who hope
in his steadfast love.
Psalm 147:11

10-7-13 MONDAY (MORNING):

What are the veils in my face that are keeping me from seeing Jesus?

Commit your way to the Lord;
Trust in him, and he will act.
He will bring forth your
righteousness as the light,
and your justice as the noonday.
Psalm 37:5-6

10-8-13 TUESDAY (MORNING):

I feel sad, but have no reason. My soul is in turmoil, and I don't know why. God is so good. And He loves and wants me so much.

Deep calls to deep. My soul yearns for the depths of God, but I feel like I've covered my face with a veil that's keeping me from seeing Him clearly.

Do I understand that I'm forgiven? Or am I holding the weight of some sins against me?

I am free. Yes, I still struggle with sin. But I'm forgiven. And God does not look at me with eternal sadness because I sin. No, He loves me, and is excited for me, and wants me closer and closer to Him.

O give thanks to the Lord, for He is good; His love endures forever!

This is the day that the Lord has made; let us rejoice and be glad in it!

IT'S OKAY. I LOVE YOU.

10-9-13 WEDNESDAY (MORNING):

It's cool that before May, I couldn't focus when I woke up early to pray. Now, I feel like I need to. Good verse:

Do not let the sun go down on your anger.
Be kind to one another,
tenderhearted, forgiving one another,
as God in Christ forgave you.
Ephesians 4:32

I will give thanks to the Lord
With my whole heart;
I will recount all of your
wonderful deeds.
Psalm 9:1

I want people to truly see how good God is and what He's doing, not just through music, but through relationships. People need to know that there's a powerful God who wants so bad to be in love with us.

I feel like this is something I may have been missing out on. Am I telling people what awesome things God has done, or am I keeping that to myself?

10-10-13 THURSDAY (MORNING):

I'm so stoked for Carley's revelation about Vietnam!

I asked God specifically to show me what it is I'm doing (or not doing) that's creating this veil, and my passage in Ephesians (which I've been reading through) for today is titled "Walk in Love." That makes me think about what I learned from Nicaragua. Am I truly loving others, or do I just appear to be? Am I truly present with people, or am I seeking my own gain?

I feel little hints of irritability, but don't show it. This isn't how I want to be . I don't want to feel those hints at all. Love isn't irritable. It doesn't say, "Love doesn't act out of irritability," but "Love isn't irritable." An irritable mindset stinks. It blocks love and feeds pride. I want to go back to love before I start running on pride again.

I'm gonna rejoice today, and I'm gonna mean it.

10-11-13 FRIDAY (MORNING):

From Matthew Henry's commentary on Song of Solomon: God doesn't want ours, He wants us. As much as our obedience and good works please Him, what He is passionate about is our broken, hungry, needy selves; He loves that!

I need to be so careful that I don't start living on the outside again; watching myself anticipating how people would view me if I did certain things. I wanna live from the inside out.

When pride comes, then
comes disgrace,
but with the humble
is wisdom.
Proverbs 11:2

God is faithful. I prayed for babies to be rescued from death, and they were. Today I'm gonna pray that He will show me today what He wants me to do mission-wise next summer. That doesn't mean He'll tell me today, but I know He cares what I say.

10-12-13 SATURDAY (MORNING):

Today I have nothing scheduled but skyping Kaitlin at noon and dinner and a movie with Carley tonight. Today I am free to create, worship, and design all the day long. God has blessed me again.

God didn't tell me yesterday where He wants me to go. But that's okay. Because He loves me and His plan is far beyond my comprehension, and I know He reveals just the right things at just the right time. Until He tells me, I will keep asking Him to and will keep worshiping Him.

Sing to the Lord, all the earth!
Tell of his salvation from day to day.
Declare his glory among the nations,
his marvelous works
among all the peoples!
1 Chronicles 16:23-24

It's so cool looking back on Nicaragua and thinking of all the amazing ways God blessed me. He literally loves me so much and encourages me and knows just the right ways to make my heart leap. When Relient K came on the kid's radio, I knew He'd put that there for me. When I saw Maria' s picture on Puente de Amistad's fridge, that was for me. And on that glorious Sunday where He broke me to pieces, the songs we sang ("The Stand", "Hosanna", other familiar ones) had been arranged because He knew I needed them. He is so good. Perfectly in control, perfectly aware of what I need. Perfectly in love with me. He blows my mind consistently.

For your servant's sake, O Lord, and
according to your own heart, you
have done all this greatness, in
making known all these great things.
1 Chronicles 17:19

NOTE: 10-13-13

"Whoever guards his mouth preserves his life; he who opens wide his lips comes to ruin." *Proverbs 13:3*

Thinking about that Sunday God broke me; I am such a sinner, but I can rejoice! God is so good and loves me so much and puts my sins out of His mind for He has paid for them.

I don't need to (and shouldn't) feel any guilt or shame. God wants me to live in crazy thankfulness and joy, because He has freed me!

Today:
—Spanish church with Carley after Redeemer, the people there were so welcoming and joyful, it was awesome
—Came home and headed out to Ben's for worship practice
—Arrived to a delicious home-cooked meal, the Mekkes family is so welcoming it's incredible
—Overwhelmed with how blessed I am. God has been so good to me, it's incredible. I don't deserve it at all. But He has given me such beautiful things. "I will sing to the Lord, because He has dealt bountifully with me!"

10-13-13 SUNDAY (MORNING):

Sin: Though I have a perfect lover, I commit adultery with lovers who only bring me pain.

Sin takes my eyes off of loving others and focuses them on my own wants.

Kaitlin brought up something really great yesterday; now that I know what I believe God's call to be on my life, I don't have to be trying to fulfill every little step and set my life up to achieve that goal. God is in control, and my goal should be to know Him and fall more in love with Him. That is what He works out of.

I will sing to the Lord
because he has dealt bountifully
with me.
Psalm 13:6

Remembering my Sundays in Nicaragua, some of the hugest, best days of my life. So thankful for how much I learned there!

10-14-13 MONDAY (MORNING):

Tremble, O earth, at the
presence of the Lord,
at the presence of the
God of Jacob...
Psalm 114:7

The Lord is on my side;
I will not fear,
what can man do to me?
Psalm 118:6

I think about this a lot: God has designed each day to be full of blessings and gifts out of His perfect love for us. This is the day He has made; it is a powerful, beautiful, intricate part of His master plan. I'm looking forward to seeing Him today.

Got to lead worship tonight for the Vision Meeting* and it went so well. God is so so good!

Note: The vision meeting was for Norfolk Christian parents and teachers and included approximately 500 attendees.

10-15-13 TUESDAY (MORNING):

You are my worth. No compliment or insult from anyone could ever change that.

For you have delivered my
soul from death,
my eyes from tears,
my feet from stumbling;
I will walk before the Lord
in the land of the living.
Psalm 116:8-9

Whoever gives thought to the
word will discover good,
and blessed is he who trusts
In the Lord.
Proverbs 16:20

I pray that I would see the impact of directly loving others today.

10-16-13 WEDNESDAY (MORNING):

You make known to me
the path of life;
In your presence there
is fullness of joy.
At your right hand are pleasures
forevermore.
Psalm 16:11

A gentle tongue is a tree of life,
but perverseness in it breaks
the spirit.
Proverbs 15:4

I want to be filled with love for others. I want to pursue relationships and pour into people. But I have to make sure I am humble. Pride and love cannot exist together, I know that full well.

AFTERNOON:

Looking over my notes from Nica (I've been home two months now) I see that my love there wasn't perfect. But it was always persevering. I strive to love others. I will give up anything and everything to love God's children. I am useless, pointless without love. But when I give up myself, I am exactly what I was made for.

I have found my fullness of joy ☺

Enseñame A Amar.

BREAK MY HEART FOR WHAT BREAKS YOURS.

It was good for me to read *1 Corinthians 13:1-8a* again. This is what I strive towards: true, selfless, joyful love.

Jesus, I pray that if there is any pride in me, You would cut me up and drain it out. I have nothing that makes it okay for me to judge others. I feel little bits of irritability and judging and jealousy pulling at the seams of my soul. But I need to consistently be drained of all selfishness so that I can love others.

10-17-13 THURSDAY (MORNING):

I do not need to live a life regretting yesterday's sins. No analyzing what I've done all the time. I'm just going to live 1 Corinthians 13 wherever I am. I'm free from those sins. I'm going to live a life of pursuing today's joys and seeking to become more like Jesus.

Life is at its absolute best when I am fully engaged with loving the people around me.

Love rejoices in the truth. It doesn't characterize people by their faults, but by their good (or potential for it!)

Whoever restrains his words
has knowledge
and he who has a cool spirit
is a man of understanding.
Proverbs 17:27

It's cool to me that even through a long day of school and homework with little to no free time, I can feel the presence of God with me the whole way through. Life is a lot better when, instead of complaining about something, I invite God in while I do it. He loves that!

10-18-13 FRIDAY (MORNING):

Jesus, if it's necessary, bring me to the point of brokenness so that I can know You better. All I want is to see You and know You more!

Love doesn't just think about good things, or agree with them, or talk about them. Love does.

For it is You who light
my lamp;
The Lord my God lightens
my darkness.
Psalm 18:28

God I earnestly pray that You would open my eyes to You. You are all around me, but I want to dive into You and see You and know You better. I want to love people powerfully by Your side. You are good, God.

10-19-13 SATURDAY (MORNING):

One of the best things about life with Jesus is that no day has to be boring, stressful, or typical. He is an active God with dynamic, active love.

Started reading *1 John*, there's some good stuff in here.

By this we know that we are in him:
whoever says he abides in him
ought to walk in the same way that
he walked.
1 John 2:5b-6

"Whoever says he is in the light and hates his brother is still in darkness. Whoever loves his brother abides in the light, and in him there is no cause for stumbling."
1 John 2:9-10

His anointing teaches you about everything…
1 John 3:27

10-20-13 SUNDAY (MORNING):

I run from You time and time again, but You always forgive me. You don't hold a thing against me; instead, You want me to fall more in love with You. Thank You.

When love does, love does it big!

"Being engaged is a way of doing life, a way of living and loving. It's about going to extremes and expressing the bright hope that life offers us, a hope that makes us brave and expels darkness with light. That's what I want my life to be all about—full of abandon, whimsy, and in love. I want to be engaged to life and with life." Bob Goff

My heart is steadfast, O God, my heart is steadfast!
I will sing and make melody!
Psalm 57:7

10-21-13 MONDAY (MORNING):

Little children, let
us not love in word or talk
but in deed and
In truth.
1 John 3:18

Jesus, I've learned that the reason I sometimes get that hurt in my heart is I'm wanting to know You more but seeking something outside of You. I'm made to go deeper in You, but I also need to be sure I'm abiding in You. It's okay for me to be living in peace. If I rest in You (while living a life of active love) I will find myself seeing You clearer and knowing Your ways better. Help me find peace in You today.

I kind of feel like I'm in a period of waiting for God's will for next summer. But instead of being frustrated about that, I need to recognize that this is a powerful opportunity for my mind to be renewed, my heart to be opened, and my love for God to grow deeper. Rest, peace, is not bad.

What if in moments of rest, instead of letting my mind wander everywhere, I prayed/thanked God?

10-22-13 (MORNING):

If we love one another,
God abides in us
and his love is perfected in us.
1 John 4:12b

There is no fear in love,
but perfect love
casts out fear.
1 John 4:18a

I don't need to be frustrated by not seeing miracles or having huge revelations all the time. I just need to be content in God. Then, in His own time, He will show Himself to me in powerful ways.

10-23-13 WEDNESDAY (MORNING):

Had an incredible worship practice with Ben last night; after finishing the big part of "You won't Relent" I told him to keep going. Then, it turned to a powerful time of prayer and spontaneous singing.

I am so blessed. Ben's so talented, and his playing flows like prayer. I'm so excited to worship more with him in the future.

10-24-13 (MORNING):

I keep thinking back to Philemon and what Paul says about him. "I have derived much joy and comfort from your love, my brother, because the hearts of the saints have been refreshed through you." Here is a man that encourages other Christian's hearts. They see God anew because of him. That's so powerful! I hope my love makes me like that.

Even youths shall faint and be weary,
and young men shall fall exhausted;
But they who wait for
The Lord shall renew their strength;
they shall mount up with wings like eagles;
They shall run and not be weary;
They shall walk and not faint.
Isaiah 40: 30-31

By the love and power of God we can go forever. Nothing can stop Him from accomplishing great things through us. In Him, we are renewed.

EVENING:

I had a very, very, valuable phone conversation with Carley tonight. One really, really important thing I realized was that I may be coming off to people like I have it all together, which can be frustrating and discouraging to someone who doesn't. Truth is, of course, I'm far from having it all together. But I live a life of knowing God is lovingly in control of every detail in my life. And the reason I don't talk a lot about how I got to that understanding is I'm trying to avoid pride, which sometimes tempts me when I talk about my spiritual life.

But I'm not okay with people being discouraged by my faith. I think it's time for me to start talking again. I know this is running towards pride's spears, but I think God wants me to share how powerful I've seen Him to be. I read again this morning about Zion proclaiming God's name and power to surrounding nations. It's time to do that. It's time to set myself on fire and display God's work.

You are so faithful and good, Jesus. Thank You for wisdom. ☺

10-25-13 FRIDAY (MORNING):

Cool thought from the book, *Love Does*: We talk about God closing doors and yes, He does that. But sometimes, He doesn't want us to walk away from that door; He wants us to kick it down.

When there is something right and good we believe God wants us to do, we shouldn't just turn away if it seems like it's not gonna happen. Love endures, pursues, fights, strives for justice. I haven't heard of a single door yet that God can't break down.

I love this idea of a "new song" in *Isaiah 42:10*. It literally means unprecedented praise.

I have blotted out your transgressions
like a cloud
and your sins like mist;
return to me,
for I have redeemed you.
Sing, O heavens,
for the Lord has done it;
shout, O depths of the earth;
break forth into singing,
O mountains,
O forest, and every tree
in it!
Isaiah 44:22-23

10-26-13 SATURDAY (MORNING):

I'm sitting in the treehouse in about 45 degree weather in awe of one of the most perfect stillnesses I've known. The morning sun beams through a cloudless sky and the fading green leaves until it hits the fort, casting long shadows on the floor. Every so often, the shadow of a bird flits across the table or a squirrel rushes up a tree, but besides these the world is almost totally at peace.

What strikes me about the stillness isn't just the calm, but the calm despite the obvious power around me. This light is strong and almost tangible, blasting through the trees like a silent cannon. But they do not run. Instead, nature seems to stand in awe of this peaceful, jealous, mysterious glory.

This is the fear of the Lord: Overwhelming awe at His power. Though man runs, the earth knows its ruler. Evil quakes in fear, and good rejoices in the peace of redemption. And someday, the world will be purged of darkness and the world will be what it was made to be: a world of worship.

Can I lie here in Your arms?
Can I lie here in Your arms?
My only aim is You.
Save me.

10-27-13 SUNDAY (MORNING):

I've been so busy this weekend and I have a lot of homework to do today. But I'm determined not to stress because I know that'll kill the joy of today and blind me to God's will for me.

"How can I stand here with You and not be moved by You?" ("Everything")

Open the eyes of my heart God. I need to see You, hear You, know You. You're everything.

It was extremely cool to see our church learn the "Came to my Rescue" chorus in sign language so they could worship with Peggy. Music is from the mouth, but worship's from the soul.

10-28-13 MONDAY (MORNING):

In romantic love you have to pursue. You have to figure out what she loves and <u>do</u> it for her, because you love <u>her</u>. When she sees how much you're doing for her, she'll realize just how much you love her.

I think God is doing just that for us. Pursuing us, setting up just the right things to blow our minds and make us realize His love for us. The sad thing is, we often turn our heads. We let stress or hate or disappointment bring us down and make us not care about love. But He keeps going. And He won't stop. "Love is strong as death, jealousy is demanding as the grave."

I don't wanna miss out on this. I will not place my goals, my responsibilities, or my passions over this. I will not make this love something I'll participate in only if I have time for it. No, I'm going to throw everything to the side like Peter did, in complete awe and joy at this love that's relentlessly passionate for me. He is the best lover, because He knows everything that makes me tick, and goes after that with all His heart.

EVENING:

The struggle will always be selfishness. The rejection of blessing and the striving after self are two of the most obviously sad, negative, detrimental things I could do. Yet I still do them, despite all He's done, how faithful He's been. Thank You, Jesus, for taking my punishment for this. You have done more than taken me in, You have dressed me up as Your desirable bride. I'm not worthy, Lord, but You have saved me. I'm sorry I run, God. I want to live in deep love with You, with eyes for no one else. Break me as much as it takes to tear down my sinful veils; refine me by fire. I am Yours.

10-29-13 TUESDAY (MORNING):

Ascribe to the Lord the
glory due his name;
Worship the Lord in the splendor
of holiness.
Psalm 29:2

You have turned for me my
mourning into dancing;
You have loosed my sackcloth
and clothed me with gladness,
that my glory may sing your
praise and not be silent.

O Lord my God, I will give
thanks to you forever.
Psalm 30:11-12

Despite my brokenness, my sin, my adultery, Jesus uses me. I'm not just a follower, I'm a participant that He has selected for specific reasons. That's really cool to know.

An evil man is
ensnared in his transgression,
but a righteous man sings
and rejoices.
Proverbs 29:6

I have been set free, now I can sing and rejoice and experience life in a beautiful way, because I'm becoming what I was meant to be. My sin does not define who I am anymore.

10-30-13 WEDNESDAY (MORNING):

God thunders wondrously
with his voice;
He does great things
we cannot comprehend.
Job 37:5

What no eye has seen,
nor ear heard,
nor the heart of man imagined,
what God has prepared
For those who love him.
1 Corinthians 2:9

I think I sometimes forget I have the legit Spirit of God in me. I love 1 Cor 2; it talks about how nobody understands someone like His Spirit. And the Spirit of the Almighty God is in me. No, I don't understand Him. But my mind is steadily being renewed to be like His.

EVENING:

I learned something very important by talking to Ben this morning. I've wanted since Nicaragua to be fully aware of how bad my sin is and how wonderful God's grace is. But I think I've been focusing too much on the sin part, to the point of almost bringing myself down and feeling down because of my sin. But that is so far from what God wants me to do. I am free. FREE!!! Free to laugh and dance because my sins are forgiven. My sins will not bring me down. Yes, I know I'm a sinner. But what's important, and what my focus should be on, is how good God has been. I'm made to praise Him, not diss myself. So that's what I'm gonna do.

10-31-13 THURSDAY (MORNING):

Oh, how abundant
is your goodness,
which you have stored
up for those who fear you
and worked for those who
take refuge in you, in the sight
of the children of mankind!
Psalm 31:19

Many are the sorrows
of the wicked,
but steadfast love surrounds
the one who trusts
in the Lord.
Psalm 32:10

I asked God for a verse I need to hear and I turned to the part in Acts 2 where the apostles are speaking and their hearers start hearing them in their own tongues. I don't know if that means that's something that'll happen, but I want to keep it in mind.

The end of Acts 2 blows my mind. That's fellowship as it's meant to be.

11-1-13 FRIDAY (MORNING):

Jeremiah 5—People often prefer false prophets to the real deal because they don't like feeling uncomfortable about their sin. However, if God's people don't preach the Word despite people's disdain for them, it will not be heard and there will be no chance for people to feel convicted of their sins.

The end of *Acts 4* reminds me of *Acts 2* from yesterday. The apostles treated each other in a way that reflected the kingdom of God: They shared everything and, in faith, received all they needed. God will reward those who give to the poor.

Read *1 Cor 13:1-8* again. Those verses will always be a challenge to me, because they perfectly show the life we are to live.

Romans 8

What do I think about? What do I focus on? Too often I let my mind wander places it shouldn't, contemplating sin in my mind.

I'm realizing something cool. Though there are sins I battle with over and over again, if from the moment I wake to the moment I sleep I am filled with love, I won't have time for self-serving sin.

I was made for more than sin. I was made for love. Made to give my life and find it by loving and encouraging and refreshing others. My sin is holding that back.

Father, I offer You all of me. Break me to pieces if You have to, but let me live in victorious love instead of the chains of sin that have been cast off. I am in love with God. There is nothing sweeter or more pleasurable than that.

Enseñame a amar.

11-2-13 SATURDAY (MORNING):

I like what I read in *Love Does* this morning: God sometimes does things in our lives that are inexplicable to us but in the end accomplish something for His glory and love that we'd never expect.

When I look at your heavens,
the work of your fingers,
the moon and the stars,
which you have set in place,
What is man that you
are mindful of him,
and the son of man
that you care for him?
Psalm 8:3-4

This is the God I worship. I see the splendor of His beauty all around me and it blows me away, but I am the sweetest thing to Him. I can't comprehend this.

11-3-13 SUNDAY (MORNING):

If I'm not loving others, I will be prideful.

I don't want a single relationship to be founded on an angle. Every relationship should be made from love, that's it. When people realize You love them, so many barriers are broken down.

I read Philemon for the third time. This guy is such a great example of love. People felt renewed and at peace because of his love and faith. I think that's really cool.

11-4-13 MONDAY (MORNING):

Pride is my greatest weakness, my greatest struggle. But I need to remember I'm free from it. I don't have to be selfish anymore. And if I fall into temptation, God will forgive me.

Isaiah 40: 9-28 Who is like God? We build ourselves wooden idols (mine is often me) and bow down to them instead of worshipping the Creator of the stars.

To whom then will
you compare me,
that I should be like him?
Says, the Holy One.
Isaiah 40:25

I know what defeats pride: love. Love forces me to put my eyes on others. And oh my gosh, it's so much more rewarding. Love is more than a perspective, it is an action.

There is so much potential in the people around me. To love them is to see that.

11-5-13 TUESDAY (MORNING):

This is what Satan would like me to believe about pride: that it is a sin that will hound so hard after me that I'll never be able to focus on loving people. But that's not true. By the power of the gospel I am free; I don't need to worry or think I can't love because of the temptation. Instead of being afraid of pride, I can be stoked on loving others. Love is the lens that makes us realize how wrong and detrimental pride is.

I don't have to live a life of guilt and depression over my sin. I have been brought to life because God died painfully for me! For this, I ought to live a life of passionate thankfulness and joy. The King of Heaven loves me, I will live out of that truth.

Psalm 119—David is overjoyed at the Lord's commands because he has found what it is to love, and that changes everything in someone's life.

Come and see what God has done;
He is awesome in His deeds toward the children of man.
Psalm 66:5

Come and hear, all you
who fear God
and I will tell what he
has done for my soul.
Psalm 66:16

I need to tell the world of God's goodness!

11-6-13 WEDNESDAY (MORNING):

Another beautiful morning in the treehouse ☺

Love is Freedom!

Love has saved us, but that's not just a cliché. It's a fact that changes everything. So much is beautiful now, because it changed the way I see the world to realize that God puts things I love in my day-to-day life as He plays the strings of my heart. As one in love with God, each day is an invitation to see Him work. I see Him in everything from how He saves the oppressed to a gentle sea breeze.

If I live fully engaged, if I commit myself to this marriage with Christ, my joy and my peace and my love will be contagious. His perfect love will burst through my actions and decisions and make people wonder about this God I worship.

Psalm 65:6-8

"You make the going out of the morning and the evening to shout for joy." v. 8

The pastures of the wilderness overflow, the hills gird themselves with joy. The meadows clothe themselves with flocks, the valleys, deck themselves with grain, they shout and sing together for joy.

"...The hope of all the ends of the earth and of the farthest seas; the one who by his strength established the mountains, being girded with might; who stills the roaring of the seas, the roaring of their waves, the tumult of the peoples, so that those who dwell at the ends of the earth are in awe at your signs." v. 6-8a

"Let us know; let us press on to know the Lord; his going out is sure as the dawn; he will come to us as the showers, as the spring rains that water the earth." *Hosea 6:3*

11-7-13 THURSDAY (MORNING):

May the God of hope fill
you with all joy and
peace in believing, so
that by the power
of the Holy Spirit you may
abound in hope.
Romans 15:13

If I believe Jesus is who He says He is, my life will abound with joy, peace, and hope.

Through him we have also
obtained access by faith into
this grace in which we stand,
and we rejoice in hope
of the glory of God.
Romans 5:2

I love that the Bible has verses like these. It's like it's saying, "Look, you're free from death! You've been given a powerful new life! Now rejoice!" His sacrifice is worthy of dancing and shouting with joy. Life springs anew.

11-8-13 FRIDAY (MORNING):

Jesus wants everything. I cannot count the costs and say, "Well... I'll just keep this one thing for my life." NO! What am I holding back?

You shall love the Lord

Your God with all
Your heart and with
All your soul
And with all your mind.

If I let go of everything for Him. He'll naturally become my obsession.

At the same time, He commands me to love others. This is a ridiculous task…if I'm living a life of self.

I prayed that God would show me what He wants me to do today. I think He wants me to avoid petty arguing and to look after those being unjustly treated. A kid in my class is being picked on and I don't know how to treat the other guys when they pick on him. I need the Lord's wisdom for that.

11-9-13 SATURDAY (MORNING):

My thing with social networking lately has been that as long as I'm not around people, I can do it. But I'm realizing that there's someone I'm always around: Jesus. He is my first love, and He loves me with all He is. I want Jesus to be my natural thought. The further I go in His love, the more He'll consume my waking moments. When I'm alone, instead of mindless ways of wasting time, I'm gonna take the opportunity to pray and spend time with my Father.

O Lord, in the morning
you hear my voice…
Psalm 5:3a

For you make him most blessed
Forever;
you make him glad in the
Joy of your presence.
Psalm 21:6

EVENING:

I'm realizing something that's a little tough. My parents (specifically Dad) are sort of like a spiritual "end" to me. Got a theological question? Go to Dad. The tough part is this: If I were to not love the same theology as Dad, or he disagreed with something I believed about Jesus, I would probably feel very alone.

This is tough because my parents are not my worth. Jesus is. "Though my father and mother forsake me, the Lord will receive me." (Ps 27:10). My parents are incredible and I don't believe for a second that they'd forsake me. But it is important for me to understand that if they would, it'd be okay. Disagreeing with my parents doesn't put my salvation in jeopardy.

Father, You are my worth. You are the one that defines me. Guide me and let me love You deeper. Teach me more about who You really are.

11-10-13 SUNDAY (MORNING):

Psalm 10 is a beautiful picture of Your justice. The wicked rejoice in beating and destroying the weak, saying , "God has forgotten, he has hidden his face, he will never see it. " They don't see God, so they believe He has abandoned the poor.

But you will "Break the arm of the wicked and the evildoer" and will "call his wickedness to account till you find none." You don't forget the poor; in fact, You love them. You want them to inherit Your kingdom.

O Lord, you hear the desire
of the afflicted;
you will strengthen their heart;
you will incline your ear to
do justice to the fatherless and the
oppressed, so
that man who is of the earth may

strike terror no more.
Psalm 10:17-18

Time and time again David sings of how You don't forget the humble. You are a just God and You arm Yourself to cast off the chains of the oppressed. Holy are You God; You defend Your sheep from the wolves. And hallelujah, You even seek to make the wolves into Your sheep.

Do I rejoice more over the destruction of the oppressor or the liberation of the oppressed?

11-11-13 MONDAY (MORNING):

Psalm 11

—You are my refuge

—Because You are my solace, evil cannot touch my soul

—You, the all-powerful God, are my protector; therefore, I can be joyful forever

—You test me. Trials will come that You will not simply take away. But, "You know the way that I take; when you have tried me, I shall come out as gold." Job 23:10. I need to be faithful. Under testing, don't let me forget who You are and what You've done for me. For if I endure, if I hold to You, I will emerge from the test as gold. Refined, strong, sound in my understanding of You. Oh come winds of testing, that I may fall more in love with God.

—You hate wickedness. You are jealous for them, but they want no part of You and wallow in adultery with other lovers. Because of this, they will receive the portion they've heaped and sought after: separation from You.

—You are righteous. There is no deception, no twisted manipulation in You. You do good and You love when I do good because it shows I'm rejecting my old lovers. It shows that I've fallen for You and am not ashamed for people to know that. And You love seeing the benefits and rewards of righteousness in my life; You love seeing the joy I receive from them.

—I will behold Your face. When I live how You've shown me, when I act out of the love we have, You rejoice. And I will feel Your wonderful smile! In the midst of darkness, of painful trials, I will be tempted to succumb to hopelessness, to bitterness. But if I have even an inkling of faith towards You. I will feel Your joy; I will feel You smiling over me. That can sustain me through anything. There is nothing greater than knowing You rejoice over me and You are proud of me. The more I abandon myself to You, the more I will see You smile.

11-12-13 TUESDAY (MORNING):

Psalm 138

—Your love and Your faithfulness never waver; every second of my life You want to be involved and engaged. You never leave, You never are tired of talking with me. You simply love unconditionally.

—You exalt Yourself. You are not selfish or sinfully prideful by doing this, for You are the only one deserving of praise. You are worthy of exultation.

—Before I even called to You, You were working and moving in my life. Your plan is so glorious Lord; for years You were working and setting things up so that when I cried out in Nicaragua, my soul was overwhelmed by the strength of Your passion for me. You were faithful to answer.

—The rulers of the earth are powerful, Lord. But when they are brought up against Your glory they will fall and worship. The prideful will be painfully humbled.

—It is amazing, God, that You regard those who are poor, weak, unattractive. In all Your holiness, Father, You reach down and want to fill the lives of the lowly. You have great love for them, Lord. You don't consider class or rank as something to affect Your love or involvement with someone. I pray, Father, that the homeless of Virginia Beach would see Your love in organizations like PIN. They are not lesser, they are not called to anything less than the wealthy. Let them know Your glory.

—You have purposes for me, Lord. You have reasons You created me, some that I may never even know. Father, I don't believe I can stop Your plans, but I do believe selfishness will stop me from becoming who You want me to be. Help me recognize it, God. You can do work through me no matter where my heart is, but I believe Your purpose involves me loving others. Humble me, Father; do whatever it takes to truly make me a servant. Fill my life; fill me simply with what I need so that I may have You as my sustenance. Thank You for giving me so much more than I deserve. Take away all idols and any sinful distractions. You want to be intimately and invasively involved in my day; I invite You in.

Capo 4
G
I'm not worthy
Dsus
You are Holy
Em7 **C2**
You have made me clean

11-13-13 WEDNESDAY (MORNING):

Psalm 45

—Your righteousness and Your glory are beautiful; my soul wants to sing of them. Out of love for You I will sing songs declaring Your majesty.

—You are far more beautiful than the idols of this world. You make it so obvious that You are the only fulfillment; no one gives grace like You.

—I love that You are a God of action. You do not hesitate to battle physically and spiritually for those You love, and when

You ride out who can stop You? I love to see how You fight to save children and how You put orphans in homes. You're so just!

—You hate wickedness. You long for the day when we will all be gathered in heaven and there will be no more injustice or hurt among Your children.

—You are a joyful God who is rejoicing. You love sincere worship, not just because we give You glory through it, but also because righteousness brings good things (love, joy, peace) in our lives.

—Abandonment is so attractive to You. When we abandon our "control" of our lives You see that we trust You,that we're surrendering any idols or distractions just to be with You. This leads to so much joy. If we trust You, we'll be able to see You at work more clearly, which is such a beautiful thing.

BREAK MY HEART
FOR WHAT
BREAKS YOURS.

11-14-13 THURSDAY (MORNING):

Matthew 10:16-38

—A couple months ago, I prayed for faith I'd have to suffer for.

—Maybe that's weird, but that's love. Take me however far You need to so I can know You better.

—You are faithful when we are persecuted. Your Holy Spirit fills us and will guide us. You will take over when we are under pressure and don't have the words to speak.

—I will be hated by many if I follow You fully. By people I don't know and people I love. But if I value people's opinions over Yours, I have some other problems.

—You speak to me and teach me. And You don't want me to keep quiet about this love I've found. You want me to sing and shout it to the world!

—I remember Nicaragua and how scared I was in the city with

Ellen and J Lo. But I also remember Your blessing of people when I prayed. I rest in the knowledge that my soul is secure in You.
—This is abandonment: to run fearlessly in the range of oppressors and proclaim Your name. If I lose my life, I'll find it.

Take Me Deeper

11-15-13 FRIDAY (MORNING):

Psalm 16:
—I've been blessed with many awesome relationships; apart from You, Father, they would crumble. If I followed an idol, any pleasure would lead to pain. But You bless me with joy that is pure and cannot be touched.
—Those who make other gods will sacrifice greatly to that idol, and will end up hurting. But You love our sacrifices, and my reward is that I know the true God better and fall more in love with You.
—You are so creative. Sometimes I have a plan for my life and it doesn't work out, but then Your plans are perfect. I love seeing how intricately Your plan is put together; how You bring me joy and bring me closer to You through means I never expected. I can be confident that if I remain faithful to You, I will see more and more of my beautiful inheritance.
—Your Holy Spirit is such a great fighter. I can feel His urging on my heart when I wonder if something is honoring to You. I feel like He sings with me as I sing for joy. The depths of God dwell inside of me!
—It is my goal to set You always before me. With You by my side, I will see corruptions and temptations for what they are. And my whole being will rejoice more and more as I live in Your presence. And You will be faithful and show me how and why to live a pure and godly life.

—When I am by Your side, I can be fearless. What can stop Your glory being shown through me if I constantly abide with the God of the universe!! In this fearlessness is everlasting joy and peace!

11-16-13 SATURDAY (MORNING):

Hosea 1-2

—Before I entered into a life of marriage to You, I chased many lovers. Far and wide I tried to find fulfillment in my sin, my adultery, thinking they had what I need.

—But I couldn't find fulfillment in my lovers. I tried to seek, but couldn't find. As soon as they were done with me, they threw me away calling me worthless.

—It came to a point of utter shame. A point of realizing my sins, realizing that even in my unfaithfulness, there was one who provided me with many good things.

—You loved me through it all. And in the heat of my shame, You spoke tenderly to me, "I forgive you, now come back to me. I have so much in store for you."

—And we were joined in marriage, betrothed in righteousness, justice, steadfast love, mercy, and faithfulness. I, an undeserving wretch, received grace and was filled with the presence of my first love. And in this marriage, You have showed me marvelous displays of love.

—I'm excited to spend the rest of life and beyond with You, Lord ☺

Today was three months since I've been home, and I was feeling kinda homesick without even knowing it had been that long. All the people there, the memories, I'll never forget them. I learned so much and was blessed so much by that month. But I really do miss it.

11-17-13 SUNDAY (MORNING):

Light is sown for righteousness
and joy for the upright in heart.
Rejoice in the Lord, O you
righteous ones,
and give thanks to his holy name!
Psalm 97:11-12

You love me so much
God I praise You! You are so worthy!

Psalm 139—YOU SEARCH ME OUT
"Where shall I flee from your Spirit?"
Even if I tried to leave you,
I wouldn't be able to!
In the depths of the sea, your
Right hand holds me. You will never
Leave

11-18-13 MONDAY (MORNING):

The Lord is on my side;
I will not fear,
what can man do to me?
Psalm 118:6

The Lord is God,
And he has made his light
to shine upon us.
Psalm 118:27

—You are not like a husband who gets bored with his wife over time. You are forever excited to be a part of my life.
—You have captured my soul. I am immune to sin unless I let it in.
—No matter how persecuted I am, no one can take away the joy of loving Jesus.

This is the day that the
Lord has made;
Let us rejoice and be
glad in it.
Psalm 118:24

I have been brought out of darkness and into the light. Am I living in purposeful acknowledgement of the latter, or dwelling on the former?

Rejoice always, pray without ceasing,
give thanks in all circumstances;
for this is the will of
God in Christ Jesus for you.
1 Thessalonians 5:16-18

This is the lifestyle I've been called to.

Why is it sometimes so easy to forget how much God loves me?

Yes, being in love with Jesus is hard sometimes. It's hard because I don't always feel His Spirit right on me. But minute by minute, ***I will seek God***. And even if I'm struggling to see Him through veils I've set up, He is pleased that I think He's worth the fight. And I will keep fighting, and He will not turn a blind eye to my striving.

11-19-13 TUESDAY (MORNING):

Can a man hide himself in
secret places so
that I cannot see him?" declares
the Lord.
"Do I not fill heaven and
earth?"
declares the Lord.
Jeremiah 23:24

I sought the Lord, and he
answered me
and delivered me from all my fears.
Psalm 34:4

For he satisfies the longing soul,
and the hungry soul He fills
with good things.
Psalm 107:9

So I decided to go on the Mexico trip. I'd been thinking how you don't always necessarily need to be called to go on a missions trip, so, for many reason I chose that one. Then, within a few hours, I found out it had been cancelled.

I guess that's a pretty straight-up answer to prayer ☺

11-20-13 WEDNESDAY (MORNING):

Job 38-39

—The temptation for hypocrisy is really great for me, but then I remembered this passage where You put man in his place…
—Where was I when You laid the foundations of the earth? I had to wait for You to create me! Even my own formation is a complete result of Your power; nothing of mine!
—Have I entered into the springs of the sea, or walked in the recesses of the deep? Only You, Lord!
—Ezra 9:6 "O my God, I am ashamed and blush to lift my face to you, my God, for our iniquities have risen higher than our heads, and our guilt has mounted up to the heavens"
—Romans 5:8 "But God showed his love for us in that while we were still sinners, Christ died for us."
—Despite all my weakness, You love me. Hallelujah ☺

11-21-13 THURSDAY (MORNING):

Micah 6:6-8

—Even today, many Christians think they have to be religious enough or righteous enough to reach Heaven/God's presence

—In 6&7, the hypothetical seeker gradually asks if more and more expensive things would be sufficient, ending with an absurd sacrifice.

—But Lord, You have told me what You want, for me to take care of the oppressed, love everyone I meet, and walk in faith and reverence before You

—You brought the sacrifice. You don't want me to be anxiously penitent, always giving things up or hurting myself in hopes of paying for my sins. You already paid for them. Now, You have work for me to do.

11-22-13 FRIDAY (MORNING):

I'm so blessed for all the lessons You've taught me. Sometimes, it's easy for me to let my mind wander back to recent moments of pride and then beat myself up over them. But something I talked to You about October 5th is that that's not how I need to treat my sins. If I've sinned and then confessed, I can learn from it and move on; if I dwell on it, it blinds my eyes to You. You have paid the price. Now I'm supposed to rejoice and praise You in this life of freedom.

I don't want to be as in love with You as I was in Nicaragua. I want to fall even more in love.

Isaiah 62 has so many beautiful signs of Your love:

V3 You shall be a crown of beauty in the hand of the Lord, and a royal diadem in the hand of your God

V4 You shall be called My Delight Is in Her, and your land Married

V5 As the bridegroom rejoices over the bride, so shall your God rejoice over you

V12 And they shall be called the Holy People. The Redeemed of the Lord; and you shall be called Sought Out, A City Not Forsaken

Open my eyes even further. Let every day be a day where I see how much I'm surrounded by blessings, how much You care for me. "When You recognize who a gift is from, it changes how You think about it." (Sept 11, 2013) And I don't even recognize many of the gifts themselves!

11-23-13 SATURDAY (MORNING):

Psalm 23

—You are my Shepherd. You are my Comforter and Protector. You know exactly what I need. At the end of the day, I can close my eyes with a smile, because I know that my God is in complete control, and will be by my side.

—You lead me into peace; when I come to You in the morning, You restore me. You open the eyes of my heart to see joy and love. There's something I've been trying to do I call the "Thankfulness Lifestyle." This means that in times of reflection and times of the day-to-day, I have my eyes open to what You've given and I'm thanking You for it.

—When I'm afraid, there's a valley. I always think of walking through Managua with Ellen and J Lo when I think of fear, because I was utterly afraid then. But when evil (stress, fear, anger) comes, I will be fine as long as I stay with You, the Shepherd. Of course, if I wander away You will find me. But first, I may feel fear and anxiety like I never have before. It is by the Shepherd's side where I can be confident.

—In the face of my enemies, You will still bring peace. Sometimes, it is at what for most would be the point of highest terror, but for me could be the point of highest peace.

11-24-13 SUNDAY (MORNING):

It's not "How much can I get away with?" but "How Holy can I be?"

I love You and want to be more in love with You. I want to lose myself in Your love, so that love is my only focus. I know the joy this brings. It's unlike anything I've felt before; this oneness with God and this passion for people.

Overflow me with Your love. I beg You to break me as many times as You need to make me as deep in You as possible. You are the cry of my heart, and when I love You above all else, everything changes.

You are so faithful! Already I can feel love welling up in my heart ☺

The Lord is my strength and
my shield;
In him my heart exults, and I am helped;
My heart exults,
and with my song I give thanks
to him.
Psalm 28:7

11-25-13 MONDAY (MORNING):

The voice of the Lord is
over the waters;
the God of glory thunders,
the Lord, over many waters.
the voice of the Lord is powerful;
The voice of the Lord is
full of majesty.
Psalm 29:3-4

This is the voice I long to hear. I'll say it plainly: I miss the way I knew God in Nicaragua. The way I constantly felt His presence, the constant joy. And it's not like that's completely gone at all. But it's almost like this is a time I need to be faithful. Sometimes, for some reason, I will not feel overpowered by the presence of God (although I feel it more than I know). But these are the times where I must have faith and must worship Him uncircumstantially. I have His word, and it tells me of His greatness. He is worthy of worship at all times. Also, I have this glorious promise:

For he satisfies the longing soul,
and the hungry soul he fills with good things.
Psalm 107:9

"Give me neither poverty nor riches; feed me with the food that is needful for me, lest I be full and deny you, and say, "Who is the Lord?" *Proverbs 30:8b-9a*

11-27-13 WEDNESDAY (MORNING):

If I truly want a deep, intimate relationship with You, I have to fight the desires of the sinful nature.

One thing have I asked of the Lord
that I will seek after:
that I may dwell in the house
of the Lord all the days
of my life,
to gaze upon the beauty of the Lord and
to inquire in His temple.
Psalm 27:4

—The "house of the Lord" is the Holy of Holies, which is as close to God as You can get
—This is my life prayer. Let me know You, Lord, let me feel You, let me speak to You. I want intimacy with this God; the joy of Your presence is unparalleled.

11-28-13 THURSDAY (MORNING): THANKSGIVING

I'm so far from understanding how much God wants to do life with me. Sometimes, I even forget or reject that fact. But this truth is the only thing that leads to everlasting joy. He loves me. He truly, deeply, passionately loves me. And sometimes, there won't be miraculous things all around me to back that up. But there are always blessings, there are always expressions of His love. It doesn't take me seeing a blind man healed to know that.

Jesus, over and over I've rejected You. I've rejected this perfect, pure intimacy for trash. I'm so, so sorry Lord. Please, be the cry of my heart, the subject of my soul. Fill me and fulfill me. Refine me and renew me. Fight with all Your love against my stubbornness: break me if You have to. You are the only thing worth living for.

Deep calls to deep.

11-29-13 FRIDAY (MORNING):

Intimacy is not something that comes easy. The human desire for indifference is what screws up love a lot; in reality, it's a selfish desire. This intimacy with You is gonna take work. I have to be all in, fully sacrificing my life to know You better. When You become my one desire (as opposed to just one of my desires), I'll find that I begin to desire and be fulfilled with pure things.

Isaiah 51

—When I'm in situations where people would expect me to curse Your name, You'll remind me of Your goodness and they'll find me rejoicing in You. Forever I can praise You with Thanksgiving.

—Everything around me will fade. People I love will pass away before my eyes; people will reject and shun me. But You will never leave, Your hand will never leave me.

—My worth is found in You. When people mock me or persecute me, I won't need to give it any mind. Because You love me,

You've forgiven and You are pursuing me. Why then should I let the lies of feeble, fading people affect me?

—We often tell You it's time for You to wake up. We're wondering why haven't You saved us from our pain? Why do You let it go on like this? When really, it's us that need to wake up. The pain we blame You for is our fault. The natural consequence of sin is pain; no sin leads to joy. Instead of blaming my pain on You, I need to remember to examine my own lifestyle.

—You comfort me. I sometimes have a fear of torture, of enduring ridiculous pain as persecution. But verses 12 & 13 remind me of something I learned in Nicaragua: Your love is worth all the pain in the world. The more of myself I have to sacrifice, the more of You I'll find. Surely You, the all-powerful bridegroom, will comfort Your bride.

—I love verse 15. "I am the Lord Your God, who stirs up the seas so that its waves roar—The Lord of hosts is His name." You are so powerful. And because of that, Your displays of affection for me are unrivaled by any lover. Mighty works of nature are put before my eyes because You know they'll blow my mind. What a love this is ☺

11-30-13 SATURDAY (MORNING):

It's painful for me to say this, but I feel very, very much like before I knew God wants intimacy with me. I want to do life with Him, but I don't feel that desire to pursue Him.

This makes me angry. Joy and peace are only found in love with God, but I feel like I'm sleepwalking through life rather than talking to Him. What I need, though, is to be one with Him. And in order to get there I need to wake up. I have these words, these expressions of His love, but its like they don't hold their original weight to me.

Jesus, I want to know You. Open my eyes God; You have done so much for me, and its like I'm just taking it, saying, "Hey thanks!" and then leaving with it. But that's not how I want life to be. I want to live in Your arms, overwhelmed by Your joy.

Break me as much as You need to bring me to You, Lord.

12-1-13 SUNDAY (MORNING):

What I feel is connected to what I do.

I don't want to talk about You if I don't talk to You.

"When You do the work of the kingdom without being connected to the King You will burn out." Anonymous

12-2-13 MONDAY (MORNING):

And by this we know that
we have come to
know him,
if we keep his
commandments.
1 John 2:3

—When we're in an intimate relationship with Jesus, His commandments are not laws, but expressions of love.

But whoever hates his brother is in the
darkness and walks in the darkness,
and does not know where he is going, because
the darkness has blinded
his eyes.
1 John 2:11

"A new commandment I give to you, that you love one another; just as I have loved you, you also are to love one another. By this all people will know that you are my disciples, if you have love for one another." *John 13:34-35*

12-3-13 TUESDAY (MORNING)

Little children, let us not love
in word or talk but
in deed and in truth.
1 John 3:18

Beloved, let us love one another, for love is from God,
and whoever loves has been born of God.
1 John 4:7

No one has ever seen God; if we love one another,
God abides in us and his love is perfected in us.
1 John 4:12

I feel God's presence when I love others. In Nicaragua, I woke up everyday to love people. I don't think I've been giving myself that mission every day recently.

EVENING:

Something I seriously need to be careful with is my tongue. In conversation, I'm quick to direct the attention to me and tell some personal anecdote or story. This isn't always a bad thing; I don't think I'm supposed to be dead quiet all the time. But this behavior is connected to that horrible pride I was shown in myself in Nicaragua.

I want to genuinely love others. I want to ask them about their lives and what they care about. I don't want to do a thing for attention.

I do believe God wants me to speak and share my story with others. But I also think it'd be wise for me to be more reserved and attentive. My worth is found in God; there is absolutely no point in trying to impress others or gain their approval.

The verses above are about love. Love is my purpose. First to love God, and then I won't be able to resist loving others. That lifestyle is the Kingdom of God manifest on earth.

12-4-13 WEDNESDAY (MORNING):

And without faith it is impossible
to please him,
for whoever would draw near
to God
must believe that he exists and that
he rewards those
who earnestly seek him.
Hebrews 11:6

Faith is the foundation of all this. I should live constantly with an awareness that You are watching, that You are with me. Just like people who are dating try to do things to please each other, so it should be with You. I can also believe that if I earnestly seek You. I will find You.

12-5-13 THURSDAY (MORNING):

I made a decision this morning that by the power of the Holy Spirit I will think only pure thoughts. It's a frequent temptation for me to dwell on impure things, but that never has good results. I want to dwell on God, I want to dwell on love. I want to be as holy as possible, becoming as much like Jesus as I can.

Zephaniah 3:14-20

The Lord your God is with you,
the mighty warrior who saves.
He will take great delight in you;
In his love he will no
longer rebuke you,
but will rejoice over you with singing.
Zephaniah 3:17

—My sins are no longer held against me; in fact, the Lord is singing with joy over me. I don't deserve any of this, but He's given it to me.

—I want to live life to the full. To do that, I need to put my full trust in God and embrace this relationship with Him.

12-6-13 FRIDAY (MORNING):

Luke 6

—v. 10-11 You knew surely that healing that man would enrage the Pharisees. Yet You healed him anyway, and that man knew love like never before.

—If I have good to do, and doing it would result in my own suffering, I can do that thing with full knowledge that I'm in the middle of God's will and my faith will be increased.

But I say to you who hear,
love your enemies,
do good to those who hate you,
bless those who curse you,
pray for those who abuse you.
Luke 6:27-28

12-7-13 SATURDAY (MORNING):

I'm determined to live out the first commandment: "You shall love the lord your God with all your heart and with all your soul and with all your mind." This should permeate everything I do.

Luke 7:36-50

—The woman in this story, out of passion for God, is willing to put herself in a shameful position to give Him praise

—Though she is looked down upon by the Pharisee, Jesus (the person who matters) is touched by her love for Him

He makes a pit, digging it out,
and falls into the hole that he has made.
His mischief returns upon his own head,
and on his own skull his violence descends.
Psalm 7:15-16

This is a perfect picture of what sin does when you embrace it.

Looking back through my "Notes from Home" Journal, I'm amazed by my experience in Nicaragua. My heart sincerely hurts out of homesickness for Casa Bernabe sometimes. Just thinking back to leading worship, and playing UNO, and working on the greenhouse, and then the fantastic things God taught me about love...what a blessing that trip was. And it gave me such a new idea of people as I came back; relationships I'd taken for granted because of my ridiculous irritability and selfishness suddenly shown like stars. I feel like coming back, I have been able to love my friends so much better. And my family; oh, how I took them for granted.

I don't want to ever lose how Nicaragua caused me to view God and people. God showed me there that He is a masterful planner, and if I just trust Him I'll see how His intricate design has so many parts made out of love for me. And with people, God showed me I am one of them. I sin. I've been dirty and felt worthless. I deserve to die. But God loves me anyway. That's how I want to love people. There is nothing anyone can do to make themselves less created by God. I've strived to let go of irritability so I can see people as God sees them: beautiful.

This trip was the most important month of my life. I am beyond blessed by it, and so so thankful. God revealed himself powerfully there, and I hope He won't stop.

12-8-13 SUNDAY (MORNING):

Psalm 8

—I love these stories of people worshiping You in China and Korea. You are the great and powerful God in every country, despite the fact that it's illegal to say that in some places. Your glory goes beyond anything human.

—Out of the months of "babies" (those who are under the oppressing anti-Christianity laws) You establish Your strength before the foe. It must enrage Kim Jong Un that the more he persecutes, the louder Your name is proclaimed. From those who should technically be afraid, praise is being shouted so that the oppressor fears.

—Look at how often my plans falter, how much I screw up. I am the perfect picture of imperfection. Yet You, this one who never fails, who has done it all perfectly from the beginning, whose glory is displayed all around me, love me. And You have given me power and authority. It's funny, because it's like, "Are You sure You want my screwed up self to be a crucial part of Your master plan? Do You really want to count on me to continue a design that's thousands of years old? That doesn't seem very smart to trust me with that." Yet You do. You've given me skills and gifts to carry out Your will. Thank goodness I have Your spirit within me, or this would go very poorly.

The thing about Nicaragua that changed everything,that made me easily let go of sins, was that I loved the Lord with all my heart, soul, and mind. I made Him my primary focus. The more I focused on Him, the more I saw His love for me.

The reward of that way of living was incredible. The joy and peace I felt were unparalleled. ***And it was not Nica that did that.*** Yes, it was there that I learned this, but it is not connected to a place. I can know God even deeper here. I can resist temptations, I can live in peace. Jesus needs to be the center of my life. He wants me. He loves when I reject the world for Him. My praise is so beautiful to Him. "He will take great delight in you; in his love he will no longer rebuke you, but will rejoice over you with singing." He sings over me.

I need to be willing to let go of things in an instant to become closer to God. He is the greatest reward. This is more than a religion; this is a life altering, earth-shaking relationship. He speaks back to me. And if I focus the eyes of my heart on Him, I will see Him.

12-9-13 MONDAY (MORNING):

It was easy to focus on You in Nicaragua because I felt like I was on a mission. But something I learned there is that I'm on a mission here as well. And that mission is to love. Life can feel so mundane, so routine, but it never truly is. At all times, there is a war for each heart around me. There are people hurting, giving up. How can I ignore that?

I have the same prayer as I did in Nicaragua as well. Enseñame a amar. Teach me how to love. I want to be a Philemon, someone who renews hearts and fills people with joy. Shake me as hard as You need to, to remove selfishness from me. Give me the strength to not fade away.

I love You,
Mark

I will not be sad because I don't feel a certain level of closeness to God. I will rejoice in who He is and pursue Him with all my heart. He has not brought me into a life of sadness, but a life of victory and salvation. I'm gonna praise Him for that.

NOTE 12-9-13

It frustrates me so much that I don't feel the oneness with You I felt in Nicaragua. It angers me how easily I forsake You.

God, I'm a mess. I am. Like a dog returning to his vomit I sin, though I've been offered incredible food. I'm so not worthy of You.

How has it come to this? I used to talk to You and see You talk back. That nearness, God, that oneness…it's worth anything.

I'm at fault. I'm selfish, I'm indifferent, I'm hypocritical…I've seen gold and pushed it away.

I'm seeking You and not finding You. That means I'm not seeking You with all my heart.

You are the bread of life. You are joy unparalleled, perfect peace.

I NEED You. Break me, God, take whatever You need. Bring me to my knees so I can love You again. Break through my stubbornness.

I am convinced that I can have that oneness again. I am convinced that I am the greatest opposition to that. But just as You have never stopped coming after me, I will get up and follow You everytime I fall.

After I wrote that above, the verse below popped into my head. I opened my Bible randomly, and I was right on the verse.

FOR YOU HAVE DELIVERED MY SOUL FROM DEATH, MY EYES FROM TEARS, MY FEET FROM STUMBLING. I WILL WALK BEFORE THE LORD IN THE LAND OF THE LIVING. *PSALM 116:8-9*

I just said, "I am convinced that I can have that oneness again." And immediately He replied, "SO AM I."

1-1-14 WEDNESDAY (MORNING):

Psalm 32

—What a great passage to start off the year with

—when I don't acknowledge my sin, I suffer its consequences

—I remember when I confessed my pride to You in Nicaragua. You forgave me, and I felt so free

—You are my hiding place in times of trouble, times of comfort, and the mundane. You are always willing to listen. It's so crucial for me to recognize the importance of the small moments I have with You.

—When I sin, it hurts. A life of sin is hell. But when I trust You God, when I strive fully to serve You, I'm surrounded by Your love. And because of that, I can rejoice. I love the idea of shouting for joy. This ecstatic love I feel when I praise You is beautiful.

—I want to know You this year. I want to come closer to You, to be so intimate with You I could almost touch You. You are awesome, Father.

MARK'S LETTER TO HIMSELF JANUARY 1, 2014:

I hope that you can look back on this year and say that you're more intimately abandoned to God than you ever have been. I hope that you can say you've loved Him and sought Him and found Him. I hope you've become skilled as a musician and that everything you create you create for God's glory. I hope you worship solely to give Him praise. In 2013, you learned the importance of loving God and others. I hope you've kept your eyes open to see the miracles that stem from that.

Mark

1-2-14
Thursday

Morning

This year, I want to love people better. I learned so much about that last year, and I also learned how selfish I'd been. I want to become more selfless and more in love.

Love is patient and kind; love does not envy or boast; it is not arrogant or rude. It does not insist on its own way; it is not irritable or resentful; it does not rejoice at wrongdoing, but rejoices with the truth. Love bears all things, believes all things, hopes all things, endures all things.
1 Cor 13

I spent a lot of last year selfishly and hypocritically. I wasted a lot of time. This year, I'm coming after your presence hard. I want to know your love, I want to understand your passion.

1-3-14 FRIDAY (MORNING):

—God, recently, I know I haven't sought You with my whole heart
—I've somehow forgotten how incredible Your love is, how much You desire intimacy with me.
—The God of this beauty all around me became a baby and died for me. And it wasn't quick. You were tortured, marked, hated. And You did it for me. Why then am I not passionately in love with You?
—I asked God for a passage that would break through to me. I opened to Nehemiah 9.
—Despite the Israelites many betrayals You were "a God ready to forgive, gracious and merciful, slow to anger and abounding in steadfast love, and did not forsake them."
—I can give into sin and reject You, and You would still bless me and welcome me whenever I returned to You. But ***I'm not okay with that life***. I want everyday to be a day obsessed with You. I want to recognize every blessing and the powerful love behind it.
—I want to really, really love You. God, open my eyes. Let me see the reason behind the sunset that looks just amazing to me. Nothing I do is worth it if it wasn't done in love with You.

1-4-13 SATURDAY (MORNING):

1 John in the Message hits me so hard
—I love verses 4-6 in Ch2. We cannot claim to have intimacy with You unless we live like You did.

Todd White—It's not about you (talk on YouTube)
Notes and thoughts:
—David screwed up, but he was a man after God's own heart
—He killed the lion and the bear in the secret place (when no one was looking)
—Shadrach, Meshack, Abednego—It's not about the fire, but who's in it with you

—When you're free from yourself, you're free of others
—When you're all about Him, He's all about you
—"You leaven the whole lump by your life lived in the midst of adversity"
—You don't live by feelings in the kingdom
—*2 Cor 3:17*—Now the Lord is the Spirit, and where the Spirit of the Lord is, there is freedom
—The Spirit's in me. I am free.
—The gospel gets the hell out of you so you can be heaven on earth
—His word dominates my experience.
—Every part of me is His
—"I'm looking foolish" It's not gonna matter, you're burning
—If I don't love God most I can't love others more
—For or against, there's no middle ground in Christ
—Any part in life I hold back from Christ is what Satan loves to thump on

Prayer for Kaitlin's missionary work
—hunger for God
—More team members
—Loneliness

1-5-14 SUNDAY (MORNING):

Great quote—Never judge the quality of Your relationship with God by how close You <u>feel</u> to Him.

1 John 5
—"The proof that we love God comes when we keep His commandments and they are not at all troublesome."
—Am I in relentless pursuit of God? Or do I just want to feel like I did in Nicaragua?
—vs 13-15 "You have eternal life, the reality and not the illusion. And how <u>bold</u> and <u>free</u> we then become in His presence..."
—If I'm in pursuit of a feeling, that's worth nothing.

1-6-14 MONDAY(MORNING):

Behold, the eye of the Lord is
on those who fear him,
On those who hope in his steadfast love,
that he may deliver their soul
from death and
keep them alive in famine.
Psalm 33:18-19

I've been thinking a lot lately. I feel like a lot of the time recently I've thought I was pursuing God, but really I was pursuing joy. But I can't have joy without God. I want to get to know Him better. I want to understand His traits more; His jealousy, His compassion. Most of all, I want to understand the lengths He went through out of love for me.

1-7-14 TUESDAY (MORNING):

Psalm 34:5
"Those who look to him are radiant,
and their faces shall never be ashamed."

—Do I radiate love? Joy? Peace? When one goes deeper in You, these start to happen on their own.

—I pray for hunger for You. I want to understand Your sacrifice better, Your unconditional love for me.

I'm gonna start working on some songs. Not really the metal ones, those are honest and all but I want to write some joyful songs. Some intimate, prayerful love songs. Heavy stuff's great, but it's kinda hard for me to just naturally connect to God through that stuff. I want to write songs that are spawned from my Secret Place, my day-to-day with God.

1-8-14 WEDNESDAY (MORNING):

There are things I really want to understand better. One of those is Your love for me. Tied to that is how badly I've committed adultery against You. I need to understand Your sacrifice as well.

God, my greatest desire is to be close to You. But Father, I can't come close if I'm selfish. What am I still holding on to? What haven't I fully surrendered to You?

I want You to break me. However messy it needs to be, please, just take away my selfishness. You bring joy. You bring peace. I want to be close to You Father; I want my day to be filled with powerful communion with You.

You've done so much for me, and I take so much of it for granted. But I don't want to anymore.

1-9-14 THURSDAY (MORNING):

Whom have I in heaven
but you?
and there is nothing on earth that I
desire besides you.
My flesh and my heart may fail,
but God is the strength of
my heart and my portion
forever.
Psalm 73: 25-26

You're all I've got.

I closed my eyes and told God I was going to just listen to Him. A reference floated through my head: *Zephaniah 3:17*

The Lord your God
Is in your midst, a mighty one who will save; he will rejoice
Over you with gladness; he will
quiet you by his love;
he will exult over you with
loud singing.

Prodigal

I took my inheritance
V1 High-tailed my way out of innocence
I ran away
I ran away

I chased after pretty things
Craving pleasures I gave up everything
Then came the pain
oh then came the pain

C You watched me run away
Prodigal I ran the path that leads astray
And still you called my name

V2 Hard-afflicted by my selfishness
Isolated by my search for bliss
Filthy with shame
oh how filthy with shame

1-10-14 FRIDAY (MORNING):

You watched me run away
Prodigal I ran the path that
Leads astray
Yet still You call my name

For with you is the fountain of life;
in your light do we
see light.
Psalm 36:9

1-11-14 SATURDAY (MORNING):

The steps of a man are established
by the Lord,
when he delights in his way;
Though he fall, he shall not be cast
headlong,
for the Lord upholds his hand.
Psalm 37:23-24

Stay in the "middle of His will"

1-12-14 SUNDAY (MORNING):

For the commandments, "'you shall not commit adultery, you shall not murder, you shall not steal, you shall not covet,'" and any other commandment, are summed up in this word: "You shall love your neighbor as yourself." *Romans 13:9*

I love this verse. Sometimes I try so hard to do what God has told me but I can't. But this summed up commandment takes care of that. If I truly love someone, I'm not gonna be jealous of them as a result of that. So if I love those around me, my last desire will be to sin against them. Sure, just because this commandment is a summary doesn't mean it's easy, but without love, all I do will be worthless.

1-15-14 WEDNESDAY (MORNING):

Psalm 41

—David had a terrible reputation full of lies and rumors, but it didn't matter because he was a man after You and defined himself by who You said he was

—I ask You to open my eyes a lot, but they are <u>my</u> eyes. If I want them to open I'm gonna need to be participating in that.

I CAN EVEN HELP YOU FORGIVE YOURSELF

INTRODUCTION TO PART 3:

Mark now enters a new season. He is going through a very difficult time, and he spends the next few months processing his actions and the loneliness that has resulted from some of his decisions. It is beautiful to see how God uses this time to call him close to Himself and really develop the intimate relationship that Mark has desired for so long. He also becomes more and more "heaven-minded," and it is as if God was preparing Mark's heart for his homecoming on May 30th, 2014.

1-17-14 (MORNING):

As tough as this current time is, and as angry as I am for screwing up, God has called me to live in a certain way. He has died for me and given me a new life.

If what you heard from the
beginning abides in you, then you
too will abide in the Son and in the Father.
1 John 2:24b

God has called me to LOVE:

Be patient	not be irritable
Be kind	not be resentful
Not envy	not rejoice at wrongdoing
Not boast	rejoice in the truth
Not be arrogant	
Not be rude	
Not insist on my own way	

Even though I only have a few days here in Roanoke, I want to spend them refueling and spending crucial time with God.

You are the great reconciler.

1-18-14 SATURDAY (MORNING):

Thinking of my "today" sections in my Nicaragua journal, I remember how everyday was unique, carrying its own sort of magic. I might start doing that again; even in the "mundane" there's adventure.

Psalm 45:

2-4—I love this picture of You. You are beautiful, with grace on Your lips. There's a peace about You. And yet, You wear a sword and ride out to war for truth, meekness, and righteousness. And when

I'm looking, I see You win daily.

6-7—You're the one perfect ruler. You see each of Your subjects and their needs, and You personally work to provide for them. You see me now, Lord.

10-11—These really hit me. If I count it all as lost in desire of You, only then will I truly know You. This goes for people too. But You are my first love. If I had nothing, if I was totally destitute and rejected would I love You? Would I still trust Your goodness? The one who has faith in You and loves You against all odds is blessed among men.

JANUARY 19, 2014 FLICKR

//thisissquareone

This photo represents a crossroads in life, when you are humbled and offset in light of your own mistakes. It represents the sudden feeling of not knowing exactly who you are, of being terrified and crushed by your own capacity for damage. But to me, this picture also represents grace. My failures, my mistakes are never enough to drive God away. In this photo, I am empty and confused, but I am ready to be restored by the light. I'm in pain, I've caused pain, but I'm loved.

Psalm 51:11-12:

11 Cast me not away from Your presence,

and take not Your Holy Spirit from me.

12 Restore to me the joy of Your salvation,

and uphold me with a willing spirit.

This is square one. I'm empty and angry at myself. I'm shocked at how unworthy I am of this grace. But when I tell God that, He looks at me, smiles, and says:

"SO WHAT?"

1-19-14 SUNDAY (MORNING):

There's a cool contrast between *Psalm 46 & 47*

46—Be still and know that I am God

47—Clap your hands, all peoples! Shout to God with loud songs of joy!

Sometimes in the midst of rejoicing and day to day life, I need to stop and think of You, and pray to You in silence.

1-21-14 TUESDAY (MORNING):

Psalm 49

I should never trust in anything I own. All will fade away. At the end of it all, when I pass through that fire, all my accolades and riches will pass away. What I want to be left is love.

1 Corinthians 13 is such an incredible passage. It directly shows who Jesus was/is and what we should be.

Right now, I don't feel close to God. I haven't for a long time. However, I asked Him to bring me close to Him no matter how painful it would be, and here I am.

I need to change. I don't want to camouflage into a new person. I want to fall in love with Jesus. I want to know Him deeply and personally. I want to give everything away and seek Him with all my heart.

God, this soul is Yours. I look at some of the things I have done and can hate myself. I want You, Lord; I need You in my life. I'm so stubborn and selfish and foolish. God, let my awareness of those things increase my understanding of grace. I'm very aware of how wretched I am right now. I don't know who I am or how to act because so much of my life I've been fake. I feel empty.

So fill me. Take me over with Your presence, wrap me in Your love. Become my everything. I'm a sinner and a wretch, but You love me anyway.

Let me understand this more.

1-22-14 WEDNESDAY (MORNING):

The one who offers thanksgiving as his
sacrifice glorifies me;
to one who orders his way rightly
I will show the salvation of God!
Psalm 50:23

I told God I wanted to read something I felt was from Him. This is what I got:

Create in me a clean heart,
O God,
and renew a right spirit within me.
Cast me not away from your
presence,
and take not your Holy Spirit from me.
Restore to me the joy of Your salvation,
and uphold me with a willing
spirit.
Psalm 51:10-12

I feel so out of God's presence. But these are the words of David after he sinned. And these are my words too.

God, forgive me. I'm so sorry for how I have messed up. Renew me, recreate me. This is square one. Restore Your joy to me, then I can rightly see You and praise You.

I need You, God, You have forgiven me. I am free. Grow me into the man I'm called to be; keep me humble.

I am Yours.

1-23-14 THURSDAY (MORNING):

I wanna be in love with You again. I want to walk with You like I did in the garden of Casa Bernabe.

Psalm 150

This passage is so beautiful. It's just praise, anexpression of love wildly shown for You. Your love is infinite, and powerful and intimate. You want me and You care about me. But God, that doesn't hit me as it should. Have I grown dull to Your love? I want my life to spill Your praises. I want to not be able to hold back my passion for You.

Most of all God, I just want that feeling of smallness in the sight of my Creator's big love. I just love sitting at Your feet. I have been brought to my knees. Please restore me in Your arms.

God, school really doesn't interest me, but I love photography and music (which I don't have enough time for with schoolwork). However, I know that You have given me the current situation I'm in. I will trust You and keep working hard. I pray that You would give me the strength to be content with what You've given me; but Lord, I also pray You would give me outlets for my creative passions.

1-25-14 SATURDAY (MORNING):

For you have delivered my soul
from death,
yes, my feet from falling,
that I may

walk before God in the light of life.
Psalm 56:13

I feel SO lost. I just feel so alone, so torn up. I feel so far from God and so, so ANGRY at myself. I don't even know who I am. I don't know how to act. My mind is in shambles. I just feel confused and purposeless and so, so sad.

I just want to walk with Jesus again. I just want to sing to Him and talk to Him and love Him. But I feel so indifferent. Doesn't it matter to me that someone DIED for me?!?!

I'm so in pain, God. I'm so rotten. Please come get me. Please wrap around me.

1-26-14 SUNDAY (MORNING):

I feel so lost and angry and worthless and traitorous and sick and wounded and wretched. But You tell me You will fill he who hungers after You.

My hands are open Lord. Please fill them.

I made an important decision today. It's time for me to stop being so shocked at the fact that I'm a sinner and embrace the truth that Jesus died for me. I'm forgiven.

I'm ready to start anew. I know who God's called me to be. I want to live joyfully in His mercy, in awe of His grace.

Thank You Jesus for Your forgiveness, I pray that You would fill me with hunger and desire for You and that You'd fill that hunger.

1-27-14 MONDAY (MORNING):

I've talked and prayed a lot about who I want to be and what I want to do. And maybe that's good, but what really needs to happen is I need to just be those things and just do what I've talked about.

"When they deliver you over, do not be anxious how you are to speak or what you are to say, for what you are to say will be given to you in that hour. For it is not you who speak, but the Spirit of your

Father speaking through you." *Matthew 10:19-20*

1-29-14 WEDNESDAY (MORNING):

Psalm 63:1-8

This passage is such a great depiction of living in the presence of God.

"I have looked upon you in the sanctuary beholding your power and glory."

"You have been my help, and in the shadow of your wings I will sing for joy."

God, I thirst for You. I want more of You. On my bed I remember the places You've taken, me the things You've shown me. I love how the Message says it: "I bless You every time I take a breath."

I wanna be that wrapped up in You.

1-30-14 THURSDAY (MORNING):

I often talk about how I want to know You better. I need to remember that You're right in front of me, all around me, begging to be known.

I love how when Jesus says, "tell no one" and the Pharisees warn people not to speak of Him, but they can't help it. "We cannot help but speak of what we have seen and heard." Acts 4:20

I DIED FOR YOU, CHILD. DESPITE HOW UNWORTHY AND FILTHY AND ADULTEROUS YOU ARE, I DIED BRUTALLY IN YOUR PLACE. SEE LIFE THROUGH THAT LENS.

2-1-14 SATURDAY (AFTERNOON):

Psalm 91– I've seen this passage referenced twice today

When he calls to me, I will answer
Him;

I will be with him in trouble;
I will rescue him and honor him
with long life I will satisfy
Him
and show him my salvation.
Psalm 91:15 –16

And me? I plan on looking
you full in the face.
When I get up, I'll see your full stature
and live heaven on Earth.
Psalm 17:15

Now that's what I want my life to be like

2-2-14 SUNDAY (MORNING):

I open up the Bible app to look at today's verse. Coincidentally, it was already highlighted, and even more coincidentally, it said this:

Love of the world squeezes out
love for the Father
practically everything that goes on
In the world – wanting
your own way; wanting everything
for yourself,
wanting to appear important –
has nothing to do with the
Father.
It just isolates you from him.
1 John 2:15- 17

I've experienced this firsthand

2-3-14 MONDAY (MORNING):

I've written about how I've recently felt far from You. A couple days ago I made a decision. Maybe I sometimes don't feel close to You, but I'm deciding to love You. When I'm tempted towards a habitual sin, I picture Your battered face on the cross dying so I don't have to sin. I'm filling the times I'd normally be listening to heavy music with worship music to remind me to focus on You throughout the day

I'm taking steps, God, because I want to look You full in the face. I want to be wrapped up in You. You were so worth it, and I confess I take so much for granted. But You were always faithful, always blessing me. You're an awesome Father. :-)

You are so good! Looking back on all journals I love seeing how You've shown up in my life. You're a great, loving father.

2-4-14 TUESDAY (MORNING):

I am a new creation. I'm not on my way to being a child of God, I am His child. I am always growing, but I do not need to wait until I'm "worthy" to come into His presence and proclaim to the world. I am my father's, and He loves me.

So this is my prayer: that your love will flourish
and that you will not only love much
but well. Learn to love appropriately.
You need to use your head and
test your feelings so that
your love is sincere and intelligent,
not sentimental gush. Live a lover's life,
circumspect and exemplary, a life Jesus
will be proud of: bountiful in fruit,
from the soul, making Jesus Christ
attractive to all, getting everyone involved in the glory and
praise of God.
Philippians 1:9- 11

Enseñame a amar.

2-6-14 THURSDAY (MORNING):

I've been reading Philippians in the Message lately, and I absolutely love seeing Paul in common language.

Yes, all the thing I once thought were so important are gone from my life. Compared to the high privilege of knowing Christ Jesus as my master, firsthand, everything I once thought I had going for me is insignificant—dog dung. I've dumped it all in the trash so that I could embrace Christ and be embraced by him.
Philippians 3:7-9

2-9-14 SUNDAY (MORNING):

Your plan is so perfect! You lead me everywhere I need to be. The people I've met, the places I've been...they all tie together into a perfect testament of how involved and how lovingly You are in my life.

Where to next, God? I think I want to go somewhere this Summer, maybe intern at Rancho el Camino. If it's Your will for me to go, please show me Lord. I love You, thank You for Your grace ☺

2-10-14 MONDAY (MORNING):

1 Peter 3 talks about putting trust in You no matter what. Sometimes, that can be really hard. I see certain things I want to happen in life, but sometimes for some reason, those things don't work out. There's a temptation there to be frustrated, but there's something You've been proving to me since Nicaragua that's really cool: If I am following You closely and I'm led somewhere I didn't particularly want to go, I can trust You. I can have peace no matter the circumstance because I have given You my life and You will give me what I need to draw close to You. I used to complain and argue when I was put in circumstances I wasn't fond of (and I confess

I sometimes still do), but when I look at all that You've done and who You've proven Yourself to be, I trust You. And I can have joy and peace.

Thank You, Father ☺

2-11-14 TUESDAY MORNING:

"So if you find life difficult because you're doing what God said, take it in stride. Trust him. He knows what he's doing, and he'll keep on doing it." 1 Peter 4:19

"And me? I'm a mess. I'm nothing and have nothing: make something out of me. You can do it; you've got what it takes but God, don't put it off." Psalm 40:17

It's nighttime, and I'm feeling a little down. I hate the idea of going to sleep with my heart in turmoil. I long to lay myself down with thoughts of my Father floating through my head.

Loneliness is what's weighing on my mind.

I opened my Bible and and landed on *Psalm 4:8* right before my eyes: "In peace I will both lie down and sleep; for you alone, O Lord, make me dwell in safety."

Oh, I am never alone, Father ☺ It's hard, coping with no longer having my best friend. But Lord, I have You. And I want more. I'm coming under Your wings, God. I don't have much to me, I'm a filthy sinner. But You see me coming after You and You love that.

Thank You for this verse, Father. Tonight, I will lie down in peace because You love me, because I can trust that despite what I face, You have me. You are my substance, my fuel, my solace.

I love You, Lord ☺

2-12-14 WEDNESDAY (MORNING):

Today, I'm gonna go out and love like crazy. My focus has been on me a lot, lately, but it gives me so much joy to build others up and show them how much they're loved. I wanna go out and love with God's love, the way He loves me.

I'll set You as a seal
Upon my heart, as a
Seal upon my arm. For there is
Love that is as strong
As death, jealousy
Demanding as
The grave.
And many waters cannot quench
This love!

["You won't relent" by Misty Edwards]

Love is selfless. I'm going out today and putting others first.

EVENING:

I absolutely love watching You move, and today, I got to see a bit of that ☺

First off, this morning, I was meditating on 1 Corinthians, and decided to consciously go out today with those verses in mind. And what do you know, when the announcements came on at school today the verses of the day were the ones from 1st Corinthians! Throughout the day, I made an effort to love, and it was cool to me how all those little questions of "who I am" faded away when my mind was on others.

Another cool thing happened at chapel today, the speaker, who I met in Nicaragua, spoke on worship and that passage I love about David dancing! Something I realized while he was talking was that I've been thinking too much about how people will think if I worship a certain way. I'm determined to change that.

It was also cool to hear Dr. Sandwell share his miraculous story again. I love watching You work Lord; thank You so much for what You're doing in him ☺

2-15-14 SATURDAY (MORNING):

In moments of quiet, strangely enough, I often try to pressure myself into being joyful.

I need to get things straight. The joy of the Lord isn't what I'm supposed to seek, I'm supposed to seek Him. Joy flows naturally from knowing the Lord, it's irresistible. But it can't be found on its own.

I'm coming after You, God. I want to know You better.

2-16-14 SUNDAY (MORNING):

Psalm 16

I know I don't feel like a "man of God" yet, but He has made known to me the path of life. He has taken me by the hand; I can come into His presence.

Jesus welcomed little children with open arms. Never should I let my age or "spiritual maturity" convince me that I can't know God yet.

2-18-14 TUESDAY (AFTERNOON):

I've had some pretty cool personal moments with You recently. Yesterday near the end of the school day I was feeling pretty alone. I didn't see my friends all day so I didn't get to connect with anyone. I was sitting in math feeling pretty bummed about this, when a verse from Nicaragua popped into my head: "They will see his face" (Rev 22:4). And I just had this image of You smiling down on me and the loneliness vanished. I'm not alone. I walk daily in the presence of my beautiful Savior ☺

Today I was feeling worried. I have a lot of work this week and I feel sick, and I've got to get up early for chapel. I was feeling overwhelmed but, strangely enough, while I was in the bathroom I remembered how pointless I learned stress was in Nicaragua. And I thought of that great verse about how You take care of the birds and will surely take care of me. And so, standing in the bathroom, I lifted my hands in the air and surrendered my worry to You. And Your peace flooded in. I don't have a thing to worry or complain about. You've got this, You've got me. That's all I need ☺

2-20-14 THURSDAY (MORNING):

...may give you the Spirit of
wisdom and of revelation
in the knowledge of
him, having the eyes
of your hearts enlightened ,
that you may know what
is the hope to which he has
called you,
what are the riches of his
glorious inheritance in the saints,
and what is the immeasurable greatness
of his power toward
us who believe...
Ephesians 1:17-19

—my eyes have been enlightened to God's beauty and love

I had a point today where I had a ton of work I needed to do and I was getting a little overwhelmed. But when I prayed, You flooded me with peace and reminded me that You're in control ☺

2-21-14 FRIDAY (MORNING):

I don't like how rushed some of my prayer times have been lately. I need to remember that these times are a need and the foundation of my life, they hold top priority in the morning.

"But God, being rich in mercy, because of the great love with which he loved us, even when we were dead in our trespasses, made us alive together with Christ—by grace you have been saved—and raised us

up with him and seated us with him in the heavenly places in Christ
Jesus, so that in the coming ages he might show the immeasurable
riches of his grace in kindness toward us in Christ Jesus."
Eph 2:4-7

God, I pray for more friends who are crazy about You. I love being around people who love You.

2-22-14 SATURDAY (MORNING):

But you, dear friends, carefully
build yourselves up in
this most holy faith by praying
In the Holy Spirit,
staying right at the center
of God's love,
keeping your arms open and outstretched,
ready for the mercy of our master
Jesus Christ.
This is the unending life, the real life!
Jude 1:20-21

Something I wrote in my "Things I learned in Nicaragua": "Love and joy go hand in hand, love begets joy, joy begets love." I can't have one without the other. God, let me see the blessings throughout today as gifts from You. I'm seeking You Lord, I am, please come close to me.

God, I'm ready to go far. I want to risk things for You so I can feel Your glory and see You at work

EVENING:

My prayer was answered. Today, I was met with some personal blessings that really showed how intimately God knows me. I had an awesome time biking with James and Anders. The weather was flawless. And I got Qdoba…twice. Not to mention I made significant progress on a music project.

I realized something today. I felt completely genuine when I hung out with James and Anders. No chameleon at all. And I legit felt like I did today with You, Lord.

Thank You so much for the changes You're enacting in my life. You're an incredible Father.

FEBRUARY 22, 2014 FLICKR

God is proving to me time and time again how good He is and how much He loves me. Little moments like the sunset catching those flowers above make me think about how God knows how much I love nature and beauty and color, and He gives it to me. I don't deserve it at all; in fact, I sometimes simply equate these moments to little coincidences in nature. But then there's that soft voice in the back of my head that says maybe if I pay a little more attention, I'll see the sunset is actually an "I love You" from a Father who perfectly understands His son.

2-23-14 SUNDAY (MORNING):

It's so cool how involved You are in my life. I'm realizing I've learned new things since some things have changed in my life. You are amazing. You're totally in control and You're right here with me.

Your beauty and love chase
after me every day
of my life.
I'm back home
in the house of God
for the rest of my life.
Psalm 23:6

Today:

God, today was killer. Straight-up gorgeous day, great photoshoot…life is great. I feel so at peace, Lord. You are doing so much for me, thank You.

2-24-14 MONDAY (MORNING):

Walk in a manner worthy of the
calling to which you have
been called,
with all humility and gentleness
with patience,
living with one another in love,
eager to maintain the
unity of the Spirit
in the bond of peace.
Eph 4:1-3

EVENING:

I'm finding my voice and I'm finding myself, but it's all pointless without You. You are the cry of my heart, Lord. You have blessed me so richly; let me not forget that You are the gift giver. I want to never lack in zeal; I want to forever live in Your wonderful presence ☺

2-25-14 TUESDAY (MORNING):

Lead me in your truth and
teach me,
for you are the God
of my salvation;
for you I wait all
the day long.
Psalm 25:5

2-26-14 WEDNESDAY (MORNING):

I'm praying that any selfishness in my life would be made known to me. Any bitterness, jealousy, pride, the things God pointed out to me in Nicaragua, need to go.

Yesterday I asked God to give me someone I could serve. And bam, one of my teachers was discouraged and I was able to thank him and encourage him for his influence in my life.

God listens and moves; He loves me.

2-27-14 THURSDAY (MORNING):

Things fall together and things fall apart, but at the end of it all Your love is unchanging.

Say not, "why were the former
days better than these?"
For it is not from wisdom
that you ask this.
Ecclesiastes 7:10

I don't exactly know why it's not wise, but the question in the above passage has gone through my head many times, almost to the letter.

Yet this is also in his word;
this is the day that
the Lord has made;
let us rejoice and be glad in it.
Psalm 118:24

It's so hard to feel this joy in times like this where my soul is in turmoil. But this day is the Creation of a God who loves and bled for me. And I should rejoice in that.

2-28-14 FRIDAY (MORNING):

Ezekiel 16 "The Lord's Faithless Bride"
—Israel's story parallels that of believers so dang well, I guess we are all God's children.
—You saw me wallowing in my blood and my pain and You tended to me.
—You saw me and thought I was beautiful; You entered into a covenant with me, and I became Yours.
—You gave me great riches and adorned me with spiritual and physical gifts
—Then, in complete rejection of You, I used those gifts for my own gain (living in pride, using my gifts to build myself up)
—I lived that way for awhile, but in Nicaragua, You handed me over to the shame of my adultery
—Overcome with shamefulness and wickedness, I lifted my hands and begged for release
—and You gave it ☺ Humbled, broken, hurting, I was welcomed back into Your arms with no hesitation
—The weight of what You've done for me is huge. You love me so much, and You rejoice when I sing to You ☺

—Running with the kids to the bus stop in the freezing cold, gazing at ridiculous sunsets…these are the jewels in the crown. I don't deserve these blessings, but You don't care. I won't take them for granted.

3-1-14 SATURDAY (MORNING):

In Your name, I bind temptations that have plagued me for years. Where Your spirit is, there is freedom. I don't want to be tossed by the tide, seeking whatever feels good. You are the <u>only</u> way to the best life imaginable. I am free in You, and I am pursuing You.

Return, o my soul,
to your rest;
for the Lord has
dealt bountifully with you.
Psalm 116:7

MARCH 2, 2014 SUNDAY (EVENING):

"The Lord upholds all who are falling, and raises up all who are bowed down." *Psalm 145:14*

"Return, O my soul, to your rest; for the Lord has dealt bountifully with you." *Psalm 116:7*

"Why are you cast down, O my soul, and why are you in turmoil with me? Hope in God; for I shall again praise him, my salvation and my God." *Psalm 42:5*

God, my soul aches a lot lately. I am a broken, messed up, sinful dude with a capacity for damage. And that's hard to stomach for me, because I want to be a guy who knows exactly what he's doing and makes everyone see Your glory. And yet here I am consistently aware of the fact that I'm blessed beyond understanding but hurting and confused because of this rift in a relationship of mine. I miss having someone to talk to, and now I feel so alone sometimes because, besides my parents, I just don't have someone close to me to pour out passion for You with.

I need You, God. I need You so dang bad. My soul rages like the sea, with a word You can calm it. Show me, God. Open my eyes, blow my mind with Your capacity to forgive and to restore. I'm bowed, please raise me. Let my soul return to rest, let me find community and friends who just can't get over You. I NEED to be around people like that.

You are in control. You are good, all the time. I want to go far for You, Lord; I want to dance wildly along with Your children in Your wonderful name. Oh God, I'm open to You. Fill me, use me as You wish. Thank You for Your goodness and grace.

MARCH 3, 2014 MONDAY (MORNING):

"Let me tell you why you are here. You're here to be salt-seasoning that brings out the God-flavors of this earth. If you lose your saltiness, how will people taste godliness? You've lost your usefulness and will end up in the garbage. Here's another way to put it: you're here to be light, bringing out the God-colors in the world. God is not a secret to be kept. We're going public with this, as public as a city on a hill. If I make you light-bearers, you don't think I'm going to hide you under a bucket, do you? I'm putting you on a light stand. Now that I've put you there on a hilltop, on a light stand—shine! Keep open house; be generouswith Your lives. By opening up to others, you'll promptpeople to open up with God, this generous Father in heaven"

Matthew 5:13-16 MSG

I'm gonna love You and I'm gonna shine because of that

MARCH 4, 2014 TUESDAY (EVENING):

I had a great day at UVA today. Honestly, the best part of it was hanging out with the RUF (Reformed University Fellowship) guys. I think my entire perspective of the reformed/Presbyterian church was opened. The RUF guys (and girls) are awesome, goofy people who seem to really love You.

I'm very thankful for the time I spent here today. UVA is amazing. I'd love to spend my college years here ☺ Thanks for blessing me so much Lord.

Note: We had entered the season of college tours, thinking ahead to what Mark would be doing after graduating high school. It never occurred to us he would not be college bound. His grades were spectacular, his SAT scores highly competitive and he had a great work ethic. But during his junior year he feel in love with leading worship, and we heard the words parents dread. "I think I am just going to join a band, tour the country and support myself that way." Luckily, we had the sense to just smile and nod, while planning visits to colleges we thought he would like. We were relieved when he fell in love with the University of Virginia.

MARCH 5TH, 2014 WEDNESDAY (AFTERNOON):

There's an epic war within me lately of shame and anger wanting to rule my heart instead of joy and grace.

I'm met with this:

"Send out your light and your truth; let them lead me; let them bring me to your holy hill and to your dwelling! Then I will go to the altar of God, to God my exceeding joy, and I will praise you with the lyre, O God, my God. Why are you cast down, O my soul, and why are you in turmoil within me? Hope in God; for I shall again praise him, my salvation and my God."

Psalm 43:3-5

—Be my exceeding joy
—Lead me to your holy hill

MARCH 6, 2014 THURSDAY (MORNING):

I like what Bob Goff does about quitting something every Thursday. I think I may start doing that.

Quitting: I'm gonna stop watching music videos at the first sign of sketchiness.

I am not defined by my sin. I am defined by the love and freedom given by my God.

Reading through Romans again. Man this book is crazy.

Claiming to be wise, they became fools,
and exchanged the glory of the immortal
God for images resembling
mortal man and birds and
animals and creeping things.
Romans 1:22-23

How sad it is that the imperfect creation is more worshipped than the perfect creator.

AFTERNOON:

I'm really fighting one of those moments of turmoil right now. I feel so alone. It's moments like this when it's tough to believe God has dealt bountifully with me. But He has. I have my wonderful family. I'm going to a wedding in June. I'm meeting with some great guys. Great music is coming out.

I'm blessed and loved, but Father, please remind me of that. I feel empty, and this is a perfect void for You to fill. Remind me how good You are, God.

MARCH 7, 2014 FRIDAY (MORNING):

Something cool I wrote in Nicaragua last year: "I need not worry about 'how intimate' or 'how developed' my relationship with God is, I just need to know how much He loves me and worship Him."

I love *Psalm 148*. It's a call to worship, but not just for people; it's for all creation. The Psalm says creation is "fulfilling His word" by worshiping Him.

Yes, the whole earth is touched by sin. But when I walk out into the world today, the creation around me is a declaration to His goodness and His glory. True beauty is from the Lord ☺

MARCH 8, 2014 SATURDAY (MORNING):

And it shall come to pass afterward,
that I will pour out my
spirit on all flesh;
your sons and your daughters
shall prophesy,
your old men shall dream dreams,
and your young men
shall see visions.
Joel 2:28

MARCH 9, 2014 SUNDAY (EVENING):

God, I just gotta thank You for showing up at worship today. During practice I was feeling feverish and crazy lightheaded, but when I found a quiet place and gave it to You and dedicated the time to Your glory, I just felt Your peace and strength wash over me. I want my whole life to be my hands raised, letting You take the wheel. You are incredible ☺ Thank You

MARCH 10, 2014 MONDAY (MORNING):

At the beginning of last week's break, I prayed that over the course of the week I'd grow closer to You. And I definitely did.

Through these last two months, You have been molding me (and sometimes pounding me) into shape. Not having someone I'm super close to has made me rely on You. Fighting off the chameleon has helped me to further find who I am. And You've been showing up, proving Your goodness and Your love for me.

I'm seeking You first, Lord. I'm not coming after zeal. I'm not coming after joy, I'm coming after You. And as I do that, I've found myself automatically becoming zealous and joyful.

You're so good, God. Thank You for Your grace ☺

MARCH 11, 2014 TUESDAY (MORNING):

When Simon Peter heard that
it was the Lord
he put on his outer garment
for he was stripped for work,
and threw himself into the sea.
John 21:7

I feel like I can relate to Peter's story. He loved Jesus so much, but under fear and pressure he completely denied Him. However, when he sees Him in the above passage he throws himself into the water, he's so excited. And though he has sinned (and repented), he lives as a powerful man of God for the rest of his life. Pretty cool.

MARCH 15, 2014 SATURDAY (MORNING):

Social media is the perfect opportunity for me to use my art for my own glory. I need to be so careful about that.

Blue Like Jazz is reminding me of some pretty important truths, including some promises I've made myself.

One of those is that I don't want to be known as a good person who just behaves and is kinda nice. I want to be known as someone who loves people. It's easy to be seen as a good person yet still be really selfish. I want to be completely selfless. I battle feelings of annoyance and jealousy sometimes, over the smallest things. What I have seen by God's hand in my life, though, is that I should never let those things have a hold in my life. I have no reason to be selfish and every reason to be thankful.

Another of those things is that I don't want to live my life governed by how I might appear in the eyes of others. I've gotten pretty over that, but every now and then I find myself face to face with the social chameleon. I'm determined to cage that thing. Nothing stops a person from accomplishing their purpose more than being self-centered.

There are a lot of other things on my mind as well as these. But at the end of the day I know what I want to be: humble, exuding love, selfless, and walking in awe of God.

Enseñame a amar.

I'm asking God to give me an opportunity to encourage someone today and show them His love. We'll see what happens ☺

THINKING IN POSTS (from www.markrodriguezphotography.com)
3-15-14

I recently read a post by a favorite singer of mine that really got me. She was talking about how she'd reached a point of shocking realization that whenever anything cool happened, she would "think in posts," basically meaning she'd start composing a tweet or pulling up Instagram to capture the moment.

I can really connect with this. I have had many moments in life where I'm just in *awe* of God's glory, oftentimes when I'm alone in nature or after being with loved ones. Those moments are so personal and sacred, but sometimes, as strange as it sounds, I kill them by beginning to devise a post in my head. I start thinking about how I'll phrase it, if people will "like" it, if I'll get any comments in response. And by the time all that's done, the moment is gone.

I've realized how simply sad it is to be a slave to social media. And I'm ashamed to say it, but I have definitely used Facebook and Instagram in the past as a place to give myself glory, to create an identity for myself that others will appreciate. And it's such a *bummer* that there have been incredible, personal moments with God in my life that have ended as a couple hundred characters and a few hashtags just because I wanted to see what other people think of me, what they think of my life.

There's a scene in the movie *The Secret Life of Walter Mitty* that struck a similar chord in me. Walter Mitty had been searching for this photographer Sean O'Connell the whole movie, and he's finally found him perched up in a mountain, scouting for snow leopards through a lens the size of a cannon. Eventually, a snow leopard is seen through the lens, framed beautifully by snow capped peaks. Walter watches in eager expectation, waiting for O'Connell to take the shot. Finally, anxious that the moment is about to pass, Walter turns and asks:

"When are you going to take it?"

To which O'Connell replies: "Sometimes I don't. If I like a moment, for me, personally, I don't like to have the distraction of the camera. I just want to stay in it."

"Stay in it?"

"Yeah. Right there. Right here."

There are so many incredible places and people all around me, so many blessings and moments that I can't even *fathom*. When I stayed on an orphanage in Nicaragua for a month last Summer, I'd go out for these prayer times where I'd sit on a work bench, all alone, and just pray surrounded by ridiculous testaments to God's wondrous ability to create. I remember one time I was just resting on that bench, relaxing in God's presence, surrounded by beautiful mango trees that rustled as a light breeze filtered by. And I am so thankful I didn't have my camera then, because there was overwhelming beauty all around me and nothing to take my attention off of it.

I don't want to think in posts. I don't want to be constantly checking to see what people think of my latest photo, or my latest status. Sometimes, I've just gotta turn off my radio, turn off my iPod, turn off my phone, and just be thankful, engaged with life and engaged with God. Because I know when I do that, I feel fulfilled in the most amazing way.

MARCH 16, 2014 SUNDAY (EVENING):

I had a great talk with Mom and Dad tonight. We talked about YWAM again, and when I asked mom why she thought I shouldn't go, her answer kinda struck a chord in me. She said that she thinks I need to go to college and face that pain and pressure of being surrounded by non-believers, of not having that safe Christian environment. She told me my mind is an amazing gift, and right now though loving people is great, the ways I could help after getting a degree are far greater. And honestly, that kinda clicked. Unless I directly feel God telling me to go to YWAM I plan on staying here.

Another thing we talked about is the loneliness I've been feeling lately. It's huge sometimes, honestly. It's been difficult, facing this loneliness in front of me, feeling like I don't have a peer who I can be close with. Mom and Dad told me they think I should find that person. They said I should pursue the mentorships I desire. And they reminded me that I WILL find those brothers I need, maybe right in front of me.

I'm reminded of God's goodness in this. He directs my path and brings me close to Him. This loneliness won't be the death of me, and I shouldn't let it make me apathetic. God's got me. I pray that this space in me longing for friendship and community would be filled, first with Him.

MARCH 17, 2014 MONDAY (AFTERNOON):

Things I'm learning lately:

—I should not feel guilty for not feeling close to God
—I should not be worried if I don't live in a constant state of euphoria
—Despite these things, I refuse to be someone who complains
—I want every expression of worship to be real and genuine
—This loneliness won't be the death of me
—One day, we'll all be together and everything will be okay. More than okay ☺

—I should never fake myself into thinking I'm feeling God's presence. That's worthless.

MARCH 18, 2014 TUESDAY (MORNING):

It's truly a blessing to wake up feeling joyful and free. ☺

Good point from *Blue Like Jazz* this morning: it's important to beware of trying to mold God and Christianity into things we want them to be.

MARCH 19, 2014 WEDNESDAY (EVENING):

God, I have so much to thank You for today. I just thank You for my time with Ryan, for his wisdom on not spreading myself too thin, the importance of this post relationship time, and pursuing my calling. Our talk was truly a huge blessing.

Something very powerful happened for me tonight. I was trying to pick worship songs for next week and it just wasn't happening. I connected with nothing vocally, and when I realized my heart wasn't in any of them, I put the guitar down.

Frustrated, I asked why nothing was working. I reflected on my previous times of worship, where I just felt You right alongside me and did everything humbly. I told You that's how I wanted this coming time of worship to be. I wanted You to be glorified, to burn like fire, to show Your awesomeness.

And then, an old favorite verse of mine floated through my head: "Will You not revive us again?" (Psalm 85:6) and the song "Everything" by Lifehouse popped into my head. Cautiously, I pulled up the chords, remembering that I've never been able to play it. And suddenly, it just began to flow. I began to sing, and partway through I began to weep. Because the song is about desiring You and seeing Your power. And the chorus is:

How can I stand

Here with You
And not be moved by You?
Would You tell me, how could it be any
Better than this?

And that just cut me to the core. Because there is literally nothing better than You. NOTHING. You have loved me so hard throughout this difficult time. And You are everything.

I feel revived, Lord. I'm ready to sing and dance and praise like crazy. I want to lead Your people in worship for the rest of my life. Keep me humble and keep my eyes on You.

I love You. Thank You.

MARCH 21, 2014 FRIDAY (MORNING):

For you were called to
freedom, brothers.
Only do not use your freedom as an
opportunity for the flesh,
but through love serve one another.
Galatians 5:13

It seems like all of Jesus's commands come down to humility and love, which I guess are pretty similar.

This passage says to walk in the Spirit, and as I do so, I will resist the sinful nature. As instead I seek to love and give of myself, and with my mind set on what grace really means, I will find myself living the best life possible.

MARCH 22, 2014 SATURDAY

God, thank You that You break every chain ☺ I'm so free in You Lord, and I love it. Of course I'm still tempted, of course I still sin, but You have proven Yourself to be the most beautiful, powerful way to live.

Thank You for this beautiful life and all the blessings in it. I pray that You would not give me so much that I think I don't need You, but just enough so that I can walk daily in the joy of Your presence.

MARCH 23, 2014 SUNDAY (MORNING):

For he satisfies the
longing soul, and
the hungry soul He fills
with good things.
Psalm 107:9

And let them offer sacrifices
of thanksgiving,
and tell of his deeds in songs
of joy.
Psalm 107:22

Psalm 107

This is just such a great passage. The whole theme of it is just "Look at what the Lord has done and praise Him for it." He's done so much, and I take so much for granted. His unconditional love makes Him the perfect Father.

MARCH 24, 2014 MONDAY

God I really, really, want this week's worship set to be done for the right reasons. I pray that You would instill a holy fear in my team and me. Lord, let us understand the magnitude of leading people in direct communication with You. Make us humble mediums for Your love, selflessly abandoning our reputation or any other chain for the sake of proclaiming Your praise.

I come humbly before You Father. Please, somehow, fill me with

Your presence. Seize hold of my tongue and guide me as a ready instrument for Your will. I'm nothing without You.

MARCH 25, 2014 TUESDAY (MORNING):

Psalm 84

—David was giddy with joy as he went to the house of the Lord because he understood that he would meet God there, he would commune with the Lord of all creation.

—As a worship leader and a worshiper, I want to have that perspective. God, let me know that I stand in Your presence when I come to worship You.

MARCH 28, 2014 FRIDAY (MORNING):

I've noticed that over about the last month or so, I've been way too lax about my prayer times; I'll make excuses and cut into them by sleeping later and I'm not okay with that. This time is a time created in response to the unconditional love of my God; it's the most important thing I'll ever do.

Matthew 1-3

—I wonder if having the story of Jesus told to me in fairy tale/ fable fashion as a kid has made it tough for me to wrap my head around the fact that His life and His death were both very painful, very real, and very important. I want to understand how real it was as I read through this book so I can truly understand how real His love is.

MARCH 29, 2014 SATURDAY (MORNING):

I'm struck by the verses about salt in the salt and light passage. I guess I feel like I've been kinda losing my saltiness recently. I can't let that be.

I want to live a life of awe and wonder. I want to be awed at how impossible to fathom God is and be perfectly okay with that. He is amazing; I want to recognize that.

4-2-14 (MORNING):

Give me neither poverty nor
riches; feed me with the
food that is needful
for me,
lest I be full and deny you
and say,
"Who is the Lord?"
Proverbs 30: 8-9a

I want to thirst for you, God. I fear being so caught up in security that I deny the wonderful life that comes from loving you. You are the best life, I see that. You bring joy and peace and those who do

Your work get to see Your power manifested on earth.

And me? I plan on
looking you full in the face.
When I get up,
I'll see your full stature and
live heaven on earth.
Psalm 17:15

From the moment I wake, I'll worship you. You are hold and you love me so much. I long to live in light of that.

Heaven (from www.markrodriguezphotography.com)

HEAVEN
4-5-14

I've been meditating on heaven a lot lately, and I must say, it wells my eyes with tears of joy every now and then. What a beautiful thought that one day, I will be completely in the presence of God and will actually be able to feel the magnitude of all His love and peace with no earthly fears or worries to distract me. The joy that I feel now, the serenity I feel now, will finally be made perfect.

The presence of God here on earth is enough to make me shudder in wonder. I've had some incredible moments in life that can only be explained as miracles where I see my Abba, my Father move in love for me so powerfully; it brings me to my knees in amazement. To think that one day I will be perfectly and totally in His presence…I'm definitely going to need a heavenly body because the joy He fills me with now sometimes makes me feel like I'm about to explode!

I love the image of Heaven because it is perfect, perfect peace. Every quarrel, every hurt, it's all gonna be resolved. All of God's children will be together and we won't hurt each other anymore; we'll finally understand how to love perfectly. And the fact that we'll all be worshiping the Lord together in one place, forever.…that amazes me.

It makes me so excited to think of the wedding feast awaiting us when we go to be with the Lord. I imagine streets filled with rejoicing, loud trumpets, wedding bells.…I'm sure it'll be far more incredible than I can comprehend now, and I love that.

God is super good. I can't wait to be with Him forever

When we arrive at eternity's shore
Where death is just a memory and tears are no more
We'll enter in as the wedding bells ring
Your bride will come together and we'll sing
You're beautiful
(Phil Wickham, "You're Beautiful")

APRIL 5, 2014 SATURDAY (MORNING):

Something I wrote in my Nicaragua journal was that beauty is a product of God's love. I wanna remember that in the midst of this incredible weather ☺

EVENING:

God, I want to be completely sold out for You. I see the words of people like some missionaries who are just totally wrapped up and wild for You.

Lord, I want to thirst for You. I want to live for Your love and I want to truly be passionate about You. I want to mean every word I sing.

Break my heart, God. Humble me. Fill me with Your spirit. I don't want to ever pretend. I just want to be in love with You. Take me over God; revive me and fill me with conviction and truth. I want You.

The Lord is good to those
who wait for him,
to the soul who seeks him.
It is good that one
should wait quietly for the
salvation of the Lord.
Lamentations 3:25-26

APRIL 8, 2014 (EVENING):

Abba, You're my one desire. I remember what it's like to walk in Your perfect peace, in the light of Your presence.

My God, I feel like I've lost that. And I want it back bad. I've prayed this so much God, and I have one conclusion: I am the problem. I remember that one quote: "If you feel far away from God, guess who moved?"

Jesus, I want to know You. I want to walk in You, to feel You burning in my heart and making me burst in laughter randomly. I want to be in love.

I'm crying out to You, God. I don't want to talk about You like You're not in the room. I want to look right at You; I want to sing right to You.

What must I do to walk in Your presence again?

April 9, 2014 Mark's 17th Birthday

APRIL 10, 2014 THURSDAY (EVENING):

I've made a decision to try something that so far has worked. I know that if I feel far away from God, I am at fault. He will never leave me. I've decided to just trust that He loves me, and even if I'm not necessarily feeling close to Him, to thank Him and pray for those things that I know touch His heart.

My greatest desire is to walk daily in the light of His presence. To feel Him and to be perfectly in tune with His will. I've never felt more alive than when I've seen through His eyes.

I am a seed, someday I'll be a tree.

APRIL 11, 2014 FRIDAY (MORNING):

6:34 am and I've already had a verse repeat! This was today's verse of the day and I also saw it last night deep in Leeland Mooring's Instagram:

Let the word of Christ
dwell in you richly, teaching
and admonishing
one another in all wisdom,
singing psalms and hymns
and spiritual songs, with
thankfulness in
your hearts to God.
Colossians 3:16

I don't want to just avoid complaining, I want to burst with thankfulness.

I feel like I can learn a lot about love as I read the story of Jesus. I love what I see in *Matthew 14:13-14*. Jesus goes to be alone, but when interrupted by an expectant crowd, He has genuine compassion on them and spends time healing and teaching them. Love isn't self-seeking.

4-12-14 SATURDAY (MORNING):

I quit Facebook indefinitely yesterday. I hate having it in the back of my head, and now I'm realizing how much I'd think about it. I'd open it several times a day and just mindlessly scroll down it.

Even after only just getting off, it feels so strange. So isolated; not really in a bad way, but everything that's right in front of me feels magnified.

I'm doing this for the glory of the Lord. I want to more effectively love people and I want more of my focus to be on Him. I pray, Jesus, that You would bless this. Open my eyes to the blessings of Your love around me.

4-13-14 SUNDAY (MORNING):

Then Jesus told his disciples,
"if anyone would come after me,
let him deny himself and
take up his cross and follow me."
Matthew 16:24

For the Lord takes pleasure
in his people;
he adorns the humble
with salvation.
Psalm 149:4

APRIL 14, 2014 MONDAY (MORNING):

I feel like I feel You the most, know You the most, rejoice in You the most when I'm doing Your work. When I'm directly serving and living humbly and treating others like Jesus did. But God, I'm oppressed by that Americanized perspective that I don't need to serve others, I don't need You.

God, teach me to love sacrificially in my daily life. I ask this specifically, Father. Please, let my eyes be opened to see what You desire from me in just the day-to-day.

APRIL 16, 2014 WEDNESDAY (MORNING):

I read a verse last night that I think I really needed:

Seek the Lord
and his strength;
seek his presence continually!
Psalm 105:4

I kind of feel like I've been pushed different ways concerning the Lord's presence. I've been convinced that it's a bad thing to seek, like it's some charismatic practice that isn't viable or something. But that's not true. That beautiful, glorious, refreshing presence of God is to be sought continually! I look forward to living with this knowledge.

"The Great God values not the service of men, if the heart be not in it. The Lord sees and judges the heart; He has no regard to outward forms of worship, if there be no inward adoration, if no devout affection be employed there in. It is therefore a matter of infinite importance, to have the whole heart engaged steadfastly for God." by Isaac Watts (writer of "When I survey the Wondrous Cross", "Joy to the World")

APRIL 17, 2014

I think I'm
about to burst
from this love
that's taking over

D# In D#
Oh my God

I'm sure that if you wanted to

A#
Untie love you could

G#
but Oh my God, you don't

G#sus
Yeah, I think I love you for it

APRIL 18, 2014 GOOD FRIDAY (MORNING):

God, what You did for me 2,000 years ago is incredible. You bore the weight of every single act of adultery I committed against You. You endured such pain, and the way we mocked You was terrible.

Thank You so, so very much for paying my price. Let me further understand how much You've done, how real Your sacrifice was. I can't even begin to understand how unworthy I am of it.

I love You, Lord.

APRIL 19, 2014 SATURDAY (MORNING):

I live such a safe life and I'm thankful for that Father, but I pray that You'd put me in risky situations in which I can glorify You, through which I can "leaven the whole lump (Galatians 5:9) through my life lived in the midst of adversity." I want to be able to show Your glory to the hopeless, to the distraught, to the mourning. Only You can save, only You can satisfy.

But God showed his love
for us in that while
we were still sinners,
Christ died for us.
Romans 5:8

APRIL 20, 2014 EASTER SUNDAY (AFTERNOON):

And behold, I am with You always to the end of the age.

APRIL 21, 2014 MONDAY (MORNING):

And as the bridegroom rejoices
over the bride,

so shall your God rejoice
over you.
Isaiah 62:5b

You rejoice over me. You delight in me; You love being involved in my daily life and You love when I recognize You in it.

You want me to see how much You love me. You want me to abound with righteousness and praise; to be constantly thanking You and acknowledging You.

I confess that I take You for granted so often, Lord. I want to dwell in Your presence to see as You see. Convict me of whatever hinders me from that.

Your dead shall live;
their bodies shall rise.
you who dwell in the dust,
awake and sing for joy!
for your dew is a dew of light,
and the earth will give birth
to the dead.
Isaiah 26:19

I remember what Mrs. Wetzel said about my prayers being like words of war. Within my peaceful, secure lifestyle, it's often hard for me to remember that God has called me to wield a sword, to hold nothing back as I sing His truth. I should not hold back any righteous anger or zeal within me, I should proclaim it loudly as a testament to my God.

APRIL 22, 2014 TUESDAY (MORNING):

You are my food, Lord. I awake and You are here eager to sustain me. Fill me up, arm me for the day ahead. I'm excited for what You have in store.

When justice is done, it is a
joy to the righteous

but terror to evildoers.
Proverbs 21:15

Whoever pursues righteousness and kindness
will find life, righteousness, and honor.
Proverbs 21:21

I would be satisfied with the presence of the Lord if all friends fell away.

DO YOU REMEMBER WHEN YOU WOULD STAY UP LATE WORKING, UNTIL IT WAS JUST YOU AND I SPEAKING TO AND LOVING EACH OTHER INTO THE NIGHT?

EVENING:

God, it's late and I have chemistry homework. I've gotta get up early tomorrow, but I just want to stop and focus on You for a sec.

I've got nothing to complain about, Lord. I'm tempted to sit here and grumble knowing how tired I'll probably be tomorrow, but that's not worth a second of being upset. I am saved, I am forgiven, and I have so many more blessings than I even know. I truly believe that if I walk in Your will, I'll have the best life possible.

Help me not to blind myself with worry and tiredness. By Your holy name Jesus, I pray that You'd crush the shame and the guilt in me and that Your joy would break miraculously through this veil. Transform me God. Revive me again; fill me with passion and desire for You.

I live for Your presence, God. Please don't leave me starving. Let me experience Your love in new ways and never take it for granted. I love You.

NOTE: APRIL 22, 2014

God, I beg that You'd help me keep from seeking my own glory when I lead worship. There is no worse hypocrisy than for my mouth to proclaim Your glory while all other parts of me seek to glorify myself. It needs to be all for You.

You are my food, my sustenance. You are all I need to be satisfied, all I need to be joyful.

One thing have I asked of the Lord, that
I will seek after;
that I may dwell in the house of the Lord
all the days of my life,
to gaze upon the beauty of the Lord
and to inquire
in his temple...
...I believe that
I shall look upon the goodness
of the Lord
in the land of the living!
Psalm 27:4, 13

APRIL 23, 2014 WEDNESDAY (MORNING):

You are a God at war. Satan violently fights back as You battle to show Your children Your love. One of his most oft-used lies is that You're not a big deal, that You're not a God who is intimately seeking to become the passion of our lives. But we didn't sign up for peace when we said yes to You. We said yes to scary, trying, heavy trouble with You as our reward if we seek You first. Christianity is not an association, a gathering or even a religion. To be a Christian, to truly be sold out on Christ, is to be at war.

...The sufferings of this
present time are
not worth comparing with the glory
that is to be revealed to us.
Romans 8:18

APRIL 24, 2014 THURSDAY (MORNING):

This is what You do, this is what You do...You MAKE me come alive!

I love hearing Brian Johnson talk about worship. He doesn't seem like a guy who's out of it and just in it to feel good; he seems to be a man who genuinely loves God.

Return, O my soul, to your rest;
for the Lord has dealt bountifully
with you.
Psalm 116:7

I will walk before
the Lord in the land
of the living.
Psalm 116:9

Psalm 116 talks about the response. The Lord has rescued me, so it is all I can do to stand either in the quiet place or in front of everybody and give Him thanks and glory.

I have two desires that are both good, positive things, but in order to achieve both I need to be very conscious and aware of both.

I have a desire to be passionate and zealous, and a desire to not be fake. The direct opponent to these is attempting to fake myself into believing I'm passionate. The fear of not being an on-fire person can tempt me to do things or say things an on-fire person would do, but to play off James, deeds without faith are dead. If I speak in the tongues of angels, but am not genuine, I'm nothing. If I do good deeds but on the inside I'm just seeking my own affirmation, I'm nothing.

The fear of not being passionate is a silly one. I grow anxious if I'm not under a distinguished assignment from the Lord at the moment. But He tells me to "be still and know" that He is God. I don't always have to be bustling about like Martha; it is far more valuable to sit at His feet like Mary.

Anxiety is an enemy to who I want to be. I must avoid hypocrisy in response to it or my desires will not be fulfilled. If I truly hunger and thirst for God, I'll be filled.

EVENING:

I swear, there are few feelings better than when I'm worshipping, leading or listening, and the Lord's presence just hits. It's like a shiver up my spine but so much more powerful. I think that feeling is truly just fear of the Lord. His hugeness, His magnitude is just suddenly so real and evident, and nobody can do a thing to stop it. So cool.

I don't know exactly why, but there's something I love about listening to worship music and dwelling on You late at night. The world is asleep, but I'm quietly humming out from my bed. The Secret Place ☺

I love the Lord. I love reflecting on where He brought me last summer, the sweetness of isolation with Him.

I want intimacy with You. A depth that can be enjoyed in times of intense quiet prayer, or simply in simple blessings. I can attribute so many wonderful things in life to You, from You as a message saying "I love you!"

APRIL 26TH

Lord God, All I want is relationship with You.

THEN HAVE IT, CHILD. IT'S RIGHT HERE, TAKE IT!

This is important: Right after I wrote those two lines above, I opened my Bible randomly and landed on *Psalm 145*. This verse was underlined:

The Lord is near to
all who call on him, to all who call
On him in truth.
Psalm 148:18

I call on the Lord. He is near me. He wouldn't hide; He wants so badly to be in a relationship with me. But I need to seize it.

I am in relationship with God. I'm never out of it. I never was out of it. But I think the entire time, He was right in front of me saying, "Come further in! Get to know me better! I want you too; I'm right here!"

APRIL 28, 2014

It's interesting looking back on a journal as it ends. The last three (including this one) that I have filled so far each seem to have a specific era of life in them. The first one contained the start of my desire of intimacy with Jesus and the months leading up to Nicaragua. The second had my month in Nicaragua and the aftermath, including my calling to be a worship leader. This third has my difficult season and the growth pains in response to that, which coincidentally are just now ending.

So where am I now? I feel like I'm coming to a place where the Lord is becoming my food, my sustenance. He has brought me to where all my close friendships have changed or they have moved away. The Lord is all I have, all I need. I look forward to the near future. I'm ready and expectant to go deeper in the Lord, and I look forward to making music to Him in the future , be it with this new band or by myself in the Secret Place ☺

I'm beyond blessed to be where God has brought me. I'm thankful for these last three chapters of life, and I'm ready to turn the page ☺

MARK'S LAST JOURNAL COVER

And me? I plan on looking you full in the face. When
I get up, I'll see your full stature and live heaven
on earth. (Ps 17:15) Seek the Lord and his strength; seek
his presence continually! (Ps 105:4) You have turned for
me my mourning into dancing; you have loosed my
sackcloth and clothed me with gladness, that my glory may
sing your praise and not be silent. O Lord My God, I
will give thanks to you forever! (Psalm 30:11-12) The Lord
your God is in your midst, a mighty one who will
save; he will rejoice over you with gladness; he will
quiet you by his love; he will exult over you with
loud singing. (Zeph. 3:17) You keep him in perfect
peace whose mind is stayed on you, because he
trusts in you. (Isaiah 26:3) For you have delivered my
soul from death, my eyes from tears, my feet from
stumbling; I will walk before the Lord in the land
of the living. (Psalm 116:9) You have captivated my heart
with one glance of your eyes... (Songs 4:9) You will seek
me and find me when you seek me with all your
heart... (Jer 29:13) For the Lord is righteous; he loves
righteous deeds; the upright shall behold his face,
(Psalm 11:7) Let the godly exult in glory; let them
sing for joy on their beds. (Psalm 149:5) Restore us,
O Lord God of hosts! Let your face shine, that we
may be saved! (Psalm 80:19) For you make him
most blessed forever; you make him glad with the
joy of your presence. (Psalm 21:6) Surely goodness and
mercy shall follow me all the days of my life, and
I shall dwell in the house of the Lord forever. Psalm 23:6)

4-28-14

Sometimes, loving Jesus is easy. The days are beautiful, people are getting along, I'm hearing a ton of good news. But sometimes, loving Him takes some serious faith. It becomes not a state of bliss, but a determined pursuit that's just as rewarding. Sometimes it's a struggle, but He'll never deny me His love.

4-29-14

The voice of the Lord...
Is over the Waters...
Is Powerful...
Is full of Majesty...
Flashes forth flames of fire...
Makes the deer give birth...
Strips the forests bare...
Psalm 29

I love Your voice.

When You speak to me clearly, either through people or creation, my heart leaps. There's something I sometimes forget, though. You are always being presented to me. All creation shouts in praise of Your glory. When it does, if I'm paying attention, I won't be able to help but to join in the song. And I should not forget that that Beauty I love, be it in creation or a friendship or a song, is a gift and an "I love you!" from You. I may not always be running giddy all over the place, but I want to live my life through the perspective that Someone so much more powerful than I loved me to the point of death. That's worth more than I know.

You have turned for me my
mourning into dancing;
you have loosed my sackcloth
and clothed me with gladness,
that my glory may sing your praise

and not be silent,
O Lord my God,
I will give thanks to you
Forever!
Psalm 30:11-12

I want to see blessings for what they are.

What kind of love would drive a perfect God to die for a sinner? Something radical...

When I run away, You do a whole lot more than just wait for me to come back. You RUN after me.

5-1-2014

One year ago last night, I began to fall in love with the Lord. What a journey it's been since ☺

I'm striving to seek and enjoy blessings rather than just recognize their existence. For example, sitting down to dinner with my entire family is a blessing and a gift from God. I can take joy from that. God has given me gifts, but it's up to me whether I enjoy them or not.

But as it is written,
what no eye has seen, nor ear heard,
nor heart of man *imagined,*
what God has prepared for those who
love Him.
1 Corinthians 2:9

The Lord is someone to be sought.

I get up and sing my love to the Lord and two hundred faces watch in bored silence. I want the love and fire of my Father to *wreck* my school, for a holy fear to shake even the most indifferent person. He dwells in these halls, and He has a plan. I hope that plan is to mess people up with His love ☺

I am willing to face shame if it means pleasing my Father ☺

What's next, God? What do You have next for me in Your plan? If it's to wait, I'll be satisfied, but I long to move for You. I long to be a part of Your plan.

5-02-14

I heard an interesting thought in *My Utmost for His Highest* yesterday. It is foolish to try to force fear of the Lord, or inspiration from Him, or the appearance of His presence. Those things are surprises He stores up in love for us.

You love me and You have a plan for me far more beautiful than I can imagine ☺

I don't want to forget the part of my calling about going into war. It's interesting to me how my prayer at Ruby's two years ago called me a sword, and then last September I was told by Mrs. Wetzel that I'm to be a warrior as well as a worship leader.

I suppose I could take the role of a traditional worship leader. But I wonder if it'll be more radical than that, more dangerous.

All is not alright. Babies lives are ended, children are raped, churches are fronts. I will praise God with my voice and by His name proclaim heaven on earth by God's grace. This is love, this is war.

Where I go, I may have to go alone. Abba, my confidence is in You. I know what You want me to do, and I know You'll qualify me for it. I've thought about how dang important my parent's approval and support is to me. What if I didn't have that?

You will take me in, Father. You see my destiny. You will protect me and give me what I need to fulfill the work before me. If I'm truly desiring You above all else, I will have peace beyond imagining.

Thank You for that.

PS. Teach me to love my brother, God. Teach me to see him as Your child who You love and who You created. You have a plan for him, and I was born being a part of it. He is a gift to me, he is a blessing. I want to treat him like one.

5-3-14

It's a wonderful, wonderful thing to know that if God is first in my heart, then wherever I am in life at that moment is where He's called me to be.

Have you not known?
Have you not heard?
The Lord is the
everlasting God,
the Creator of the ends of
the earth.
He does not faint or grow weary;
his understanding
is unsearchable.
Isaiah 40:28

EVENING:

I think I may do what I did when I came back from Nica and talk a little less for a while. Coupled with that, I want to check how centered my daily focus is on myself. The words I speak are how others define me. I want them to come from pure and glorifying intentions.

By this I seek Your peace, Father.

"You keep in perfect peace him whose mind is stayed on you, because he trusts in you." *Isaiah 26:3*

Fasts:

Fasting, when done with holy, true intentions, is guaranteed to lead the one fasting into deeper relationship with the Father. He loves to see us sacrifice, to see us show that He is our first love.

I'm fasting from Facebook and kind of from talking a lot right now. Through these fasts, my focus is put more on the Lord and I have more opportunities to focus on Him. And they're working ☺

You will seek me and
find me,

when you seek me
With all your heart.
Jeremiah 29:13

Quiet me by Your love in this fast, Father. I long to hear Your strong, gentle voice, to feel the direction of Your Spirit.

5-3-14 (CON'T)

Dad just told me he believes Song of Songs is a picture of Christ's love for the church. And I don't know why, but that really, really hit me.

I love my Papa, but he's a theologian and I guess sometimes that makes me feel like he doesn't really feel that whimsy or have a fire of love for the Lord. Which is a skewed view. But to hear the Presbyterian minister say that about Song of Songs is huge to me

I think over the last few months, I've let that unsureness about the meaning of the book make me not view God's love through its lens. And suddenly, it feels verified, because my super educated father believes it is. Truly, I'm overjoyed.

He says it's not just God's love for the church, but also for the individual. He mentioned how we don't completely get it, kind of like how we don't completely get the love between a man and a woman. And it's a beautiful picture because it doesn't make sense why the Lord would love us this much. And I love my Dad's response, "It must be love."

You are altogether
beautiful
my love,
there is no flaw in you
Songs 4:7

5-4-14 MORNING:

Song of Songs

1:4 "The King has brought me into his chambers." The Secret Place, an intimate place where He tells me things only for me to hear.

It's such an encouraging thing to look back on my life and see how God used hard things for good. They have all led me to a place where I don't even have someone to be fake for if I wanted to. And it's here, at this lonely place, that the Father meets me and I see how easy it is to fall deeper in love with Him. It's a beautiful thing ☺

EVENING:

The Lord is fascinated with me. Like Misty Edwards sings, I am always on His mind. He doesn't just get reminded of me every now and then. No, He's smiling now, watching as I write out of love.

He is *passionate* for me.

5-5-14 (MORNING):

It adds so much color to life to be in love with God. I've written before that our feelings about a gift completely change depending on who gave it to us. It's the same with God. The sun filtering through the trees outside my window right now is beautiful, yes, but to know that the Lord made that beauty out of love for me blows my mind.

Suddenly, the world is a love song, and I realize that the Lord knows exactly how to blow my mind, what it takes. And when I look around and see that beauty, I realize just how close God is :)

"You have captivated my heart with one glance of your eyes..." *Song of Songs 4:9*

There are a couple of things I set out to change when I came back from Nicaragua that I've backslid on a bit. I think the main one has to do with love and being self-centered, honestly. I wrote in my Nicaragua journal that if I love others more than myself, I'll find I don't talk as much. And if I think of how things are now, I'm sliding back into monopolizing conversations and trying to be funny all the time. That's not good. I think that kind of behavior destroys my peace and takes my focus off the Lord. I want to live a life of being constantly engaged and present, but I also want to be constantly at peace and tuned in with the Lord. I think pulling in the reigns on my tongue in this fast will be really good for me. I'm seeking You in this Lord, to grow more intimate and close with You. That's something I know I'll be rewarded for.

MAY 6, 2014 (EVENING):

I realized tonight when I'm deliberately silent and deliberately listening, I learn to love. When someone's speaking and I care about them and their story and I'm not trying to come up with a joke or anecdote then I begin to love them. Because then I value them above myself.

I feel so unsure of how to act in social situations. Not necessarily in an awkward way, and definitely not out of shyness or something like that; it's more because I'm still learning how to be selfless and loving and in tune with You in public. It's pretty difficult, honestly, but I think that being intentional about this fast of stepping back and listening and getting "back to the basics" will help.

I don't want to do anything out of trying to be like someone else or trying to fit in. What I want first and foremost is to establish this Secret Place, this Eden, and carry it around with me. I want to love on a mission spawned out of intimacy with my Jesus.

Coming after You, Lord ☺ Thanks for loving me and showing me that You do.

MAY 7, 2014 (MORNING):

But I have calmed and
quieted my soul
like a weaned child with
its mother,
like a weaned child is my soul
within me.
Psalm 131:2

EVENING:

I'VE BROUGHT YOU OUT INTO THE DESERT SO THAT YOU MIGHT RETURN KNOWING ME BETTER THAN EVER.

MAY 8TH, 2014 (MORNING):

The steadfast love of the Lord
never ceases;
his mercies never come to an end;
they are new every morning;
Great is your faithfulness.
Lamentations 3:22-23

God thunders wondrously with
His voice;
he does great things
that we cannot comprehend.
Job 37:5

I want to love deliberately. Selfless love makes incredible things happen.

You are so at work, so prevalent, and we ignore it. We sit down and fold our hands out of tradition, not recognizing that we're in the presence of God. Open my own eyes God. I will be grateful for how much of a miracle it is to step into Your presence.

MAY 9TH, 2014 (MORNING):

Kind of a cool little miracle this morning...today and tomorrow Ben and I are helping at Sonrise Music Festival but I woke up feeling crazy sick. I couldn't even really think straight, and I knew prayer time would be a struggle. So I asked God for clarity so that I could spend time with Him, and I suddenly just cleared mentally and joy washed through me. God recognized my sincerity and love for Him and blessed me as a result. I have an incredible Father ☺

Note: Mark found himself being the main driver for recording artist Francesca Battistelli. When I called him to check in, he said, "Can't talk, Mom, Fransesca and her band want to go to Tropical Smoothie. She needs a smoothie, gotta go!" He was so energized.

MAY 10, 2014

Here's the issue. I've struggled so much in the past with basing the way I act off of pleasing other people. I've felt startlingly unsure recently of how to act, who I am. I felt this way when I came back from Nicaragua, but I'm realizing I think I reattached to my friends and used them a bit as my personality anchors.

I believe You've brought me into a place that's lonely but necessary recently (I kind of think of it as the desert Jesus was led into). I've lost those "anchors." But maybe that's a good thing. Because now, like Jesus, it's me and You. And in this sort of lonely time, I want to cultivate an intimate and overwhelming relationship with You in the Secret Place that invades the rest of my life.

You are my first love, I want my only anchor, my only love (for now) to be You.

And God, I plead that You'll teach me who I am. It's such a strange request, but I think You get it. Please help me.

I love You, Lord,
Mark

MAY 11, 2014

Never underestimate the level of nostalgia contained in a long-uncleaned closet.

Wondering if God has something in *Psalm 11* for me. I was gonna look it up and opened right to it, still checking it out.

There's a temptation that can arise in the midst of a fast that's important to recognize; and that's to focus on myself and my own pleasure as opposed to taking advantage of the time I've given myself to fall further into God.

There's something so enticing to me about overseas mission. I feel like both my trips to Nicaragua just backed my calling so well. I was seeing people at war. James Belt and the Jaentschke's and the Adams and so many more people waging the war of God to help His precious children. Such a beautiful sight to see and such a wonderful thing to be a part of.

I'd like to go back there. Or somewhere. Just to remind my stubborn eyes that all is not well in the world...

Thank You for grieving with me when I grieve. Thank You for rejoicing with me when I rejoice.

I sometimes doubt that God can use me. I think, how can I lead His people in singing to Him, in being in direct connection to Him if I don't have a spotless record?

I fail to see that I am the crown jewel of God's creation, over mountains and oceans and sunrises and starry skies. I fail to recognize that no leader of His is perfect, none were chosen because they were spotless. And I fail to comprehend the magnitude of His love for me. Lacey Storm (Flyleaf) says it well, that it's the saddest thing for people to be so loved by God and not recognize it, not see how far He'd go, how far He did go for us.

I am loved. I am chosen to sing words of war from my imperfect mouth, chosen to lead an army into battle. And I can't do a thing to separate myself from the love that assigned this to me.

Glory to the God who calls the name of the lost, we are all unfaithful. Holy is the one who knows my deepest sin, but calls me beautiful.

MAY 12, 2014

It's a gorgeous day ☺
What a killer, blessed life I have.

Restore, us, O Lord God of hosts!
Let your face shine, that
we may be saved!
Psalm 80:19

Time to be free from worries about who I am or who I was or who I'm supposed to be. Time to be just wrapped up and grateful in God. All stains are gone, my eyes are open. Time to just enjoy what God's given me and fight for Him.

This place of few close friends that God has brought me to recently is such a fantastic testament to His love. He wants me ***all to himself***.

I keep thinking about taking a 2-3 day trip after school lets out. Just heading out and maybe making camp in some woods near the water with my guitar, my Bible, and my journal. I want to take that time to just be still and pray and sing and dwell in the Secret Place. Here's hoping ☺

How long, O Lord? Will you forget me forever?
How long will you hide your face from me?
How long must I take counsel in my soul
and have sorrow in my heart all the day?
How long shall my enemy be exalted over me?
Consider and answer me, O Lord my God;
light up my eyes, lest I sleep the sleep of death,
lest my enemy say "I have prevailed over him"
lest my foes rejoice because I am shaken
But I have trusted in Your steadfast love;
My heart shall rejoice in Your salvation.
I will sing to the Lord,
Because He has dealt beautifully with me.
Psalm 13

MAY 14, 2014 (MORNING):

The fact that I can trust God with my life is such a beautiful thing. On the beach last night, I was bummed and lonely. And then the faith hit, and I was reminded that God will use the points in life to which my circumstances have brought me as tools to give me the best life possible. And that's a wonderful thing.

In him you also are
being built together
into a dwelling place for God
by the Spirit.
Ephesians 2:22

Jesus, thank You for letting me take this kid home last night. People were saying I'd hate him because he's so different from me, but I love that. I pray that You would make Your love and grace so evident to him while he is with our group.

MAY 15, 2014 (MORNING):

I was having a conversation yesterday with someone about what God's been doing in my life lately, and it moved her to tears.

My testimony, no matter how crazy I think it is or isn't, is a weapon. The pain and the joy I've felt as I've walked with Jesus can speak to people.

I want more of these conversations. I want to hear people's testimonies and I want to share mine. As I was seeing this person with her tears of joy yesterday, I was seeing God work. And that is my absolute favorite thing.

MAY 16TH, 2014 (MORNING):

The lines have fallen for me
in pleasant places;
Indeed, I have a beautiful
inheritance...
Psalm 16:6

MAY 17, 2014 (MORNING):

I feel kind of mentally out of it right now, like I'm watching someone else live my life. It's a very uncomfortable feeling. I pray, in

Jesus's name, that I'd be present with people and in passion.

Life is *beautiful*. Life is a love gift from my Father that is daily filled with opportunities to thank Him and feel Him smiling at me. Life is meant to be enjoyed and shared.

God's love is wild, but we blind ourselves from it for some reason sometimes. I don't want to do that. I want to throw up my sails and let the wind of His love mess me up and cause my heart to burn like fire. In the day to day, I'll seek to recognize the warmth of His smile.

You are eternally faithful. I feel like lately You've really impressed the idea of my weakness and Your sovereignty upon me. It's such a beautiful thing that You've shown me: that I can find comfort in giving up control, in trusting You. It's proven so true. Your plans are so beautiful, so worth believing in. You love me so much and You know exactly what thrills my heart the most. I believe that though I may face gigantic trials, I will know joy like I never have before.

Watching "Father of Lights" is reminding me how awesome it is to listen to someone talk bout how incredible Jesus is. The overwhelming love He creates is so beautiful.

NOTE: Father of Lights is a documentary

MAY 18TH, 2014 (MORNING):

And the glory of the Lord shall
be revealed,
and all flesh shall see it
together,
for the mouth of the Lord
has spoken.
Isaiah 40:5

Open the eyes of my heart, Lord. I want to see You.

EVENING:

I was hit with an important realization tonight; I've been worrying. About relationship stuff, school, even whether or not I'm close to God.

Tonight, Jesus reminded me that I'm free. That He's got me and worry will only destroy me. A lot of my worries are so selfish too; I still sometimes worry whether or not I'm a good person in the world's eyes. Oh what a lie that is to buy into. I'm beyond messed up.

But, my Papa loves me anyways. And He wants me to get to work loving others. It saddens Him to see me putting back on the chains He took off when I'm made to dance and sing.

Lord Jesus, fill me up. Empty me of my selfish thoughts and make me a vessel of love. Thank You for giving me a new life.

MAY 19, 2014 (MORNING):

The heavens declare the glory
of God,
and the sky above proclaims his
handiwork.
Day to day pours out speech,
and night to night reveals
knowledge.
Psalm 19:1-2

I love this part about the day-to-day. I struggle sometimes with doubting God's presence when I don't feel directly assigned to something by Him. Yet this verse says the day-to-day pours speech about Him.

MAY 20, 2014 (MORNING):

The peace You offer is one of my favorite things about You. To be able to know that You will take me where I need to go, and to know that I can experience this beautiful joy and freedom along the way, is such a blessing. ☺

I am blessed richly.

For you make him most
blessed forever;
You make him glad with the
joy of your
presence.
Psalm 21:6

MAY 21, 2014 (MORNING):

God, I can be so impulsive and defiant and ignorant to what You've done for me. But You love me far past that. My sin won't stop You from loving me. Lord, help me understand the magnitude of that.

MAY 22, 2014 (MORNING):

O Love of God, teach me to love! Teach me to see those around me as masterful, beautiful creations with bits of You in them. Show me how to put others before myself.

For the sake of Christ, then,
I am content with weaknesses,
insults, hardships, persecutions,
and calamities.
For when I am weak,
then I am strong.
2 Corinthians 12:10

"Think of how much suffering it's taken for him to earn that kind of faith," Mom.

Let me suffer for Your sake, God. If that's what it takes to fall more in love with You, I'm in.

MAY 23, 2014 (MORNING):

So thankful for what the Lord did at band practice last night. "Mercy Blinding" took on a new form in a beautiful way, and I began to realize how easy and comfortable it is to be myself around these guys. I am very excited to see what He continues to do in our group.

MAY 24, 2014 (MORNING):

What a beautiful first day of Summer You've blessed me with today, Lord ☺ I pray that You would be glorified through these next three months. I want to find You and know You and fall for You more and more each day ☺

Blessed are the people who know the
festal shout,
who walk, O Lord, in
the light of your face,
who exalt in your
name all the day
And in your righteousness
are exalted.
Psalm 89:15-16

Teach me to walk in the light of Your face.

Give me the strength and the initiative to share the great works of Your hand with those around me.

MAY 26, 2014

There are a couple of things I need to get straight if I'm gonna draw closer to God this summer. First off, it is worthless if my prayer times are when I come and talk about how I'm gonna seek Jesus, but then kinda forget about what I read as soon as it's done. I'm going to stop during the day to pray and dwell in the Lord's smile...

Another thing has to do with social media. I ditched Facebook, but that's worthless if I just use Instagram twice as much. I must remember why I quit Facebook: so that my five minutes between activities are spent doing something I actually enjoy or just being in God's presence. This is very important.

The third thing just has to do with sin in general. If I let myself fall into being selfish, I am defying God's beautiful love and pushing Him away. I pray that Jesus would cultivate such a heart for loving others in me that I wouldn't even start to take that step.

The last thing has to do with love. Love must be a priority; it is my weapon and my war. I want to love and respect my parents, I want to love my siblings. I want to show love to every single person I run into and I want to understand how much God loves them.

I want to fade away. My selfish desires have to go. My hunger for recognition, compliments and being the center of attention is meaningless.

Let this be the summer of the Secret Place, where I create things for You God, You and You alone. Where I truly listen and You tell me beautiful things. Where You become more and more my passion, and I become more and more Your bride.

I am excited for this.

Psalm 17:15 "And me? I plan on looking you full in the face. When I get up, I'll see your full stature and live heaven on earth." (MSG)

Mark's Secret Place

MAY 26, 2014

What an idea that the Lord would store up surprises, blessings of love for me throughout the day. And what an idea that He'd be excited for me to find them.

OH, SEEK ME FIRST CHILD, AND I WILL GUIDE YOU INTO A LIFE BEAUTIFUL BEYOND IMAGINING.

Every blessing is a love song. And I am oh so blessed.

Oh to think of this Giant Love plan at work.

MAY 27, 2014

Every day has the potential to be incredible if I would choose to love.

> He has told you, O man, what is good;
> and what does the Lord require of you
> but to do justice, and to love kindness,
> and to walk humbly with your God?
> *Micah 6:8*

He does not retain his anger forever,
because he *delights* in steadfast love
Micah 7:18b

God does not have to love. He isn't forcing Himself to love. He delights in loving me. Because truly, I'm beautiful to Him.

MAY 28, 2014 (MORNING):

Sing aloud, O daughter of Zion;
shout, O Israel!
rejoice and exult with all your heart,
O daughter of Jerusalem!
Zephaniah 3:14

Teach me to love, God. Teach me how to show people they're valued and how to bless them. Give me Your eyes of perfect love so that I may see what You see and feel what You feel toward those around me

Humble me, Father. If I have a selfish perspective God, break it. The most fulfilling life is a life of loving You and others so much that I don't have time to be self-centered.

MAY 29TH, 2014 (MORNING):

Was hit by the realization last night that I don't really view myself as God's child very well. I think pretty low of myself, and though we're called to be humble, I'm realizing the way I've been thinking has actually been kinda selfish. I've been so caught up in the idea that I'm weak and unworthy of God's love that I've forgotten to fully live in the light of what He's done for me. Yes, I'm a sinner, and it's important to acknowledge that. But I'm also beloved to the Creator of the earth, sky and sea. That's cause to live with wild joy! I don't need to live in shame of my sin anymore. My cage door's been unlocked and I can live in joy of my freedom. I'm not filthy. I'm white as snow.

I love how passionately my Dad advocates the will of God ☺ I'm so blessed to have the parents I have.

I love how in *Psalm 107*, both people dealing with tough circumstances and those who've blatantly denied You are quickly met with grace when they cry out. You show no partiality.

Mark's Last entry…

MAY 30TH, 2014 (MORNING):

Do all things without grumbling or disputing,
that you may be blameless and innocent,
children of God without
blemish
In the midst of a crooked and twisted
generation
among who you shine as
lights in the world.
Philippians 2:14

THE CABIN

I open the cabin's front door and am greeted with one of the most beautiful good mornings I've ever known. All around me, the mighty forest brims with gentle light as the sun crests the horizon somewhere behind the trees. The cleansing scent of pine fills my nostrils, then my lungs, then my soul, and then flows back out as gently as it came.

The trees are silent as they are old; the sweet calm is only broken by the satisfying crush of September leaves as I step barefooted from the porch to the earth. A breeze flows over my skin, and as the tree branches ride it, I spot something in the distance.

Light. Fierce, glorious, powerful light. And suddenly, I hear a quiet, yet strong voice that caresses my heart.

"Come, find me."

The thrill of that eager voice spreads my mouth into a smile, then bursts through my lips in a laugh.

The branches sway again, and another golden ray pushes through a gap in the trees.

"Come, find me."

Without a thought, I sprint into the forest.

The wind on my face as I run exhilarates me. Leaves and pine straw are left fluttering in my wake. All I can think of is that voice, that strong, passionate, joyful voice calling me towards it.

The light becomes less and less blocked by the trees. All around, branches seem to burst into flame as the light pours through the once-muted Autumn leaves.

The closer I get, the more the world seems to stir. On my left, a herd of deer prances forward, the orange rays beaming brilliantly off their coats. I hear birds chirping and watch in wonder as a blue jay zips past me.

Suddenly, I dodge a tree, and my feet land on cool, soft sand. And then I see the light.

Above a flat mirror of a lake burns the most vibrant, intense gorgeous sunrise I've ever seen. The sun blasts fantastically into clouds that seem like waves, turning them into romantic pinks and laughing oranges. The sun is just over the far side of the lake, creating a fantastic copy on the watery canvas below.

I sink to my knees as I gaze at what lies before me. And as my soul burns in wonder, that lovely voice speaks again. Just three tiny words, but they mean more to me than any I've ever heard.

"I love you!"

And suddenly, Creation bursts forth in worship. And I leap to my feet, spinning and dancing before the Lord as I sing of His awesome power, His goodness, His mind-blowing love. And then, I hear that Mighty Voice join me, and the world becomes Eden as it returns to its true purpose of glorifying its Creator.

And in this moment, all is as it should be, and I am what I was designed to be.

EPILOGUE

As I continued alone in Bald Head Island Maritime Classic Road Race, I was so curious to know how Mark had placed, and I couldn't wait to see him at the finish line. As I finally came out of the hills, my body loosened up, and I picked up my pace. In the final stretch into the harbor area, I could hear the crowd cheering their loved ones in. There! I spotted my family and Mark, excitedly cheering for me. "Go, MOM! Run it in! Almost there! Go!" It was awesome. There is nothing quite like reaching the finish line and having the ones closest to you rooting you on.

While the larger group headed back to the house to make lunch, Mark and I decided to stick around for the awards. We were hoping that Mark had placed somewhere. When the race coordinator announced that Mark Rodriguez had won first flace in his age bracket, we went nuts. This was the first and only race he would win on this earth. We reveled in the glory. As he walked back through the small crowd with his "trophy," we were beaming at each other. Who knew it would turn out like this? What a day!

And then we heard the next surprise… "The first-place winner in the 35-40 age bracket for the 25th Annual Bald Head Island Maritime Classic Road Race is Leigh Ellen Rodriguez!" ***What?*** That can't be. I have run my whole life and have never won a race. NEVER. Not even close. Mark and I whooped, jumped, victory danced our way home with our trophies in hand. Team Rodriguez owned that race.

Today, I am reminded that while Mark finished his race earlier than I have, I still have some miles to go—my own race. The terrain is hilly, and I can get really tired and lonely without him. Mark ran his race so well, and he finished so strong. With God's help, I hope to do the same in mine.

I am so thankful that I have a crowd on my sidelines continuing to spur me on.

Mark is now out of my sight, but I know we run after the same goal. And in the words of his journals, I hear his voice continuing to push me forward toward the prize.

I cannot wait to see him at the finish line, where we will marvel at the trophies. We will dance, jump, and whoop together again.

In honor of him, to the glory of Christ, I will push on.

CPSIA information can be obtained
at www.ICGtesting.com
Printed in the USA
BVOW09s1042160617
486873BV00002B/103/P